THE

SECOND ADMINISTRATION

OF

JAMES MADISON

1813—1817

HISTORY OF THE UNITED STATES.

BY

HENRY ADAMS.

HISTORY

OF THE

UNITED STATES OF AMERICA

DURING THE SECOND ADMINISTRATION OF

JAMES MADISON

By HENRY ADAMS

VOL. I.

ANTIQUARIAN PRESS LTD.
New York
1962

First Published
1891-1896
by
Charles Scribner's Sons

———

Reprinted 1962
by
Antiquarian Press, Ltd.
New York, N.Y.

Edition Limited to 750 Sets

Library of Congress Catalog Card Number: 61-8054

Printed in the U.S.A.
———
NOBLE OFFSET PRINTERS, INC.
NEW YORK 3, N.Y.

CONTENTS OF VOL. I.

HISTORY OF THE UNITED STATES.

CHAPTER I.

THE American declaration of war against England,
July 18, 1812, annoyed those European nations that
were gathering their utmost resources for resistance
to Napoleon's attack. Russia could not but regard
it as an unfriendly act, equally bad for political and
commercial interests. Spain and Portugal, whose
armies were fed largely if not chiefly on American
grain imported by British money under British protection, dreaded to see their supplies cut off. Germany, waiting only for strength to recover her
freedom, had to reckon against one more element
in Napoleon's vast military resources. England
needed to make greater efforts in order to maintain
the advantages she had gained in Russia and Spain.
Even in America, no one doubted the earnestness
of England's wish for peace ; and if Madison and
Monroe insisted on her acquiescence in their terms,
they insisted because they believed that their military position entitled them to expect it. The recon-

quest of Russia and Spain by Napoleon, an event almost certain to happen, could hardly fail to force from England the concessions, not in themselves unreasonable, which the United States required.

This was, as Madison to the end of his life maintained, " a fair calculation ; " [1] but it was exasperating to England, who thought that America ought to be equally interested with Europe in overthrowing the military despotism of Napoleon, and should not conspire with him for gain. At first the new war disconcerted the feeble Ministry that remained in office on the death of Spencer Perceval : they counted on preventing it, and did their utmost to stop it after it was begun. The tone of arrogance which had so long characterized government and press, disappeared for the moment. Obscure newspapers, like the London " Evening Star," still sneered at the idea that Great Britain was to be " driven from the proud pre-eminence which the blood and treasure of her sons have attained for her among the nations, by a piece of striped bunting flying at the mastheads of a few fir-built frigates, manned by a handful of bastards and outlaws," — a phrase which had great success in America, — but such defiances expressed a temper studiously held in restraint previous to the moment when the war was seen to be inevitable.

Castlereagh did not abandon the hope of peace until Jonathan Russell, August 24, reported to him the concessions which the President required ante-

[1] Madison to Wheaton, Feb. 26, 1827; Works, iii. 553.

cedent to negotiation, — the stoppage of impressments, dismissal of impressed seamen, indemnity
for spoliations, and abandonment of paper blockades.
The British secretary intimated that he thought
these demands, as conditions precedent to an armistice, somewhat insulting;[1] and in conversation he
explained to Russell that such concessions would
merely cost the Ministry their places without result.
" You are not aware," he said,[2] " of the great sensibility and jealousy of the people of England on
this subject; and no administration could expect to
remain in power that should consent to renounce
the right of impressment or to suspend the practice,
without certainty of an arrangement which should ob-
viously be calculated to secure its object." Russell
then proposed an informal understanding, — adding of
his own accord, without authority from his Government, a proposal, afterward adopted by Congress,
that the United States should naturalize no more
British seamen. Castlereagh made the obvious reply that an informal understanding offered no more
guaranty to England than a formal one; that it
had the additional disadvantage of bearing on its
face a character of disguise; that in any case the
discussion of guaranties must precede the understanding; and that Russell had on this subject neither authority nor instructions.[3]

[1] Castlereagh to Russell, Aug. 29, 1812; State Papers, iii. 589.
[2] Russell to Monroe, Sept. 17, 1812; State Papers, iii. 593.
[3] Castlereagh to Russell, Sept. 18, 1812; State Papers, iii. 592.

The correspondence closed September 19, and Russell left England; but not until October 13, after learning that the President had refused to ratify the armistice made by Prevost with Dearborn, did the British government order general reprisals, — and even this order closed with a proviso that nothing therein contained should affect the previous authority given to Admiral Sir John Borlase Warren to arrange a cessation of hostilities.

The realization that no escape could be found from an American war was forced on the British public at a moment of much discouragement. Almost simultaneously a series of misfortunes occurred which brought the stoutest and most intelligent Englishmen to the verge of despair. In Spain Wellington, after winning the battle of Salamanca in July, occupied Madrid in August, and obliged Soult to evacuate Andalusia; but his siege of Burgos failed, and as the French generals concentrated their scattered forces, Wellington was obliged to abandon Madrid once more. October 21, he was again in full retreat on Portugal. The apparent failure of his campaign was almost simultaneous with the apparent success of Napoleon's; for the Emperor entered Moscow September 14, and the news of this triumph, probably decisive of Russian submission, reached England about October 3. Three days later arrived intelligence of William Hull's surrender at Detroit; but this success was counterbalanced by simultaneous news of Isaac Hull's startling capture of the " Guerriere," and the certainty of a prolonged war.

In the desponding condition of the British people, — with a deficient harvest, bad weather, wheat at nearly five dollars a bushel, and the American supply likely to be cut off; consols at $57\frac{1}{2}$, gold at thirty per cent premium; a Ministry without credit or authority, and a general consciousness of blunders, incompetence, and corruption, — every new tale of disaster sank the hopes of England and called out wails of despair. In that state of mind the loss of the " Guerriere" assumed portentous dimensions. The " Times" was especially loud in lamenting the capture : —

"We witnessed the gloom which that event cast over high and honorable minds. . . . Never before in the history of the world did an English frigate strike to an American ; and though we cannot say that Captain Dacres, under all circumstances, is punishable for this act, yet we do say there are commanders in the English navy who would a thousand times rather have gone down with their colors flying, than have set their fellow sailors so fatal an example."

No country newspaper in America, railing at Hull's cowardice and treachery, showed less knowledge or judgment than the London "Times," which had written of nothing but war since its name had been known in England. Any American could have assured the English press that British frigates before the " Guerriere" had struck to American ; and even

in England men had not forgotten the name of the
British frigate "Serapis," or that of the American
captain Paul Jones. Yet the "Times's" ignorance
was less unreasonable than its requirement that
Dacres should have gone down with his ship, — a
cry of passion the more unjust to Dacres because
he fought his ship as long as she could float. Such
sensitiveness seemed extravagant in a society which
had been hardened by centuries of warfare; yet the
"Times" reflected fairly the feelings of Englishmen.
George Canning, speaking in open Parliament not
long afterward,[1] said that the loss of the "Guerriere"
and the "Macedonian" produced a sensation in the
country scarcely to be equalled by the most violent
convulsions of Nature. "Neither can I agree with
those who complain of the shock of consternation
throughout Great Britain as having been greater
than the occasion required. . . . It cannot be too
deeply felt that the sacred spell of the invincibility
of the British navy was broken by those unfortunate
captures."

Of all spells that could be cast on a nation, that of
believing itself invincible was perhaps the one most
profitably broken; but the process of recovering its
senses was agreeable to no nation, and to England,
at that moment of distress, it was as painful as Canning described. The matter was not mended by the
"Courier" and "Morning Post," who, taking their
tone from the Admiralty, complained of the enor-

[1] Cobbett's Debates, xxiv. 463; Feb. 18, 1813.

mous superiority of the American frigates, and called
them "line-of-battle ships in disguise." Certainly
the American forty-four was a much heavier ship
than the British thirty-eight, but the difference had
been as well known in the British navy before these
actions as it was afterward; and Captain Dacres
himself, the Englishman who best knew the relative
force of the ships, told his court of inquiry a different story:[1] "I am so well aware that the success
of my opponent was owing to fortune, that it is my
earnest wish, and would be the happiest period of
my life, to be once more opposed to the 'Constitution,' with them [the old crew] under my command,
in a frigate of similar force with the 'Guerriere.'"
After all had been said, the unpleasant result remained that in future British frigates, like other
frigates, could safely fight only their inferiors in
force. What applied to the "Guerriere" and "Macedonian" against the "Constitution" and "United
States," where the British force was inferior, applied
equally to the "Frolic" against the "Wasp," where
no inferiority could be shown. The British newspapers thenceforward admitted what America wished
to prove, that, ship for ship, British were no more
than the equals of Americans.

Society soon learned to take a more sensible view
of the subject, but as the first depression passed
away a consciousness of personal wrong took its
place. The United States were supposed to have

[1] James, App. No. 77.

stabbed England in the back at the moment when
her hands were tied, when her existence was in the
most deadly peril and her anxieties were most heavy.
England never could forgive treason so base and
cowardice so vile. That Madison had been from the
first a tool and accomplice of Bonaparte was thenceforward so fixed an idea in British history that time
could not shake it. Indeed, so complicated and so
historical had the causes of war become that no
one even in America could explain or understand
them, while Englishmen could see only that America
required England as the price of peace to destroy
herself by abandoning her naval power, and that
England preferred to die fighting rather than to die
by her own hand. The American party in England
was extinguished; no further protest was heard
against the war; and the British people thought
moodily of revenge.

This result was unfortunate for both parties, but
was doubly unfortunate for America, because her
mode of making the issue told in her enemy's favor.
The same impressions which silenced in England
open sympathy with America, stimulated in America
acute sympathy with England. Argument was useless against people in a passion, convinced of their
own injuries. Neither Englishmen nor Federalists
were open to reasoning. They found their action
easy from the moment they classed the United States
as an ally of France, like Bavaria or Saxony; and
they had no scruples of conscience, for the practical

alliance was clear, and the fact proved sufficiently the intent.

This outbreak of feeling took place in the month of October, when the hopes of England were lowest. While Wellington retreated from Madrid and Burgos to Ciudad Rodrigo; while Napoleon was supposed to be still victorious at Moscow, although his retreat began October 19, two days before Wellington abandoned the siege of Burgos; and while, October 18, the " Wasp" captured the " Frolic," and October 25 the " United States " captured the " Macedonian," — in England public opinion broke into outcry against the temporizing conduct of the government toward America, and demanded vigorous prosecution of the war.

" In any other times than the present," said the " Times " of October 30, " it would appear utterly incredible that men should adopt so drivelling a line of conduct as to think of waging a war of conciliation and forbearance, and that with enemies whom they themselves represent as alike faithless and implacable."

The Government hastened to pacify these complaints. Orders were given to hurry an overwhelming force of ships-of-the-line and frigates to the American coast. Almost immediately England recovered from her dismay ; for November 11 news arrived that the Russians were again masters of Moscow, and that Napoleon was retreating. Day after day the posts arrived from Russia, bringing accounts more and more encouraging, until when Parliament met, November 24, the hope that Napoleon might never escape from Russia had become strong.

Thus the new Ministry found themselves able to face opposition with unexpected strength. Madison's calculations, reasonable as they seemed to be, were overthrown, and the glow of English delight over the success of Russia made the burden of the American war seem easy to bear. In Parliament hardly a voice was raised for peace. The Marquess Wellesley in the debate on the King's speech attacked ministers, not because they had brought the country into war with America, but because they had been unprepared for it; "they ought as statesmen to have known that the American government had been long infected with a deadly hatred toward this country, and, if he might be allowed an unusual application of a word, with a deadly affection toward France." [1] America had been suffered to carry on hostilities without danger to herself, and must be convinced of her folly and desperation. Lord Grenville also asserted that the American government was always hostile to England, but that only the conduct of ministers had enabled it to pluck up courage to show its enmity. [2] Canning, in the Commons, attacked still more sharply the forbearance of the Ministry and their silence toward America:

" It never entered into my mind that the mighty naval power of England would be allowed to sleep while our

[1] Cobbett's Debates, xxiv. 34; Nov. 30, 1812.
[2] Cobbett's Debates, xxiv. 47, 48; Nov. 30, 1812.

commerce was swept from the surface of the Atlantic; and that at the end of six months' war it would be proclaimed in a speech from the throne that the time was now at length come when the long-withheld thunder of Britain must be launched against an implacable foe, and the fulness of her power at length drawn out. It never entered into my mind that we should send a fleet to take rest and shelter in our own ports in North America, and that we should then attack the American ports with a flag of truce." [1]

From such criticisms Lord Castlereagh had no difficulty in defending himself. Whitbread alone maintained that injustice had been done to America, and that measures ought to be taken for peace.

This debate took place November 30, two days after the destruction of Napoleon's army in passing the Beresina. From that moment, and during the next eighteen months, England had other matters to occupy her mind than the disagreeable subject of the American war. Napoleon arrived in Paris December 18, and set himself to the task of renewing the army of half a million men which had been lost in Russia, and of strengthening his hold on Germany, where a violent popular emotion threatened to break into open alliance with the Russian Czar. December 30 the Prussian corps of the Grand Army deserted to the Russians; and soon afterward the French abandoned Poland and the province of old Prussia, and with difficulty, no enemy attacking, held Berlin. The interest of England turned to the

[1] Cobbett's Debates, xxiv. 72; Nov. 30, 1812.

negotiations and military movements of the Continent. After January 1, 1813, Englishmen never willingly thought of the American war, or gave attention to terms of peace. They regarded the result in America as dependent on the result in Germany; and they would have ignored the war altogether had not the American frigates and privateers from time to time compelled their attention.

With the prospect of a great trade about to open with the continent of Europe, as the French garrisons were driven out of Germany and Spain, English manufacturers could afford to wait with patience for better times ; but although a nation so long accustomed to the chances of war could adapt itself quickly to changes in the course of trade, England felt more than it liked to admit the annoyance of American hostilities on the ocean. During the first few months this annoyance was the greater because it was thought to be the result of official negligence. December 30, a merchant writing to the "Times" declared that "the Americans have taken upward of two hundred sail of British merchantmen and three or four packets from the West Indies. Recent advices from the Windward Islands state that the Admiral is mortified at the depredations of the American privateers, it not being in his power to prevent them, most of the few cruisers under his orders having been out so long from England that their copper is nearly off, — so that the privateers remain unmolested, as they can sail round our ships whenever they think proper; they are in consequence become so daring as even to cut vessels out of harbors, though protected by batteries, and to land and carry off cattle from plantations. The accounts from Jamaica by the mail which arrived on Friday represent that island to be literally blockaded by American privateers."

When the press spoke at all of naval matters, it talked wildly about the American frigates. " Such fearful odds," said the " Morning Post" in regard to the "Macedonian," December 26, "would break the heart and spirit of our sailors, and dissolve that charm, that spell, which has made our navy invincible." " The land-spell of the French is broken, and so is our sea-spell," said the "Times." The American frigates were exaggerated into ships-of-the-line, and were to be treated as such, British frigates keeping out of their way. At first, the British naval officers hesitated to accept this view of a subject which had never before been suggested. Neither Captain Dacres nor his court-martial attributed his defeat to this cause ; but before long, nearly all England agreed to rate the American frigates as seventy-fours, and complained that the Americans, with their accustomed duplicity, should have deceived the British navy by representing the " Constitution" and " United States " to be frigates. The " Times " protested in vain against this weakness : —

" Good God! that a few short months should have so altered the tone of British sentiments! Is it true, or is it not, that our navy was accustomed to hold the Americans in utter contempt? Is it true, or is it not, that the 'Guerriere' sailed up and down the American coast with her name painted in large characters on her sails, in boyish defiance of Commodore Rodgers? Would any captain, however young, have indulged such a foolish piece of vain-boasting if he had not been carried forward by the almost unanimous feeling of his associates?" [1]

To the charge that the British Admiralty had been taken unprepared by the war, the Admiralty replied that its naval force on the American station at the outbreak of hostilities exceeded the American in the proportion of eighty-five to fourteen.

" We have since sent out more line-of-battle ships and heavier frigates," added the " Times," January 4, 1813. " Surely we must now mean to smother the American navy. . . A very short time before the capture of the 'Guerriere' an American frigate was an object of ridicule to our honest tars. Now the prejudice is actually setting the other way, and great pains seem to be taken by the friends of ministers to prepare the public for the surrender of a British seventy-four to an opponent lately so much contemned."

The loss of two or three thirty-eight gun frigates on the ocean was a matter of trifling consequence to the British government, which had a force of four ships-of-the-line and six or eight frigates in Chesapeake Bay alone, and which built every year dozens of ships-of-the-line and frigates to replace those lost or worn out; but although the American

[1] The Times, Jan. 2, 1813.

privateers wrought more injury to British interests
than was caused or could be caused by the American
navy, the pride of England cared little about mercantile losses, and cared immensely for its fighting
reputation.   The theory that the American was a
degenerate Englishman, — a theory chiefly due to
American teachings, — lay at the bottom of British
politics.   Even the late British minister at Washington, Foster, a man of average intelligence, thought
it manifest good taste and good sense to say of the
Americans in his speech of February 18, 1813, in
Parliament, that "generally speaking, they were not
a people we should be proud to acknowledge as our
relations."[1]   Decatur and Hull were engaged in a
social rather than in a political contest, and were
aware that the serious work on their hands had little
to do with England's power, but much to do with
her manners.   The mortification of England at the
capture of her frigates was the measure of her previous arrogance.

The process of acquiring knowledge in such light
as was furnished by the cannon of Hull, Decatur,
and Bainbridge could not be rendered easy or rapid.
News of the American victories dropped in at inter-
vals, as though American captains intentionally prolonged the enjoyment of their certain success, in
order to keep England in constant ill temper.   News
of the "Java" arrived about the middle of March,
and once more the press broke into a chorus of

[1] Cobbett's Debates, xxiv. 625 ; Feb. 13, 1813.

complaints. The " Times " renewed its outcry ; the
" Courier " abused the " Time. " for its " tone of
whining lamentation, of affected sensibility, and
puerile grief," but admitted that the behavior of
the American frigates seemed extraordinary ; while
the " Pilot," the chief naval authority, lamented in
set periods the incomprehensible event : —

" The public will learn, with sentiments which we shall
not presume to anticipate, that a third British frigate has
struck to an American. This is an occurrence that calls
for serious reflection, — this, and the fact stated in our
paper of yesterday, that Loyd's list contains notices of
upwards of five hundred British vessels captured in seven
months by the Americans. Five hundred merchantmen
and three frigates ! Can these statements be true ; and
can the English people hear them unmoved? Any one
who had predicted such a result of an American war this
time last year would have been treated as a madman or
a traitor. He would have been told, if his opponents
had condescended to argue with him, that long ere seven
months had elapsed the American flag would be swept
from the seas, the contemptible navy of the United States
annihilated, and their maritime arsenals rendered a heap
of ruins. Yet down to this moment not a single American frigate has struck her flag. They insult and laugh at
our want of enterprise and vigor. They leave their ports
when they please, and return to them when it suits their
convenience ; they traverse the Atlantic ; they beset the
West India Islands ; they advance to the very chops of
the Channel ; they parade along the coasts of South
America ; nothing chases, nothing intercepts, nothing en-
gages them but to yield them triumph."

The immediate moral drawn from these complaints was the necessity of punishing the United States; but no one could longer deny that the necessary punishment was likely to prove tedious and costly. February 18 Parliament took up the subject of the American war, and both Houses debated it. In the Lords, Bathurst made a temperate speech devoted to showing that America in claiming immunity from impressments claimed more than England could afford to yield, — "a right hitherto exercised without dispute, and of the most essential importance to our maritime superiority." Lord Lansdowne replied with tact and judgment, rather hinting than saying that the right was becoming too costly for assertion. "Some time ago it was imagined on all hands that in the event of a war with America, the first operation would be the destruction of her navy. What the fact had turned out to be, he was almost ashamed to mention. If any one were asked what had been the success of our navy in this war, he would unfortunately find some difficulty in giving an answer." [1] Lord Liverpool, while defending his administration from the charge of imbecility, tended to strengthen the prevailing impression by the tone of his complaints against America: "Although she might have had wrongs, although she might have had grounds for complaint, although she might have had pressing provocations, yet she ought to have looked to this country as the guardian power to which she was indebted not only

[1] Cobbett's Debates, xxiv. 582.

for her comforts, not only for her rank in the scale of civilization, but for her very existence." [1]   Perhaps these words offered as good an explanation as the Prime Minister could give of the war itself, for apart from the unconscious sarcasm they contained, they implied that England assumed to act as guardian to the United States, and had hitherto denied to the United States the right to act independently.

Both Lord Holland and Lord Erskine gently glanced at this assumption; and Erskine went so far as to intimate that sooner or later England must give way. " It has been said that this war, if the Americans persist in their claims, must be eternal. If so, our prospects are disheartening. America is a growing country, — increasing every day in numbers, in strength, in resources of every kind. In a lengthened contest all the advantages are on her side, and against this country." The warning lost none of its point from Lord Eldon, who, always ready to meet any logical necessity by an equally logical absurdity, granted that " unless America should think proper to alter her tone, he did not see how the national differences could be settled."

Such a debate was little likely to discourage America. Every country must begin war by asserting that it will never give way, and of all countries England, which had waged innumerable wars, knew best when perseverance cost more than concession. Even at that early moment Parliament was evi-

[1] Cobbett's Debates, xxiv. 586.

dently perplexed, and would willingly have yielded
had it seen means of escape from its naval fetich,
impressment. Perhaps the perplexity was more evident in the Commons than in the Lords, for Castlereagh, while defending his own course with elaborate
care, visibly stumbled over the right of impressment.
Even while claiming that its abandonment would have
been " vitally dangerous if not fatal " to England's
security, he added that he " would be the last man in
the world to underrate the inconvenience which the
Americans sustained in consequence of our assertion
of the right of search." The embarrassment became
still plainer when he narrowed the question to one of
statistics, and showed that the whole contest was
waged over the forcible retention of some eight hundred seamen among one hundred and forty-five thousand employed in British service. Granting the
number were twice as great, he continued, " could the
House believe that there was any man so infatuated,
or that the British empire was driven to such straits,
that for such a paltry consideration as seventeen
hundred sailors, his Majesty's government would
needlessly irritate the pride of a neutral nation or
violate that justice which was due to one country
from another ? " If Liverpool's argument explained
the causes of war, Castlereagh's explained its inevitable result, for since the war must cost England at
least ten million pounds a year, could Parliament be
so infatuated as to pay ten thousand pounds a year
for each American sailor detained in service, when

one tenth of the amount, if employed in raising the wages of the British sailor, would bring any required number of seamen back to their ships? The whole British navy in 1812 cost twenty million pounds; the pay-roll amounted to only three million pounds; the common sailor was paid four pounds bounty and eighteen pounds a year, which might have been trebled at half the cost of an American war.

No one rose in the House to press this reasoning. Castlereagh completed his argument, showing, with more temper than logic, that England was wholly in the right and America altogether in the wrong; the American government and people were infatuated; they had an inordinate and insolent spirit of encroachment and unreasonable hostility; had prostituted their character and showed an unexampled degeneracy of feeling. "For America he confessed that he deeply lamented the injury which her character had sustained by the conduct of her government; it was conduct unworthy of any State calling itself civilized and free."

Castlereagh's invective had the merit of being as little serious as his logic, and left as little sting; but what Castlereagh could say without causing more than a smile, never failed to exasperate Americans like drops of vitriol when it came from the lips of George Canning. Canning had not hitherto succeeded better in winning the confidence of England than in curbing the insolence of America; he was still in opposition, while the man whom in 1807 he could hardly condescend to consider a rival was Secretary for Foreign Affairs and leader of the House. Worst of all, Canning could not escape the necessity of supporting him, for Castlereagh's position in regard to America was strong, while Canning's own position was weak and needed constant excuse. In the debate of Feb. 18, 1813, he undertook the difficult task of appearing to attack Castlereagh while defending himself.

Canning's speech began by an argument so characteristic as to win the praise of John Wilson Croker, Secretary to the Admiralty, — a man less than most politicians prone to waste praise on opponents. Whitbread had quoted, in excuse of the American practice of naturalization, two Acts of Parliament, — one the 6th Anne, according to which any foreigner who served two years in any British vessel, military or merchant, without further condition or even oath, or more than the statement of the fact of service, became entitled to every protection of a natural subject of the realm. No words could be more emphatic than those of the statutes. " Such foreign mariner," said the 6th Anne, " shall to all intents and purposes be deemed and taken to be a natural-born subject of his Majesty's kingdom of Great Britain, and have and enjoy all the privileges, powers, rights, and capacities " which a native could enjoy. Again, by the 13th George II. every foreign seaman who in time of war served two years on board an English ship by virtue of the king's proclamation was *ipso facto* naturalized. Other naturalization laws existed, guaranteeing all the privileges of a natural-born subject to foreigners under certain conditions ; but the Acts of Anne and George II. were most in point, as they referred to foreign sailors alone; and with these laws on the statute-book Parliament seemed to stand in an unfavorable position for disputing the right of America to adopt a similar system. Canning's argument on the meaning of these statutes was interesting, not only as an example of his own mind, but as the only legal justification of a long war which England fought against America at prodigious expense,— a justification which she maintained for years to be sound.

" My construction of the Acts of Anne was altogether different," said Canning in reply to these quotations. " I understood that by it this country professed to give that only which it is competent to bestow without interfering in any degree with the rights or claims of other Powers ; that it imparted to foreigners on certain conditions certain municipal privileges, but leaves untouched and unimpaired their native allegiance. . . . The enactments of this statute are a testimony of national gratitude to brave men of whatever country who may lend their aid in fighting the battles of Great Britain, but not an invitation to them to abandon the cause of their own country when it may want their aid ; not an encouragement to them to deny or to undervalue the sacred and indestructible duty which they owe to their own sovereign and to their native soil."

Something peculiarly sacred must have inhered in the statute of Anne which thus conferred naturalization on Dutch or Swedish seamen as " a testimony of national gratitude " for " fighting the battles of Great Britain " for two years in the British merchant service in time of peace, and converted them into citizens enjoying " all the privileges, powers, rights, and capacities " of natural-born subjects of Great Britain, which consisted, according to Canning, only in " certain municipal privileges " in England, subject to the will of a foreign sovereign. Such a definition of the " privileges, powers, rights, and capacities " of a natural-born subject of his Majesty's kingdom of Great Britain seemed new to American lawyers; but it was received with applause by the House, and was further developed by Croker, who laid down the principle, new to the popular view of England's pride, that the naturalized citizen, who was by the law required " to all intents and purposes " to " be deemed and taken to be a natural-born subject," was in fact by the Admiralty " considered as having two countries, — the voluntary service of the one being looked upon as unable to debar the natural allegiance to the other."

The rest of Canning's speech consisted in defence of impressment and of paper blockades, and in panegyric upon European republics at the expense of " the hard features of transatlantic democracy." While assailing the British government because " the arm which should have launched the thunderbolt was oc-

cupied in guiding the pen," he expressed his devout
wish that the war might not be concluded until
England had smothered in victories the disasters to
which she was so little habituated. If an harangue
of this character served in any degree to guide or
aid the councils of England, it served much more
effectually the war-party of America, where Canning
was held in singular antipathy, and where every admission he made in regard to "the shock of consternation" caused by the American frigates gave
pleasure more acute than any pain his sarcastic
phrases could thenceforward inflict.

Alexander Baring spoke with his usual good sense,
pointing out that Castlereagh's speech proved chiefly
the greater interest of England to call for and court
negotiation on the subject of impressments. Whitbread challenged public opinion by going to the verge
of actual sympathy with America. The debate ended
in an unopposed vote for a vigorous prosecution of
the war, leaving the subject in truth untouched, except that England had avowed an extreme desire
to punish America, and naturally felt an extreme
irritation because America showed ability to bear
punishment.

The spring came, bringing no new prospects. England refused to make a suggestion on which the
governments could discuss terms of peace. She refused even to think upon the problem, but massed
a huge armament in Chesapeake Bay and Delaware
River to restore her naval invincibility. Yet reflec-

tion seemed still to be silently at work, for, March 22, the "Times" interrupted its outcry over the loss of the "Java" by publishing a temperate article on the new Foreign Seamen Bill of Congress, — an article in which the suggestion first appeared that peace might after all be restored by simply omitting in the pacification any mention of impressment. The idea found support nowhere; but while, insufficient as it seemed, the human imagination could hardly conceive of any other expedient, at the same moment the uselessness of trying to obtain peace on any terms was made clear by the interference of the Russian Czar.

CHAPTER. II.

NAPOLEON declared war against Russia June 22, four days after the American declaration against England; crossed the Niemen June 24, and August 1 was already at Vitebsk, about three hundred miles south of St. Petersburg, and about equally distant from the frontier and from Moscow. There, in the heart of Russia, he paused to collect his strength for some blow that should lay the Russian empire at his feet; and while he hesitated, the Czar, August 3, returned to his capital to wait. At that moment the chances of war favored Napoleon. Nothing was more likely than his success in destroying the Russian army, and in dictating terms of peace in St. Petersburg.

News of the American declaration of war reached St. Petersburg August 6, and added a new anxiety to the overburdened mind of Alexander. The American minister at that court found himself in a delicate position. His Government declared war against England and became for military purposes an ally of France at the moment when Russia entered into formal alliance with England and went to war with France. If Napoleon caught and crushed the Russian army and marched on St. Petersburg, the American minister would certainly be no favorite with Russians; if Napoleon were beaten, the American minister need expect no consideration, for in that case every influence at the Russian Court was certain to be English, and from England could come no favors.

At the moment when Brock, with his force of a few hundred men attacked Detroit, Napoleon with two hundred thousand men moved upon Smolensk and the Russian army. August 15, he celebrated his fête-day on the banks of the Dnieper; and while Hull was surrendering the fort of Detroit, the Russian army, hardly in better humor than the Ohio militia, were preparing to abandon Smolensk to save themselves from Hull's fate. Napoleon took possession of the town August 18, but failed to destroy the Russian army, and then, turning away from St. Petersburg, pursued his retreating enemy toward Moscow. The battle of Borodino, or Moscowa, followed, September 6, and the French army entered Moscow September 14. There it remained more than a month.

During these weeks of alarm and incessant fighting, the Czar still found time to think of American affairs. The influence of Count Roumanzoff, though lessening every day, still controlled the regular course of foreign relations. September 21 Roumanzoff sent for Adams, and said that the Emperor had been much concerned to find the interests of his subjects defeated and lost by the new war, and it had occurred to him that perhaps an arrangement might be more easily made by an indirect than by a direct negotiation : he wished to know whether an offer of mediation on his part would meet with any difficulty on the part of the United States.[1] Adams replied that his Government could not fail to consider it as a new evidence of the Czar's friendship, but suggested that there was a third party to be consulted, — the British government. Roumanzoff answered that he had already sounded the British minister, who had written to Lord Castlereagh on the subject.

The British minister, lately arrived in Russia, was not a person calculated to aid Roumanzoff. Lord Cathcart, who had been chosen by Castlereagh for the post of ambassador at St. Petersburg, was best known as the commander of the Copenhagen expedition in 1807. Some Americans might perhaps remember that he had served in America during the Revolutionary War. A well-informed writer in the London " Times," who belonged to the Wellesley interest, seemed to doubt Lord Cathcart's qualifications for his new post. " He is only better fitted for it than the horse he rides," was the criticism ; [2] but the better he had been fitted for it, the worse he would have suited Roumanzoff's purpose, for his first object could be no other than to overthrow Roumanzoff and thwart his policy. No serious support of Russian mediation could be expected from him. He began his

---

[1] Diary of J. Q. Adams, Sept. 21, 1812; ii. 401.

[2] VETUS, in the " Times," Oct. 26, 1812.

career by seeking access to the Emperor through other channels than the chancellor.[1]

Adams, September 30, advised his Government of the Czar's proposed mediation. October 15, Roumanzoff announced that his proposal was ready, and would be sent at once to Washington, — which was actually done, before receiving a reply from London. The step could hardly please the British government; but Roumanzoff seemed almost to take pleasure in disregarding England, and perhaps felt that the course of events must either remove him entirely from the government, or make him independent of British support. He clung to the American mediation as the last remnant of his anti-British policy.

The British government would have preferred to make no answer to the Russian offer of mediation. To English statesmen the idea was absurd that England could allow Russia, more than France or the United States themselves, to mediate on blockade and impressment, or upon points of neutrality in any form ; but Castlereagh had every reason to conciliate the Czar, and rather than flatly reject a suggestion from such a source, he replied that he thought the time had not yet come, and that the offer would not be accepted by America.[2] So it happened that the offer of Russian mediation went to America without positive objection from England,

[1] Diary of J. Q. Adams, Oct. 21, 1812 ; ii. 414.

[2] Diary of J. Q. Adams, ii. 433. Adams to Monroe, Dec. 11, 1812 ; State Papers, iii. 626.

finding its way slowly across the Atlantic during the winter months.

With it went the tale of Napoleon's immense disaster. October 23 he began his retreat; November 23 he succeeded in crossing the Beresina and escaping capture; December 5 he abandoned what was still left of his army; and December 19, after travelling secretly and without rest across Europe, he appeared suddenly in Paris, still powerful, but in danger. Nothing could be better calculated to support the Russian mediation in the President's mind. The possibility of remaining without a friend in the world while carrying on a war without hope of success, gave to the Czar's friendship a value altogether new.

Other news crossed the ocean at the same time, but encouraged no hope that England would give way. First in importance, and not to be trifled with, was the British official announcement, dated December 26, 1812, of the blockade of the Chesapeake and Delaware. Americans held that this blockade was illegal,[1] — a blockade of a coast, not of a port; a paper-blockade, one of the grievances against which the war was waged; but whatever they might choose to call it, they could not successfully disprove its efficiency, or deny that it made Chesapeake Bay, Delaware River, and the Vineyard Sound little better than British waters. Export of American produce from the Chesapeake and Delaware ceased.

[1] Diary of J. Q. Adams, Feb. 1, 1813; ii. 440.

The blockade, though serious beyond all other military measures, roused less attention and less protest than another measure of the British government which had the character of a profitable insult. A circular dated November 9, addressed to the governors of West Indian colonies by the British government, authorized them to issue licenses for importation of necessary supplies during the war, — a precaution commonly taken to meet the risk of famine in those regions. The Governor of the Bermudas, in issuing a proclamation January 14, 1813, published the circular, which contained one unusual provision : [1] —

" Whatever importations are proposed to be made, under the order, from the United States of America, should be by your licenses confined to the ports in the Eastern States exclusively, unless you have reason to suppose that the object of the order would not be fulfilled if licenses are not also granted for the importations from the other ports in the United States."

Probably the discrimination was intended, like the exemption from blockade, as a favor to New England, and must have been meant to be more or less secret, since publication was likely to counteract its effect ; but in time of war the British government was at liberty to seek supplies where it chose.

Madison thought differently. He sent to Congress, February 24, 1813, a special Message expressing indignation at the conduct of England.

[1] State Papers, iii. 608.

"The policy now proclaimed to the world," he charged, "introduces into her modes of warfare a system equally distinguished by the deformity of its features and the depravity of its character, — having for its object to dissolve the ties of allegiance and the sentiments of loyalty in the adversary nation, and to seduce and separate its component parts the one from the other. The general tendency of these demoralizing and disorganizing contrivances will be reprobated by the civilized world."

Although many persons shared Madison's view of war as a compulsory process of international law, Federalists and Republicans were at a loss to understand his view of " deformity " and " depravity " in modes of warfare. The whole truth in regard to West and East Florida was not known, but so much was notorious, even in 1811, as to warrant the British minister in protesting " against an attempt so contrary to every principle of public justice, faith, and national honor." [1] What the United States could do in Florida in time of peace, England could surely do in Massachusetts in time of war ; but if England's conduct was in reality deformed and depraved, as charged, the celebrated proclamation of William Hull to the Canadians in 1812, inviting them to quit their allegiance and to " choose wisely " the side of the United States, should have been previously disavowed by the United States government. No little ridicule was caused by the contrast between Madison's attitude toward Canada and his denunciation of England's attitude toward Massachusetts.

[1] Foster to Monroe, July 2, 1811; State Papers, iii. 542.

Taken together, the news from Europe in the last days of winter gave ground for deep reflection. With the overthrow of Napoleon's authority and the close alliance between Great Britain and Russia, the last chance of forcing concessions from England vanished. A long war, with no prospect of success, lay before the United States. New York harbor, the Delaware River, and Chesapeake Bay were already so nearly closed to commerce as to foreshadow complete stoppage; and if Boston was still open, its privileges must soon cease unless Great Britain deliberately intended to regard New England as neutral. All this, though alarming enough, might be met with courage; but against the pronounced disaffection of Massachusetts and Connecticut no defence existed; and whenever those States should pass from stolid inertia into the stage of active resistance to the war, the situation would become hopeless. Under such circumstances England would have a strong motive for refusing peace on any terms.

The shadow of these fears lay over the Inaugural Address which the President pronounced March 4, 1813, after taking for a second time the oath of office at the Capitol. His speech contained only the defence of a war that needed no defence, and complaints against England which were drowned in the tumult of war, the loudest complaint that man could make. Every tone showed that Madison felt doubtful of support, and that in proving the war to be just he betrayed consciousness that it was not ener-

getic.   Perhaps the most characteristic sentence in
the Address was that in which he congratulated the
country " with a proud satisfaction," that in carrying
on the war, "no principle of justice or honor, no usage
of civilized nations, no precept of courtesy or humanity, have been infringed ; the war has been waged on
our part with scrupulous regard to all these relations,
and in a spirit of liberality which was never surpassed."   Madison's phrases were the more remarkable because at about the same time the British
government announced its intention of making America feel what war meant.   The courtesy and humanity
of the war were to be all on the American side ;
while not a word in the Inaugural Address gave the
pledge which could win victories, — the assurance
that the President himself had energy and meant
to exert it.

Besides the alarming difficulties which rose partly
from failure of military calculations at home and
abroad, but chiefly from want of national experience
in the business of war, other annoyances surrounded
the President, and could not fail to make him wish
for peace.   Armstrong had not been six weeks in
the War Department before he set the members of
Administration at odds.   The factious days of Robert
Smith returned, and the President found the task of
maintaining discipline as great in the Cabinet as it
was in the army.   One of the strongest characters
called into prominence by the war, who was himself
destined to have charge of the War Department,

spoke of Armstrong, four months later, in language hinting impatient consciousness of something too complicated to describe. " And Armstrong! — he was the devil from the beginning, is now, and ever will be." [1]   Only by studying what Armstrong did, could the causes be understood of the passion which he excited in every man he crossed.

Monroe was the first to resent Armstrong's proceedings. Monroe's character, the opposite of Armstrong's, was transparent; no one could mistake his motives, except by supposing them to be complex; and in his relations with Armstrong his motives were simpler than usual, for Armstrong's views could not be carried into effect without loss of pride to Monroe. Already Monroe had surrendered the War Department to him, with the expectation that if any one was to have general command of the armies in the field, Monroe was to be the man. Down to the time when Armstrong took control, the idea was universal that the next campaign was to be fought by Monroe. Jan. 13, 1813, Serurier wrote to his Government: [2]

" There is much talk of Mr. Monroe for the command of the army, and he has shown a zeal in organizing his Department which tends to confirm me in that belief. . . . Mr. Monroe is not a brilliant man, and no one expects to find a great captain in him; but he served through the War of Independence with much bravery under the orders and by the side of Washington. He is a man of great

[1] Adams's Gallatin, p. 488.

[2] Serurier to Bassano, Jan. 13, 1813 ; Archives des Aff. Étr. MSS.

good sense, of the most austere honor, the purest patriotism, and the most universally admitted integrity.   He
is loved and respected by all parties, and it is believed
that he would soon gain the hearts of all his officers and
soldiers.   He would be given a staff as good as possible,
and with this assistance as well as all his own recognized
resources, it is believed that he would be perfectly suited
to carry on the campaign about to open against the last
continental possession of England in America."

As acting Secretary of War, Monroe had urged
Congress to increase the number of major-generals ;
and after Armstrong took charge of the Department
Congress passed the Act of February 24, 1813, authorizing the increase.   February 27 the nominations
were sent to the Senate.   In a letter to Jefferson,
Monroe told the story : [1] —

" On the day that the nomination of these officers was
made to the Senate the President sent for me and stated
that the Secretary of War had placed me in his list
of major-generals, at their head, and wished to know
whether I would accept the appointment, intimating that
he did not think I ought to do it, nor did he wish me to
leave my present station.   I asked where I was to serve.
He supposed it would be with the Northern army under
General Dearborn.   I replied that if I left my present
office for such a command it would be inferred that I had
a passion for military life, which I had not ; that in such
a station I could be of no service in any view to the
general cause or to military operations, even perhaps
with the army in which I might serve ; that with a view
to the public interest the commander ought to receive all

[1] Monroe to Jefferson, June 7, 1813 ; Jefferson MSS.

the support which the government could give him, and by accepting the station proposed, I might take from General Dearborn without aiding the cause by anything that I might add. I stated, however, that the grade made no difficulty with me, a desire to be useful being my only object; and that if the command was given me even with a lower grade than that suggested, admitting the possibility, I would accept it. The difficulty related to General Dearborn, who could not well be removed to an inactive station."

Monroe said, in effect, that he would have the command in chief or nothing. Armstrong said, in effect, that he meant to be commander-in-chief himself. The new major-generals were James Wilkinson, Wade Hampton, William R. Davy of South Carolina, Morgan Lewis of New York, William Henry Harrison of Indiana Territory, and Aaron Ogden of New Jersey. The command of the Northern army was left to Dearborn, and as the world knew Dearborn's incompetence to conduct a campaign, no one was surprised to learn that Armstrong meant to conduct it as Secretary of War, at the army headquarters in the field, performing the duties of lieutenant-general.

No sooner was Monroe satisfied that Armstrong meant to follow this course than he took the unusual step of writing to the President a formal remonstrance against his colleague's supposed plan. The act appointing six major-generals was approved February 24. The same evening Monroe had a conversation on the subject with the President, and the next day, February 25, submitted the substance of his remarks in writing.[1] His argument chiefly regarded the inconvenience and unconstitutionality of separating the War Department from the President and of mixing military with civil functions : —

" As soon as General Armstrong took charge of the Department at War, I thought I saw his plan; that is, after he had held it a few days. I saw distinctly that he intended to have no grade in the army which should be competent to a general control of military operations; that he meant to keep the whole in his own hands; that each operation should be distinct and separate, with distinct and separate objects, and of course to be directed by himself, not simply in outline but in detail. I anticipated mischief from this, because I knew that the movements could not be directed from this place. I did not then anticipate the remedy which he had in mind."

From that moment began a feud between the two Cabinet ministers. The cause was obvious. Armstrong had found that if a general command were to be created, it must be given to Monroe. Probably he felt no more confidence in Monroe's military abilities than in those of Dearborn; but determined that his hand should not be thus forced, Armstrong decided to retain Dearborn, although his opinion of Dearborn, as shown afterward,[2] made the retention an act of grave responsibility. The decision once taken, he had no choice but to supply Dearborn's wants by his own presence with the army, — a course

[1] Monroe to Madison, Feb. 25, 1813; Monroe MSS. State Department Archives ; Gilman's Monroe, p. 108.

[2] Armstrong's Notices of the War, i. 113–116.

certain to challenge attack from all Virginia. Had
Armstrong been bent on destroying his rival by
means which the world could have found no chance
to oppose or criticise, he would have removed Dearborn, and would have sent Monroe to waste his
reputation in the task of conquering and holding
Canada.   The retention of Dearborn was an unfortunate beginning for the new Secretary of War.

The first effect of Armstrong's administration was
to turn Monroe into a vindictive enemy; the second
was to alienate Gallatin. Of all the old Republican
leaders, Gallatin cared least for office and most. for
consistency. Under any reasonable distribution of
party favors, the Presidency should have fallen to
him after Madison, not only because he was the fittest
man, the oldest, ablest, and most useful member of
the Executive government, but also because he represented Pennsylvania; and if any State in the Union
had power to select a President, it was she. Madison
would have been glad to secure for Gallatin the succession; he had no special love or admiration for
Monroe, while his regard for Gallatin was strong and
constant; but Pennsylvania cared more for interests
than for men, while Virginia cared so much for men
that she became prodigal of interests. Pennsylvania
allowed Virginia, through the agency of William B.
Giles, Samuel Smith, and Michael Leib, to thrust
Gallatin aside and to open the path for a third
Virginian at the risk of the Union itself. Gallatin,
too proud to complain, had no longer an object of

ambition; and from the moment ambition ceased
abstract ideas of duty alone remained to counteract
the disgusts of disappointment.

Gallatin's abstract ideas were those of 1801, —
simplicity, economy, and purity. Financiering — the
providing of money for wasteful expenditure — was
his abhorrence. "I cannot consent to act the part
of a mere financier," he wrote to Jefferson in 1809; [1]
"to become a contriver of taxes, a dealer of loans,
a seeker of resources for the purpose of supporting
useless baubles, of increasing the number of idle and
dissipated members of the community, of fattening
contractors, pursers, and agents, and of introducing
in all its ramifications that system of patronage,
corruption, and rottenness which you so justly exe-
crate." These words were meant to apply only to
a state of peace, but they applied equally well to a
state of war from the moment war became useless.
In the beginning of Madison's second term, no man
of intelligence denied that the war had failed; that
its avowed objects could not be gained; that every
month of war increased the danger of disunion,
brought national bankruptcy nearer, and fastened
habits of extravagance and corruption on the country.
From his post at the Treasury, Gallatin could see
better than most men the dangers, both financial and
political, engendered by the war, while his acquaint-
ance with European affairs showed him the need of
rapid diplomacy.

[1] Adams's Gallatin, p. 408.

Armstrong represented everything antagonistic to Gallatin; his methods were arbitrary and underhand; his political training was that of the New York school, tempered by personal contact with the court of Napoleon; from him economy could hardly be expected. Yet perhaps the worst feature of his administration was likely to be his use of patronage. The number of Gallatin's personal enemies was small, and the use of patronage in a way that would outrage him seemed difficult; yet within a few weeks Armstrong offended him deeply. March 18, 1813, William Duane, of the "Aurora" newspaper, was appointed to the post of adjutant-general. The appointment was improper, and the motives to which it was sure to be attributed made it more scandalous than the unfitness of the person made it harmful to the service. Gallatin's anger was deep: "Duane's last appointment has disgusted me so far as to make me desirous of not being any longer associated with those who have appointed him."[1]

Into this embroglio of national and personal difficulties Daschkoff, the Russian *chargé* at Washington, suddenly dropped the Czar's offer to mediate a peace. Of its prompt acceptance, under such circumstances, no one could doubt, and on this point the Administration was united. Daschkoff's letter bore date March 8, and Monroe's reply was sent March 11. The letter of reply was a civil and somewhat flatter-

[1] Gallatin to Nicholson, May 5, 1813; Adams's Gallatin, p. 482.

ing compliment to Alexander ; [1] the mission itself was
a matter to be more deliberately arranged.

The next decision regarded the character of the
mission.   The necessary powers might have been
sent, without further form, to Minister Adams at
St. Petersburg, but the President and his advisers
thought with reason that the addition of other negotiators to the mission would give more weight and political effect to the measure.[2]   They decided to send
two new envoys to join Adams ; and on the same
reasoning to select prominent men.   As a guaranty
of their wish for peace, they decided that one of
these men should be a Federalist, and they chose
James A. Bayard of Delaware for the post.   For
the other, Monroe thought of naming some Western
man, to secure the confidence of the Western country, and reconcile it to the result; but a different
turn was given to the measure by Gallatin, who
asked the appointment for himself.   Gallatin's exceptional fitness for the task outweighed all objections.   The President consented to appoint him ; and
Monroe, who had from the first attached himself to
Gallatin, acquiesced, although he saw the consequences to the Cabinet and the Treasury.

A question less easy to decide was whether the new
mission should be despatched at once, or should wait
until England should formally accept the mediation.
There again political motives dictated immediate ac-

[1] State Papers, iii. 624.

[2] Monroe to Jefferson, June 7, 1813 ; Jefferson MSS.

tion. If England should accept, much time might be saved if the mission were on the spot; if she did not accept, the peace-party in America would be more effectually silenced. In either case, Russia would be deeply pledged to support her own undertaking.

The President did not intend to lose Gallatin in the Treasury. Abundant precedents warranted the double employment of government officers. In 1794 John Jay, then chief-justice, had been sent to negotiate with England, and the Senate had approved the appointment. In 1799 Oliver Ellsworth, also chief-justice, was sent to negotiate with France, and the Senate had again approved. These were Federalist precedents, supposed to be binding, at least on the Federalist party. If the chief-justice, the head of an independent branch of government, could be sent abroad as an Envoy Extraordinary in Executive employment, no objection could exist to sending an Executive officer on a temporary service of the same kind, unless on the score of expediency. To prevent difficulty on that account, the Secretary of the Navy consented to act as head of the Treasury until Gallatin's return. Gallatin himself inclined to look on his separation from the Treasury as final,[1] but made his arrangements in agreement with the President's views, which looked to his return in the autumn.

Before he could depart he was obliged to complete the necessary financial arrangements for the coming year, on which he was busily engaged at the moment

[1] Adams's Gallatin. p. 483.

when Daschkoff's letter arrived. First in importance
was the loan of sixteen million dollars. March 12,
subscription books were opened in all the principal
towns, and the public was invited to take the whole
amount at seven per cent interest, to be reduced to
six per cent at the end of thirteen years. About four
million dollars were offered on these terms. Propo-
sals in writing were then invited by a Treasury circular, dated March 18, and after an active negotiation
between Gallatin and three or four capitalists of New
York and Philadelphia, — John Jacob Astor, Stephen
Girard, David Parish, — the remainder of the loan
was provided. In all about eighteen millions were
offered. Fifteen and a half millions were taken, in
the form of six per cent stock, issued at eighty-
eight dollars for every hundred-dollar certificate, re-
deemable after the year 1825. About half a million
was taken at par, with an annuity of 1 1–2 per cent
for thirteen years, in addition to the six per cent
interest.

Calculated as a perpetual annuity, as English bor-
rowers would have viewed it, the rate of this loan was
less than seven per cent; but if the nominal capital
must or should be repaid after twelve years, the rate
was about 7.50 per cent. In the end, the government
paid 7.487 per cent, for the use of these sixteen millions for thirteen years. The terms were not excessive when it was considered that New England in
effect refused to subscribe. Perhaps the loan could
not have been taken at all, had not credit and cur-

rency been already expanded to the danger-point, as
the allotment showed ; for while New England, where
most of the specie was held, subscribed less than half
a million, and Boston took but seventy-five thousand,
Pennsylvania, where banking had become a frenzy,
took seven million dollars.   New York and Baltimore
together contributed only half a million more than
was given by Philadelphia alone.   Ten million dollars
were taken by Astor, Girard, and Parish, — three for-
eign-born Americans, without whose aid the money
could not have been obtained on these terms, if at all.
Doubtless they were bold operators ; but Americans
were supposed to be not wanting in the taste for
speculation, and the question could not but rise how
these men knew the secret of distributing the load
which no native American dared carry.

The bargain was completed April 7.   At that moment the Treasury was empty, and could not meet
the drafts of the other departments ; but with sixteen
millions in hand, five millions of Treasury notes, and
an estimated revenue of something more than nine
millions, Gallatin collected about thirty million dollars, and April 17 wrote to the Secretaries of War
and Navy,[1] allotting to the one thirteen millions and
a quarter, to the other four and a half millions,
which could not be exceeded without the consent of
Congress.   This done, and every question having
been settled that could be foreseen, — the tax-bills
ready to be laid before Congress, and even the draft

[1] Gallatin's Writings, i. 535.

for a new bank-charter prepared, — Gallatin bade fare-
well to the Treasury, and May 9 sailed from the
Delaware River, with Bayard, for the Baltic.

Twelve years had passed since Gallatin took charge
of the finances, and his retirement was an event
hardly less serious than a change of President; for
it implied that the political system he had done so
much to create and support stood so near the brink
of disaster as to call him from the chosen field of
his duties into a new career, where, if anywhere, he
could save it. As Monroe felt called to the army, so
Gallatin turned naturally to diplomacy. He knew
that after another year of war the finances must be
thrown into disorder like that of the Revolutionary
War, beyond the reach of financial skill ; and he
believed that if any one could smooth the path of
negotiation, that person was likely to serve best the
needs of the Treasury. Yet he took grave responsibility, of which he was fully aware, in quitting his
peculiar post at a moment so serious. Success alone
could save him from universal censure ; and perhaps
nothing in his career better proved the high character
he bore, and the extraordinary abilities he possessed,
than the ease with which he supported responsibility
for this almost desperate venture.

The task he had set for himself was hopeless, not
so much because of the concessions he was to require,
as on account of the change in European affairs which
made England indifferent for the moment to any
injury the United States could inflict. Monroe's in-

structions to the new commission, though long, consisted largely in arguments against the legality of impressment as a part of the *jus gentium;* although the legality of European war-measures had long ceased to be worth discussing. As the solution of the dispute, Monroe could offer only the new Foreign Seamen Act, which England had refused from the first to consider, and which was certainly open to objections, — on the American side because it offered too much ; on the British side because it offered more than could in practice be performed. To make the utmost possible concession, Monroe proposed that no native-born British subject, thenceforward naturalized in America, should be allowed to serve either in the national or the private vessels of the United States, — a provision which carried one step further the offer to naturalize no British seamen except on condition of leaving the sea, and which went to the ·verge of conceding the right of impressment. Notwithstanding these concessions, the instructions were still positive on the main point. Without a clear and distinct stipulation against impressments, no treaty was to be signed ; negotiations must cease, and the negotiators must return home.[1]

[1] Monroe to the Plenipotentiaries, April 15, 1813 ; State Papers, iii. 695.

CHAPTER III.

During the winter the Republican legislature of
New York chose Rufus King, the chief Federalist in
the country, to succeed John Smith as United States
senator. Some Republicans charged that this election was the price paid by De Witt Clinton for
Federalist votes in the Presidential contest; but
Clinton's friends declared it to be the price paid by
the Administration Republicans for Federalist aid in
granting a corrupt bank charter. That the choice
was due to a bargain of some kind no one denied,
and possibly both stories were true. Rufus King
himself stood above suspicion, and had been considered an opponent of the Federalist alliance with
Clinton; but he was a powerful recruit to the opposition in the Senate, which numbered thenceforward
nine votes, or precisely one fourth of the body. The
annoyance to the Administration was the greater because King's Republican colleague, Obadiah German,
belonged to the Clintonian opposition, and voted with
the Federalists. At the same time Charles Cutts of
New Hampshire was succeeded by Jeremiah Mason,
a very able and extreme Federalist. Three more
senators — Giles, Samuel Smith, and Michael Leib —

could be counted as personally hostile to the President. Jesse Franklin of North Carolina was succeeded by David Stone, an independent, opposed to the war. Already the opposition threatened to outweigh the votes on which the President could depend. As though legislation had become a matter of inferior importance, William H. Crawford of Georgia, the only vigorous Republican leader in the Senate, resigned his seat, and followed Gallatin to Europe. He was sent to take the place of Joel Barlow at Paris, and hurried to his post. In this condition of party weakness, the election of Rufus King and Jeremiah Mason to the Senate was a disaster to the Administration ; and all the more anxiously the President feared lest the popular election in May should convert New York altogether into a Federalist State, and give Massachusetts the necessary strength to stop the war.

This election, on which the fate of the war was believed to turn, took place as usual, May 1, and began by a Federalist success in the city of New York, followed by another in Kings, Queens, and Westchester counties. These counties before the century ended had a voting population of near half a million, but in 1813 they cast in State elections about eight thousand votes, and gave a majority of eight hundred for the Federalist candidate Stephen Van Rensselaer, the unfortunate general of the Niagara campaign. Throughout the eastern and central counties the election was disputed ; three of the four districts into which the State was divided left the result so close — within about three hundred votes — that only the western counties of Cayuga, Seneca, and Genesee turned the scale. Governor Tompkins was re-elected by the moderate majority of three thousand in a total vote of eighty-three thousand; but the Federalists obtained a majority of ten in the Assembly, and gained confidence with their strength. In this election, for the first time, the issue was distinct between those who supported and those who opposed the war. The chief towns, New York, Hudson, and Albany, were strong in opposition; the country districts tended to support.

In Massachusetts the Federalist governor Caleb Strong, who had made himself peculiarly obnoxious by refusing to call out the State's quota of militia, received nearly fifty-seven thousand votes, while Senator Varnum, the Republican candidate, received forty-three thousand. Considering that the population of Massachusetts was about one fourth smaller than that of New York, the vote of one hundred thousand persons in the smaller State, and only eighty-three thousand in the larger, seemed a proof of popular indifference ; but in truth the vote of New York was larger than usual, and only one thousand less than at the next election of governor, in 1816. The difference was due to the unequal suffrage, which in New York State elections was restricted to one hundred pound free-holds, while in Massachusetts all citizens worth sixty pounds were entitled to vote.

At the same time John Randolph met with defeat, for the only time in his life. John W. Eppes, one of Jefferson's sons-in-law, took residence within Randolph's district for the purpose of contesting it; and after a struggle succeeded in winning the seat, on the war-issue, by a vote of eleven hundred and twelve to nine hundred and forty-three.[1] This change of membership tended, like the New York election, to show that the people were yielding to the necessity of supporting the war. Yet the process was alarmingly slow. In the second year of hostilities, New Hampshire, Massachusetts, Rhode Island, Connecticut, and New Jersey were Federal in all branches of their State governments; New York, Delaware, and Maryland were partly Republican and partly Federalist; of the eighteen States only ten were wholly Republican, and seven of these were Southern. In the United States Senate the Administration could count upon twenty-two votes, with reasonable certainty; the other fourteen senators were more or less lukewarm or hostile. In the House, one hundred and fourteen members supported the Administration, and sixty-eight opposed it. As far as concerned numbers, the Administration was strong enough in Congress; but the universal want of faith in its capacity to conduct a war of such consequence gave the Federalists an advantage beyond proportion to their numerical strength. The task of opposition was easy, and its force irresistible when the ablest and oldest Repub-

[1] Niles, iv. 168.

lican in office — the Secretary of the Treasury — felt
himself helpless in face of the Government's inapti-
tude for war, and wrote to his closest intimates that
no one could " expect much improvement in the
manner of making it more efficient. I think that
there exists real incapacity in that respect, — an incapacity which must necessarily exhaust our resources
within a very short time." [1]

Fortunately for the Government the same slowness
of movement which counteracted its undertakings, affected equally its internal enemies in their hostility.
The New England extremists wished and expected
to act energetically against the war. Chief-Justice
Parsons quieted Pickering in the autumn of 1812 by
assuring him that the Massachusetts House of Representatives would act at its winter session ; [2] yet the
legislature met and adjourned without action. The
party waited for the spring election of 1813, which
was to give them control of New York. Their disappointment at the re-election of Governor Tompkins
was extreme, and the temptation to wait until the
national government should become bankrupt and
disgraced became irresistible. Another campaign was
likely to answer their purpose. While England grew
stronger every day, America grew weaker ; the
struggle became more and more unequal, the result
more and more certain ; and the hope of peaceably

[1] Gallatin to William Few, May 9, 1813 ; Gallatin MSS.
[2] Pickering to Lowell, Nov. 7, 1814; New England Federalism,
p. 404.

restoring the Federalist party to power diminished
the temptation to adopt measures of force.

Thus when the Thirteenth Congress met for its
extra session, May 24, the Government felt stronger
than on March 5, when the old Congress expired.
The elections were safely passed ; the peace negotiations might be considered as begun ; taxation was
no longer a matter of taste.   The majority liked
taxation as little in 1813 as they had liked it in 1812
or in 1801 ; but they could no longer dispute or even
discuss it.   Gallatin had gone, leaving the bills for
them to pass ; and Congress, which at any other
time would have rebelled, had no choice but to pass
them.

Once more Henry Clay was chosen Speaker, and
setting Cheves aside he placed John W. Eppes at the
head of the Ways and Means Committee.   The House
missed John Randolph, but gained John Forsyth of
Georgia, and Daniel Webster, — a new member from
New Hampshire, of the same age as Calhoun and
Lowndes, but five years younger than Clay.   Otherwise the members varied little from the usual type,
and showed more than their usual faculty for discussing topics no longer worth discussion.

President Madison's Message of May 25 challenged
no angry comment.   Its allusion to the Russian
mediation and the terms of peace had an accent of
self-excuse, as though he were anxious to convince
England of her true interests ; its allusion to France
contained the usual complaint of delays " so unrea-

sonably spun out ; " and its reference to the war and
the finances was rather cheerful than cheering.   Daring as Madison's policy had been, he commonly spoke
in tones hardly to be called bold ; and this Message
had the disadvantage, which under the circumstances
could not be called a fault, of addressing itself rather
to Europe and to enemies, than to a spirited and
united nation.   It had also the merit of directing
Congress strictly to necessary business ; and Congress acted on the direction.

Nothing less than necessity could at that moment
of early summer have induced the members of Congress to remain in session at all.   Stout as the majority might be in support of the war, the stoutest
were depressed and despondent.   They saw themselves disappointed in every hope and calculation on
which they had counted a year before.   Even their
unexpected naval glory was lost for the moment by
the victory of Broke's frigate the " Shannon " over
the " Chesapeake," June 1, as Congress began its
work.   Disaster after disaster, disgrace upon disgrace, had come and were every moment multiply-
ing.   Suffocated with heat, members were forced to
sit day by day in the half-finished Capitol, with a
Southern village about them, their nearest neighbor
a British fleet.   " Defeated and disgraced everywhere," said one of the stanchest war members describing the scene, " Congress was to impose the
burden of taxes on a divided people, who had been
taught by leaders of the war party to look upon a

tax-gatherer as a thief, if not to shoot him as a burg-
lar." [1] According to the same authority, " the country was at the lowest point of depression, where fear
is too apt to introduce despair." In this condition
of spirits, Gallatin's tax-bills were reported to the
House June 10, — measures such as the Republican
party had, till very lately, not conceived as within
the range of its possible legislation. They included
a direct tax of three million dollars ; taxes on salt,
licenses, spirits, carriages, auctions, sugar refineries ;
a stamp tax, and a complete machinery for the as-
sessment and collection of these odious and oppres-
sive imposts.

At the same moment, Daniel Webster began his
career in Congress by moving Resolutions which
caused a long and unprofitable debate on the conduct
of France and the character of the French repealing
Decree of April 28, 1811, — a debate that could have
no other result or object than to mortify and annoy
the President, who had been, like so many other
rulers, the victim of Napoleon's audacity. Pending
this debate, June 13, the President took to his bed
with a remittent fever, and for five weeks his recovery
was doubtful. Madison was still confined to his bed,
when, July 15, messengers from the lower Potomac
brought news that the British fleet, consisting of
eight or ten ships-of-the-line and frigates, was in the
river, sixty miles below, making its way up the difficult channel to Washington. A reasonable and well-

[1] Ingersoll's History, i. 120.

grounded fear took possession of the city.   July 21,
Serurier wrote to his Government: [1] —

" Every one is making ready to move. I know that
they are secretly packing up at the Departments. I have
as yet sent nothing away, in order not to show distrust of
the Government's power; but I have got ready my most
valuable papers, and from the moment the President shall
quit his residence, I shall follow where he goes, with my
principal portfolios in one of my carriages."

The British ships were approaching the city; the
sound of their guns was believed to be heard; and
the Government had little means of stopping them.
Every man prepared for volunteer duty; other work
was suspended. About three thousand militia and volunteers, among whom were all the Cabinet and many
members of Congress, were mustered, and marched to
Fort Washington, which was occupied by some six
hundred regular troops, with the Secretary of War at
their head; while the Secretary of the Navy took his
post on the 28-gun frigate " Adams " in the river
beneath, and the Secretary of State rode down the
river shore with a cavalry scouting party to recon-
noitre the British ships.[2]   July 15 and 16 the House
of Representatives ordered a Fast, and went into
secret session to consider modes of defence.

Unfortunately the motion for inquiry was made by
a Federalist. The majority, determined to make no

[1] Serurier to Bassano, July 21, 1813; Archives des Aff. Étr.
MSS.

[2] National Intelligencer, July 17, 20, 22, 1813.

admissions, referred the subject to the Military Committee, which reported the next day through its chairman, Troup of Georgia, that the preparation was "in every respect adequate to the emergence." When a majority could benefit only its enemies by telling the truth, history showed that honorable men often preferred to tell what was untrue. In this case the British ships made their soundings, and obtained whatever knowledge they sought; then left the river to visit other parts of the Bay, but never were so far distant that they might not, with energy and a fair wind, within four-and-twenty hours, have raided the defenceless village. They had but to choose their own time and path. Not a defensible fort or a picket-fence stood within ten miles of Washington, nor could a sufficient garrison be summoned in time for defence. Armstrong, Jones, and Monroe doubtless assured Congress that their means of defence were "in every respect adequate," but Congress took the responsibility on its own shoulders when it accepted their assurance.

Perhaps of all the incompetence shown in the war this example most exasperated patriotic citizens, because it was shared by every branch of the government. For six months the Administration and its friends had denounced Hull, Van Rensselaer, and Smyth for betraying the government, while the Clintonians and peace Democrats had denounced the President for imbecility; but in regard to the city of Washington the generals were not in question, for no generals were there, while the President was dangerously ill in bed. The Legislature and Cabinet were chiefly responsible for whatever should happen, — the more because their warning was ample, even if under such circumstances warning was needed. If Jefferson assumed as a matter of course that William Hull was to be shot and Stephen Van Rensselaer broken for their mistakes, Republicans might properly ask what punishment should be reserved for Armstrong, Jones, and Monroe of the Cabinet, Troup of Georgia, Sevier of Tennessee, Wright of Maryland, and other members of the Military Committees of the House and Senate for their neglect of the national capital.

The debate on Webster's Resolutions, and the report made in consequence by Monroe, July 12, tended to throw additional discredit on the Government. In no respect did Madison's Administration make an appearance less creditable than in its attitude toward Napoleon's Decrees, again and again solemnly asserted by it to have been repealed, in the face of proof that the assertion was unfounded. No Federalist rhetoric was necessary to make this mortification felt. Madison seldom expressed himself with more bitterness of temper than in regard to the Emperor's conduct, and with Monroe the subject drew forth recurrent outbursts of anger and disgust. His report tacitly admitted everything that the Federalists charged, except that the Administration had a secret engagement with France: it had deceived itself, but it had not wilfully deceived the public.

While the House was busied with these unpleasant subjects, the Senate took up the President's recent nominations. May 29, four names were sent to it for diplomatic appointments, — those of Albert Gallatin, J. Q. Adams, and James A. Bayard, to negotiate treaties of peace and commerce with Great Britain, and a treaty of commerce with Russia; that of Jonathan Russell to be Minister Plenipotentiary to Sweden. Rufus King immediately began opposition by moving three Resolutions of inquiry in regard to the nature of the Russian appointments and the authority under which the Treasury was to be administered in the Secretary's absence. The President replied, June 3, that the duties of the Secretary of the Treasury were discharged by the Secretary of the Navy under the provisions of the Act of 1792. The Senate, by a vote of twenty to fourteen, referred the matter to a committee consisting of Anderson of Tennessee, Rufus King, Brown of Louisiana, and Bledsoe of Kentucky. Anderson, the chairman, wrote to the President and went to see him on behalf of the committee, but received only the answer that the President declined to discuss the matter with them in their official character. The Senate then adopted a Resolution that the functions of Secretary of the Treasury and Envoy Extraordinary were incompatible. The Federalists obtained on this vote the support of Giles, Leib, and Samuel Smith, German of New York, and Gilman of New Hampshire, all of whom were disaffected Republicans; but even with

this aid they would have failed without the votes of
Anderson, Bledsoe, and the two Louisiana senators,
who joined the malcontents.

Madison was then slowly recovering strength, and
greatly harassed by anxieties. He would not sacrifice Gallatin to the Senate; he hoped that firm-
ness would carry the point,[1] and at worst he could
throw upon senators the charge of factious opposition. This he succeeded in doing. July 16 the
Senate committee, naturally expecting Madison to
suggest some arrangement, once more sought and
obtained a conference, — "when the President was
pleased to observe," said their report,[2] " that he was
sorry that the Senate had not taken the same view
of the subject which he had done; and that he regretted that the measure had been taken under circumstances which deprived him of the aid or advice
of the Senate. After the committee had remained
a reasonable time for the President to make any
other observations if he thought proper to do so,
and observing no disposition manifested by him to
enter into further remarks, the committee retired
without making any observations on the matter of
the Resolutions, or in reply to those made by the
President."

Finding itself thus defied, the Senate, without more
discussion, rejected Gallatin's nomination by eighteen votes to seventeen, Anderson and the two Lou-

[1] Madison to Gallatin, Aug. 2, 1813; Works, ii. 566.
[2] Executive Journal, ii. 388.

isiana senators still adhering to the hostile interest.
Adams and Bayard were then confirmed with little
opposition.

After the passage of many years, the propriety of
the decision may still be left open to debate. As far
as the Federalists were concerned, their votes contradicted their own precedents; and if they conceded,
as their precedents required, that the question was
not one of law but of expediency, they assumed responsibility in acting as final judges. The incompatibility asserted by them was a matter of dispute.
Two successive chief-justices had been sent as envoys abroad. No one could doubt that the Secretary of the Treasury, or any other member of the
Executive or Judicial departments, might be appointed to negotiate a treaty in Washington. Temporary
absence from Washington had never implied incompatibility. Every one knew that the Secretary of War
meant in person to conduct the war on the frontier.
No one could question the President's right to appoint acting secretaries. If convenience alone was
the point at issue, surely the President knew best
the demands of his own Executive departments, and
might be trusted with the responsibility which belonged to him. That he should fail to see, as soon
as the Senate could discover, an incompatibility that
would work only against himself, need not be taken
for granted by his own party, whatever might be the
case with the opposition.

On the other hand every one might admit that as

the country grew, Secretaries of the Treasury were likely to find work in their own Department that would effectually limit their capacity for foreign travel; and if the Senate thought that stage to be already reached, senators were right in insisting upon the appointment of a new secretary in Gallatin's place. Unfortunately for their argument, their power did not extend so far. Gallatin remained Secretary of the Treasury, and continued to negotiate as such, without paying attention to the Senate or its theories.

The Senate further weakened its position in acting on the nomination of Jonathan Russell as Minister to Sweden. The subject was referred, June 2, to a committee consisting of Senator Goldsborough of Maryland, together with Anderson and Rufus King. Jonathan Russell had made himself obnoxious to the peace party by eagerness shown, while he was in charge at London, to bring on the war. The committee not only entered on an investigation of his doings at Paris, but also introduced a Resolution declaring that any mission to Sweden at that time was inexpedient, and by order of the Senate asked a conference with the President. Monroe, angry at this conduct, declared privately that a faction in the Senate, counting on the death not only of President Madison but of Vice-President Gerry, and the election of Giles as President of the Senate, were scheming to usurp the Executive power.[1]

[1] Monroe to Jefferson, June 28, 1813; Adams's Gallatin, p 484.

In order to counteract their manœuvre, and also to relieve the President, who was then dangerously ill, Monroe took the ground that the Executive would not confer with a co-ordinate branch of government except through an agent, because his dignity would not allow him to meet a committee except by a committee of his own. Monroe thus expressed this somewhat unrepublican doctrine: "A committee of the Senate ought to confer with a committee of the President through a head of a Department, and not with the Chief Magistrate; for in the latter case a committee of that House is equal to the President."[1] As a necessary conclusion, Monroe's argument seemed to the Senate not beyond dispute; but they answered it, three days afterward, still less logically, by passing Goldsborough's Resolution that it was inexpedient at that time to send a Minister Plenipotentiary to Sweden.

Whatever might have been the case with Gallatin's rejection, no one could doubt that the vote on Russell's appointment was factious. When twenty-two senators, including Jeremiah Mason, Christopher Gore, Samuel Dana, Rufus King, and William B. Giles, declared that a minister resident in Sweden was inexpedient in the summer of 1813, they declared what every other well-informed man knew to be an error. If any American envoy was ever expedient, it was

[1] Monroe to Jefferson, June 28, 1813; Adams's Gallatin, p. 484. Cf. Madison to the Senate, July 6, 1813; Executive Journal, ii. 381.

an envoy to Sweden in 1813; for ·in Sweden at that moment all that was left of American commerce centred after being driven from England, and the political interests of Sweden were greatly involved with those of the United States. The error was the less to be denied, because, only six months afterward, the Senate admitted itself in the wrong, and approved the appointment of Russell.

These votes of the Senate made a deep impression. In time of peace and safety the Senate might show factiousness without necessarily exciting public anger, although at no time was the experiment quite safe; but at a moment like July, 1813, when public opinion tended toward a serious temper, factiousness was out of place, and was the more dangerous because President Madison, though never showing great power as a popular leader, had still a clear perception of the moment when to strike an enemy. He rarely failed to destroy when he struck. The time had come when the Republican party, with one voice, would be obliged to insist that party discipline must be restored; and this result was precipitated by the Senate's conduct in regard to the diplomatic nominations.

An illustration of the dangers into which the spirit of faction at that excited moment led the factious, was furnished by the legislature of Massachusetts, which met, May 26, and after listening to a long speech from Governor Strong arraigning the national government for its injustice to England and

partiality to France, referred the subject to committees which lost no time in reporting. One of these
reports, presented June 4 by Josiah Quincy of the
State Senate, closed with a Resolution that the Act
admitting Louisiana into the Union violated the Constitution, and that the Massachusetts senators in Congress should use their utmost endeavors to obtain its
repeal. Another report, by a joint committee, contained a remonstrance addressed to Congress against
the war, couched in terms of strong sectional hostility to the Southern States, and marked throughout
by a covert argument for disunion. A third report,
also by Josiah Quincy, on a naval victory lately
won by Captain James Lawrence of the " Hornet,"
contained a phrase even longer remembered than
Quincy's assertion that the Government could not be
kicked into a war. The Government had in fact been
kicked into the war, but Quincy was not the better
pleased. He reported that in order not to give offence to many of the good people of the Common-
wealth by appearing to encourage the continuance of
an unjust, unnecessary, and iniquitous war, the Massachusetts senate while admiring Lawrence's virtues
refrained from approving his acts, —

" And to the end that all misrepresentations on this
subject may be obviated, —

Resolved, as the sense of the Senate of Massachusetts,
that in a war like the present, waged without justifiable
cause, and prosecuted in a manner which indicates that
conquest and ambition are its real motives, it is not

becoming a moral and religious people to express any
approbation of military or naval exploits which are not
immediately connected with the defence of our sea-coast
and soil."

Such tactics, whether in or out of Congress, were
more dangerous to their authors than any blunders
of the Administration could ever be to the party in
power. If the nation should be successful in the
war, it might perhaps in good nature leave unpun-
ished the conduct of its malcontents; but if by
their means the nation should be conquered or
forced into a humiliating peace, the people would
never forget, and never forego revenge. Mere opposition to foreign war rarely injured public men,
except while the war-fever lasted. Many distinguished statesmen of Europe and America had been,
at one time or another, in opposition to some special
war, — as was the case with Talleyrand, Charles James
Fox, Lord Grey, Jefferson, and Madison; but opposition became unpardonable when it took a form
which could have no apparent object except national
ruin. The Federalists who held the ideas expressed
by the legislature of Massachusetts could explain or
defend their future course only by the conviction that
the inevitable and long-expected "crisis" was at
hand, which must end either in disunion or in reconstruction of the Union on new ground. As "a moral
and religious people," they separated from the common stock, and thenceforward, if the Union lasted,
could expect no pardon.

The extravagance of the Massachusetts Federalists was counterbalanced by the same national disasters which caused it. Nothing showed that the war was popular in any of the sea-board States; but the pressure of circumstances, little by little, obliged lukewarm and even hostile communities to support it. Virginia and the Southern States were drawn into relations toward the government which they had never intended to accept. Pennsylvania, Kentucky, and Tennessee submitted to exactions that would at any previous stage of their history have produced a revolution. Perhaps the strongest proof of change in popular prejudices was furnished by the taxes. Tax-bills which were supposed to have already overthrown one great political party, — bills which inflicted the evils so hotly and persistently denounced by Jefferson, Gallatin, and John Randolph in opposition, and which had been long delayed by fear of their popular effect, — were passed by Congress quickly, by decided votes, and with less debate than was given to the discussion whether the President had or had not told all he knew about Bassano's Decree of April 28, 1811. From the time they were approved by the President, in July and August, 1813, to the time of their repeal, neither the President nor his party was troubled by popular discontent on account of the passage of these Acts. They were accepted as a necessary part of the national system, and of a war-policy.

The most curious symptom, and the one which

most perplexed the Federalists, was that this popular movement of concentration acted in direct resistance to the movement of events. In every respect as the Federalists looked back at the past twelve years their prophecies had come true. The Republican party, they argued, had proved itself incompetent, and had admitted the failure of its principles; it had been forced to abandon them in practice, to replace the government where the Federalists had put it, and to adopt all the Federalists' methods; and even then the party failed. Equally imbecile in peace and war, the democratic movement had ended in such disgrace and helplessness as few governments had ever outlived, and such as no nation with a near and powerful neighbor could have survived. In 1813 the evidence of downfall had become patent. The government was ruined in credit and character; bankrupt, broken, and powerless, it continued to exist merely because of habit, and must succumb to the first shock. All this the Federalists had long foreseen. Fisher Ames in the press, scores of clergymen in the pulpit, numberless politicians in Congress, had made no other use of their leisure than to point out, step by step, every succeeding stage in the coming decline. The catastrophe was no longer far away, it was actually about them, — they touched and felt it at every moment of their lives. Society held itself together merely because it knew not what else to do.

Under circumstances following each other in necessity so stringent, no Federalist could doubt that society would pursue the predicted course; but it did not. Illogical and perverse, society persisted in extending itself in lines which ran into chaos. The threatened " crisis " had arrived, wanting no characteristic of those so long foretold; but society made no effort to save itself. A vaster ruin and still more terrible retribution lay beyond. The Federalists were greatly and naturally perplexed at discovering the silent under-current which tended to grow in strength precisely as it encountered most resistance from events. They tried to explain the phenomenon in their own way,— the clergy according to religious conceptions, the politicians according to their ideas of popular character. The political theory was the more plausible and less respectable. A. C. Hanson, the extreme Maryland Federalist, mobbed and nearly killed in Baltimore in June, 1812, only to be elected to Congress in November, thought that the national movement of 1813 was due to military glory. Hanson wrote to Pickering on the subject, in the autumn : [1] —

" The war is becoming more popular every day in this State [Maryland]. Our successes, and the weak manner in which it is conducted by the enemy make it so. . . . It would seem that after a while, unless the British can gather the sense and courage to strike some severe blows, the war by its own generative powers will create the means for its support. The vanity of a people can-

[1] Hanson to Pickering, Oct. 16, 1813; Pickering MSS.

not bear these brilliant naval victories, and there is no
passion to which the rulers of a people can address themselves with greater effect. Even in my district the active opposers of the war are falling off every day, and
unless we shortly meet with some reverses, the Administration will shortly find more friends than enemies in this
State by a great deal. . . . The impression is becoming
universal that the enemy cannot harm us if he would.
A few hard blows struck in the right place would be of
great service to the country."

A people that could feel its vanity flattered by such
glories as the war gave in 1813 must have felt the
want of flattery to an unusual degree. The idea was
extravagant. Not so much the glories as the dis-
graces of the war roused public sympathy; not so
much the love of victory as the ignominy of defeat,
and the grinding necessity of supporting government
at any cost of private judgment. At such a moment any success was keenly felt, and covered every
failure. The slow conviction that come what would
the nation must be preserved, brought one man after
another into support of the war, until the Federalists
found their feet in a quicksand. The " crisis " produced the opposite effect to that which Burke's phi-
losophy predicted.

Congress finished its work, and August 2 adjourned. Immediately afterward the President went
to Montpelier to recover his strength in the air of
the Blue Ridge. The session had not been unsatisfactory, for although the Senate refused to impose
an embargo, wanted by the President in order to cut

off illegitimate trade with England's dependencies, and although the same body put its negative on the appointments of Gallatin and Jonathan Russell, yet Congress passed the tax-bills, authorized another loan of seven and a half millions, and made the business of trading under a British license a penal offence. The operations of war alone remained to burden the President's mind.

CHAPTER IV.

The fall of Detroit and Chicago in August, 1812, threw the American frontier back to the line of the Wabash and the Maumee, and threatened to throw it still farther back to the Indian boundary itself. The Miami or Maumee River was defended by Fort Wayne; the Wabash had no other defence than the little fort or blockhouse which Harrison built during the Tippecanoe campaign, and named after himself. Fort Harrison stood near the later city of Terre Haute, close to the border of Illinois; Fort Wayne stood within twenty miles of the Ohio border. The width of Indiana lay between the two.

Had Brock been able, after the capture of Detroit, to lead his little army into Ohio, he might have cleared not only the Maumee River, but the whole western end of Lake Erie from American possession. Recalled in haste to defend Niagara, Brock left only two or three companies of troops as garrison at Detroit and Malden. The Indians could do little without the aid of regular forces, but they tried to carry both Fort Wayne and Fort Harrison by stratagem. The attacks were made almost simultaneously a few days after September 1, and not without skill.

In the case of Fort Harrison the Indians were nearly
successful, not so much in fighting as in burning it.
With great difficulty its young captain, Zachary Taylor, of the Seventh Infantry, succeeded in saving his
post. Fort Wayne was held by Captain James Rhea
of the First Infantry until reinforcements arrived,
September 12. Except the usual massacres of scattered families, the Indians accomplished nothing.

Upon the State of Ohio, with its quarter of a million
inhabitants, and of Kentucky with four hundred
thousand, fell the immediate burden of defending the
border between the Ohio and the Lakes. Governor
William Henry Harrison of the Indiana Territory
leaving Vincennes June 19, the day after the declaration of war, was at Cincinnati when threatening news
began to arrive from Detroit. Harrison had military
knowledge and instincts. He saw that after the capture of Mackinaw Detroit must fall, and that Hull
could save himself only by evacuating it.[1] Harrison's
ambition, which had drawn him to Tippecanoe, drew
him also to lead the new crusade for the relief or
recovery of Detroit. He went to Kentucky at the
invitation of Governor Scott, and under the patronage of Scott and Henry Clay he took the direction
of military affairs. August 24 news reached Kentucky that Hull was shut in Detroit, and must surrender unless immediately relieved.[2] The Governor
of Kentucky at once summoned what was then called

[1] Harrison to Eustis, Aug. 10, 1812 ; Dawson, p. 273.
[2] Harrison to Eustis, Aug. 28, 1812 ; Dawson, p. 283.

a *caucus*, composed of himself, his successor elect
Governor Shelby, Henry Clay, Justice Todd of the
United States Supreme Court, Major-General Hopkins of the Kentucky militia, various Congressmen,
judges, and other citizens,[1] whose whole authority
was needed to warrant giving to Harrison, who was
not a citizen of Kentucky, the commission of major-
general and the command of the expedition to Detroit.   By general acclamation, and on the warm
assurances of universal popular approval, the measure was taken ; and Harrison started at once for
Cincinnati and Detroit to organize the campaign.
The news of Hull's surrender met him as he left
Frankfort.

By this combination of skill and accident, Harrison
reached the object of his ambition, — the conduct of
war on a scale equal to his faith in his own powers ; but
the torrent of Western enthusiasm swept him forward
faster than his secret judgment approved.   Appointed
by caucus the general of volunteers, he could keep
his position only by keeping his popularity.   Without
deciding precisely where to march, or what military
object to pursue, he talked and acted on the idea that
he should recover Detroit by a *coup-de-main*.[2]   He
knew that the idea was baseless as a practical plan,
and futile as a military measure ; but nothing less
would satisfy the enthusiasm of his Kentucky volunteers, and the national government almost com-

[1] Harrison to Eustis, Aug 28, 1812 ; Dawson, p. 283.
[2] Dawson, p. 296.

pelled him to pretend what he did not at heart believe possible.

The confusion thus created was troublesome. First, Harrison insisted on commanding the troops marching to relieve Fort Wayne, and obliged the good-natured General Winchester, who outranked him, to yield the point.[1] Then after a forced march with the Kentuckians down the St. Mary's River, having relieved Fort Wayne, Harrison was obliged, September 19, to surrender the command to Winchester, who arrived with orders from the Secretary of War to take general charge of the northwestern army. Harrison then left Fort Wayne for Piqua. Meanwhile the President and Eustis, learning what had been done in Kentucky, September 17, after much debate decided to give to Harrison the commission of brigadier-general, with the command of the northwestern army, to consist of ten thousand men, with unlimited means and no orders except to retake Detroit.[2] Brigadier-General Winchester, who was already at Fort Wayne, was given the option of serving under Harrison, or of joining the army at Niagara.

These new orders reached Harrison September 25 at Piqua. Harrison then resumed command, and two days afterward, September 27, wrote to the secretary, announcing his plan for the autumn campaign. Three columns of troops, from widely distant quar-

[1] Winchester to the "National Intelligencer," Sept. 16, 1816.
[2] Eustis to Harrison, Sept. 17, 1812 ; Dawson, p. 299. Eustis to Governor Shelby, Sept. 17, 1812. McAffee, p. 117.

ters, were to move to the Maumee Rapids, — the
right column, consisting of Virginia and Pennsylvania troops, by way of the Sandusky River; the
centre column, of twelve hundred Ohio militia, by
Hull's road ; the left column, consisting of four
Kentucky regiments and the Seventeenth U. S. Infantry, was to descend the Auglaize River to Fort
Defiance on the Maumee, and thence to fall down
that river to the point of junction with the two
other columns.

Compared with Hull's resources, Harrison's were
immense ; and that he had no serious enemy to fear
was evident from his dividing the army into three
columns, which marched by lines far beyond supporting distance of each other. At the same time he
ordered Major-General Hopkins of the Kentucky
militia to march with two thousand men up the
Wabash into the Indian country, and to destroy the
Indian settlements on the Wabash and Illinois rivers.
Had a British force been opposed to the Americans,
its general would have had little difficulty in destroying some one of these four isolated columns, and
driving Harrison back to central Ohio ; but only
bands of Indians, not exceeding five hundred at most,
were to be feared before the army should cross the
Maumee, and little anxiety existed on account of
enemies, unless for the safety of Fort Wayne.

Harrison's anxieties bore a different character.
September 23 he wrote to the Secretary of War :
"If the fall should be very dry, I will take Detroit

before the winter sets in; but if we should have much
rain, it will be necessary to wait at the rapids until
the Miami of the Lakes is sufficiently frozen to bear
the army and its baggage." [1] The promise was rash.
However dry the season might be, the task of marching an army with siege-artillery past Malden to Detroit, and of keeping it supplied from a base two hundred miles distant, with the British commanding the
Lake, was one which Harrison had too much sense
to attempt. Nothing but disaster could have resulted
from it, even if Detroit had been taken. In the
actual condition of that territory, no army could be
maintained beyond the Maumee River without con-
trolling the Lake. Perhaps Harrison was fortunate
that constant rains throughout the month of October
brought the army to a halt long before it reached the
Maumee. Only the left division of five Kentucky
regiments succeeded in getting to the river, and
camped in the neighborhood of old Fort Defiance,
waiting for the other columns to reach the rapids.
There the Kentuckians remained, under the command
of General Winchester, without food, clothing, or
sufficient shelter, in a state of increasing discontent
and threatening mutiny, till the year closed.

Within a month after assuming command Harrison
found himself helpless either to advance or to retreat,
or to remain in any fixed position. The supplies required for ten thousand troops could not be sent
forward by any means then known. October 22 the

[1] Dawson, p. 312.

left column, consisting of the Kentucky regiments
and some regulars, was at Defiance on the Maumee;
the central column of a thousand Ohio troops under
General Tupper was on Hull's road, a hundred miles
from the Maumee, unable to march beyond Urbana,
where its supplies were collecting; the right column
of Pennsylvanians and Virginians was still farther
from the front, slowly approaching the Sandusky
River from the southeast, but far out of reach. General Hopkins's expedition up the Wabash ended in
failure, his troops becoming a mere mob, and at last
disbanding, leaving their general to follow them home.
Harrison himself was riding indefatigably through the
mud, from one end to the other of his vast concave
line, — now at Defiance, making speeches to pacify
Winchester's Kentuckians; then at Piqua and Urbana with the Ohioans; soon a hundred miles away
at the river Huron, east of Sandusky; next at Woos-
ter, Delaware, or Franklinton, afterward Columbus,
in the centre of Ohio, looking for his right wing;
but always searching for a passable ridge of dry
land, on which his supplies could go forward to the
Maumee Rapids. The result of his search was given
in a letter of October 22, from Franklinton, to the
Secretary of War: —

"I am not able to fix any period for the advance of
the troops to Detroit. It is pretty evident that it cannot
be done upon proper principles until the frost shall become so severe as to enable us to use the rivers and the
margin of the Lake for transportation of the baggage and

artillery upon the ice. To get them forward through a swampy wilderness of near two hundred miles, in wagons or on packhorses which are to carry their own provisions, is absolutely impossible."

The obstacle which brought Harrison's autumn campaign to this sudden close was the vast swamp that extended from the Sandusky River on his right to the Auglaize River on his left, and for the moment barred the passage of his necessary supplies as effectually as though it had been the Andes. Hull had crossed it, cutting a road as he went, and no one had then appreciated his effort ; but he had marched with a small force in May and June. Harrison tried to transport supplies, heavy guns, military stores, and all the material for an army of ten thousand men on a long campaign, as the autumn rains set in. On the extreme right, with great effort and expense, a considerable quantity of rations was accumulated on the Sandusky River, to be sent to the Maumee Rapids whenever the frosts should harden the swamps. On the extreme left, desperate efforts were made to carry supplies to Winchester's army at Defiance by way of the Auglaize and St. Mary's rivers. Hull's road was impassable, and for that reason the column of Ohio troops and their supplies were stopped in the neighborhood of Urbana.

Throughout the months of October and November Harrison's army stood still, scattered over the State of Ohio, while wagons and packhorses wallowed in mud toward the Maumee Rapids. None arrived.

Sometimes the wagons were abandoned in the mud ; sometimes the packhorses broke down ; sometimes the rivers were too low for boats ; then they froze and stopped water-transport. Universal confusion, want of oversight and organization, added to physical diffi- culties, gave play to laziness, incapacity, and dishon- esty. No bills of lading were used ; no accounts were kept with the wagoners ; and the teams were valued so high, on coming into service, that the owners were willing to destroy them for the price to be received.[1] The waste of government funds was appalling, for nothing short of a million rations at the Maumee Rapids could serve Harrison's objects, and after two months of effort not a ration had been carried with- in fifty miles of the spot. In Winchester's camp at Defiance the men were always on half rations, except when they had none at all. During the greater part of December they had no flour, but lived on poor beef and hickory roots. Typhus swept them away by scores ; their numbers were reduced to about one thousand. The exact force which Harrison had in the field was matter of conjecture, for he sent no return of any description to the adjutant-general's office.[2] The Government gave him *carte blanche*, and he used it.[3] Chaos and misconduct reigned in every department, while he, floundering through the

[1] McAffee, p. 184.

[2] Armstrong to Harrison, April 4, 1813 ; Armstrong's Notices, i. 245.

[3] Harrison to Secretary of War, Jan. 4, 1813 ; Dawson, p. 337.

mud along his line of two hundred miles front, sought in vain for a road.

For the train of errors and disasters in the northwest Secretary Eustis was chiefly responsible, and his resignation, Dec. 3, 1812, left the campaign in this hopeless condition. From Dec. 3, 1812, until Jan. 13, 1813, Monroe acted as Secretary of War; and to him Harrison next wrote from Delaware, December 12, a letter which not only disheartened the Government, but was calculated to create a prejudice against the writer in the mind of any Secretary of War who was not invincibly prejudiced in his favor.[1]

"If there were not some important political reason," said Harrison, "urging the recovery of the Michigan Territory and the capture of Malden as soon as those objects can possibly be effected, and that to accomplish them a few weeks sooner expense was to be disregarded, I should not hesitate to say that if a small proportion of the sums which will be expended in the quartermaster's department in the active prosecution of the campaign during the winter was devoted to obtaining the command of Lake Erie, the wishes of the Government, in their utmost extent, could be accomplished without difficulty in the months of April and May. Malden, Detroit, and Mackinaw would fall in rapid succession. On the contrary, all that I can certainly promise to accomplish during the winter, unless the strait should afford us a passage on the ice, is to recover Detroit. I must further observe that no military man would think of retaining Detroit, Malden being in possession of the enemy, unless his army

[1] Dawson, p. 333. Armstrong's Notices, i. 63, 86.

was at least twice as strong as the disposable force of the enemy. An army advancing to Detroit along a line of operation passing so near the principal force of the enemy as to allow them access to it whenever they think proper, must be covered by another army more considerable than the disposable force of the enemy. I mention this circumstance to show that the attack ought not to be directed against Detroit, but against Malden ; and that it depends upon the ice affording a safe passage across the strait, whether I shall be able to proceed in this way or not. Detroit is not tenable. Were I to take it without having it in my power to occupy the opposite shore, I should be under the necessity of hiding the army in the adjacent swamp to preserve it from the effects of the shot and shells which the enemy would throw with impunity from the opposite shore. This result is so obvious to every man who has the least military information, that it appears to me as extraordinary as any other part of General Hull's conduct that he should choose to defend Detroit rather than attack Malden."

Hull could have asked no better apology for his surrender. Harrison did not know that the insubordination and refusal of the Ohio colonels to evacuate Detroit had forced Hull to remain there ; but that Detroit was not tenable came at last to the surface as a self-evident truth of the campaign, — which Hull had always seen, and which Harrison himself announced almost as clearly in August as in December, but which he ignored in the interval.

" If it should be asked," he continued, " why these statements were not made sooner, — I answer that although I was always sensible that there were great difficulties to be encountered in the accomplishment of the wishes of the President in relation to the recovery of Detroit and the conquest of the adjacent part of Upper Canada in the manner proposed, I did not make sufficient allowance for the imbecility and inexperience of the public agents and the villany of the contractors. I am still, however, very far from believing that the original plan is impracticable. I believe on the contrary that it can be effected."

The excuse did not satisfy the Cabinet, who thought they saw that Harrison wished to throw upon Government the responsibility for a military failure fatal to himself. Perhaps a simpler motive guided Harrison, who from the first never had known precisely what to do, or had seen any clear path to success. He wrote, January 4, from Franklinton, —

" When I was directed to take the command in the latter end of September, I thought it possible by great exertions to effect the objects of the campaign before the setting in of winter. . . The experience of a few days was sufficient to convince me that the supplies of provisions could not be procured for our autumnal advance; and even if this difficulty was removed, another of equal magnitude existed in the want of artillery. There remained then no alternative but to prepare for a winter campaign."

According to this account he had seen early in October that advance was impossible, yet he wasted millions of money and many of his best troops in attempting it. Winter had come, and he was pledged to a winter campaign as impracticable as the autumn campaign had proved to be. Without the control of the Lake, any army beyond the Maumee must starve or surrender. The government had already paid a vast price in money and men in order to obtain this knowledge ; yet Harrison proposed a winter campaign, with full persuasion of its uselessness.

December 20 he sent orders [1] to Winchester to descend the Maumee River from Defiance to the rapids, there to prepare sleds for an expedition against Malden, to be made by a choice detachment when the whole army should concentrate at the rapids. Early in January, the ground being at last frozen, provisions in large quantities were hurried to the Maumee River. Artillery was sent forward. The Pennsylvania and Virginia brigades moved to the Sandusky River, making an effective force of fifteen hundred men at that point. The whole effective force on the frontier amounted to six thousand three hundred infantry.[2] Harrison intended to move his headquarters forward from the Sandusky, and to reach the Maumee Rapids January 20, to which point he supposed General Winchester already in motion from Defiance.[3]

This was the situation January 12 ; and although

[1] Dawson, p. 454.

[2] Harrison to the Secretary of War, Jan. 4, 1813 ; Dawson, p. 339.

[3] Harrison to the Secretary of War, Jan. 4, 1813 ; Dawson, p. 339.

Harrison hinted in his reports of January 4 and 8
that his winter campaign would probably fail,[1] he
showed the intention of advancing at least as far
as the strait opposite Malden, about thirty-five miles
beyond the Maumee. This he might venture without
much danger; and if he reached that point, supposing
the straits to be frozen, the enemy to show little sign
of resistance, and the weather to favor, he might
attack Malden. Hull had been expected to take
Malden with twelve or fourteen hundred men, with
an open river behind him, a British fleet on his flank,
fifty miles of road to cover, and supplies for only a
few days at Detroit; but Harrison with six thousand
men, the river frozen and the British fleet frozen in
it, a secure base, with a million rations close in his
rear, and no Isaac Brock in his front, still spoke
with extreme doubt of his prospects, and said that
" most of the well-informed men who knew the character of the country "[2] expected a suspension of
operations for the winter.

Aware that from a military point of view no land-
campaign could, except by accident, effect any result
proportionate to its cost, Harrison had placed himself
at the head of a popular movement so strong that
he would have met the fate of Hull and Alexander
Smyth, had he not made at least a demonstration

[1] Harrison to the Secretary of War, Jan. 4, 1813 ; Dawson, p. 339.

[2] Harrison to the Secretary of War, Jan. 8, 1813 ; Dawson, p. 339.

against an enemy whose face he had not yet seen. Forced by his own pledges and the public discontent to enter on an unmilitary campaign, he was anxious to risk as little as possible where he could hardly expect to gain anything; and he would probably have contented himself with his first scheme of a *coup-de-main* against Malden or Detroit, without attempting to hold either place, had not his subordinate, General Winchester, rescued him from an awkward position by a blunder that relieved Harrison of further responsibility.

Brigadier-General Winchester was a planter of Tennessee, sixty-one years old, and formerly an officer in the Revolutionary War. Though outranking Harrison, he had allowed himself to be set aside by what he thought intrigue,[1] and consented to conduct the left wing of the force under Harrison's command. Winchester was not a favorite with his Kentucky militia-men, who had no choice in electing him to their command. Their term of service was to expire in February; they had been imprisoned since September in a wilderness at Defiance, — hungry, cold, sick, and mutinous, able to find no enemy willing to fight them, and disgusted with idleness. No sooner was the ground frozen and the general movement of concentration possible, than Winchester's command by common consent, under Harrison's or-

[1] Winchester to the "National Intelligencer," Sept. 16, 1817; Major Eves's Statement; Armstrong's Notices, i. 203. Cf. Dawson, p. 443.

ders, broke up their camp near Defiance and marched
to the rapids, where Hull's road crossed the Maumee.
There they arrived January 10, as Harrison expected.
They fortified themselves on the north bank, and
waited for the arrival of Harrison, who intended to
join them January 20.

Winchester's force included three regiments of
Kentucky militia, numbering nine hundred effectives,[1] and the Seventeenth United States Infantry,
numbering three hundred men, also Kentuckians.
Altogether he had under his command at the rapids
about thirteen hundred men,[2] — a force barely sufficient to hold the exposed position it had taken on
the north bank of the river. The three Kentucky
militia regiments were soon to go home. The other
columns were not yet within supporting distance. If
Colonel Proctor, who commanded at Malden, were
capable of imitating Brock's enterprise, he would
hardly throw away an opportunity, which might
never recur, to strike a blow at the Kentuckians,
and by defeating them to drive Harrison's army behind the Sandusky River. Every military motive
warned Winchester not to divide, detach, or ex-
pose his troops without caution. He was himself
a detachment, and he had no support nearer than
the Sandusky.

While the troops were busily engaged in building a
store-house and throwing up log-works in an injudi-

[1] Winchester's Statement; Armstrong's Notices, i. 197.
[2] McAffee, p. 230.

cious and untenable position,[1] two Frenchmen came
into camp, begging protection for the inhabitants of
Frenchtown on the river Raisin, thirty miles in front,
and within the British lines. Thirty-three families,
or about one hundred and fifty persons, were resident
at Frenchtown, and the place was held by a few Canadian militia, supposed to consist of two companies,
with about as many Indians, — in all, some three
hundred men.[2] This force might easily be destroyed,
and the loss to the British would be serious. Winchester's troops became eager to dash at them. A
council of war decided, January 16, without a voice
in remonstrance, that the movement should be made.
The most ardent supporter of the adventure was Col.
John Allen of the Kentucky Rifle regiment; but no
one offered opposition, and Winchester agreed to the
council's opinion.[3]

The next morning, Jan. 17, 1813, Col. William
Lewis, of the Fifth Kentucky militia, started for the
river Raisin, with four hundred and fifty men.[4] A
few hours afterward he was followed by Colonel
Allen with one hundred and ten men. No reports
told what regiments were taken, or where they were
at any moment stationed; but Lewis and Allen probably led twelve companies, drawn from four Kentucky regiments, — the Seventeenth United States

---

[1] McAffee, p. 237.

[2] Winchester's Statement; Armstrong's Notices, i. 199.

[3] Winchester to the " National Intelligencer," Dec. 13, 1817.

[4] Winchester to the " National Intelligencer," Dec. 13, 1817.

Infantry, recruited in Kentucky, commanded by Col. Samuel Wells; the Kentucky Rifles, Col. John Allen; the First Kentucky Infantry; and Colonel Lewis's regiment, the Fifth Kentucky Infantry, — in all, six hundred and sixty men, representing the flower of Kentucky.

They marched on the ice, along the shore of Maumee Bay and Lake Erie, until nightfall, when they camped, and at two o'clock the next afternoon, January 18, reached without meeting resistance the houses on the south bank of the river Raisin. The north bank was occupied, according to British authority,[1] by fifty Canadian militia and two hundred Indians. The British force opened fire with a three-pound howitzer. The action began at three o'clock and lasted till dark, when the enemy after an obstinate resistance was driven about two miles into the woods with inconsiderable loss.[2] The action was sharp, and cost the Americans not less than twelve killed and fifty-five wounded, reducing their effective number to six hundred.

Colonel Lewis had orders to take possession of Frenchtown, and hold it. He reported his success to General Winchester at the rapids, and remained at Frenchtown waiting further orders. Winchester became then aware that the situation was hazardous. Six hundred men were with him in a half-fortified camp on the north bank of the Maumee; six hun-

---

[1] James, i. 185; Richardson, p. 74.

[2] Richardson, p. 75.

dred more were thirty miles in advance, at the Raisin
River; while fully two thousand — or, according to
Harrison's estimate, four thousand [1] — enemies held
two fortresses only eighteen miles beyond the Raisin.
The Kentuckians at the Maumee, equally aware of
their comrades' peril, insisted on going to their aid.
Winchester promptly started on the evening of January 19, and arrived at Frenchtown the next morning.   Colonel Wells's Seventeenth United States
Infantry, two hundred and fifty men, followed, arriving at Frenchtown in the evening.[2]

Winchester, before leaving the Maumee Rapids,
sent a despatch to Harrison with a report of the
battle of the 18th, which met Harrison on the road
hurrying to the Maumee Rapids.   The next morning, January 20, Harrison arrived at the camp on
the Maumee, and found there about three hundred
Kentucky troops,[3] the remainder being all with Winchester at the river Raisin.   Probably Harrison, whose
own caution was great, felt the peril of Winchester's
situation,[4] but he sent his inspector-general, Captain
Hart, forward with orders to Winchester " to hold the
ground we had got at any rate," [5] while he wrote to
the Secretary of War : —

[1] Winchester's Statement; Armstrong's Notices, i. 198.

[2] Winchester to the "National Intelligencer," Dec. 17, 1817.

[3] Harrison to the Secretary of War, Jan. 26, 1813; Official
Letters, p. 125.

[4] Harrison to Governor Meigs, Jan. 19, 1813; "National Intelligencer," Feb. 11, 1813.

[5] McAffee, p. 210 ; Armstrong's Notices, i. 200.

" Upon my way to this place [Maumee Rapids] last evening, I received the letter from the General [Winchester] of which the enclosed is a copy, informing me of the complete success of the enterprise in the defeat of the enemy and taking the stores they had collected. The detachment under Colonel Lewis remain at the river Raisin, and General Winchester very properly marched yesterday with two hundred and fifty men to reinforce him and take the command. . . . It is absolutely necessary to maintain the position at the river Raisin, and I am assembling the troops as fast as possible for the purpose." [1]

Harrison added that his only fear was lest Winchester should be overpowered. He waited at the Maumee Rapids two days, until at noon, January 22, a messenger arrived with disastrous tidings from the front.

Winchester afterward told the story of his own proceedings with so much candor that his narrative became a necessary part of any explanation of his disaster : —

" Suspecting that Proctor would make an attempt to avenge this stroke, and knowing that our wounded men could not be removed, I hastened to reinforce Colonel Lewis with Wells's regiment, two hundred and fifty men ; and set out myself to join him, and arrived on the morning of the 20th. The town, lying on the north side of the river, was picketed on three sides, the longest facing the north, and making the front. Within these pickets Colonel Lewis's corps was found. Not thinking the posi-

---

[1] Harrison to the Secretary of War, Feb. [Jan.] 20, 1813; MSS. War Department Archives.

tion eligible, nor the pickets a sufficient defence against artillery, I would have retreated but for the wounded, of whom there were fifty-five ; but having no sufficient means for transporting these, and being equally destitute of those necessary for fortifying strongly, I issued an order for putting the place in the best condition for defence that might be practicable, intending to construct some new works as soon as the means for getting out timber might be had.   On the evening of the 20th Wells arrived, and was directed to encamp on the right, in an open field, immediately without the picketing.   On the 21st a patrol as far as Brownstown [opposite Malden] was sent out, and returned without seeing anything of an enemy.   On the same day a man from Malden came in who reported that the enemy were preparing to attack us ; but knowing nothing of the kind or extent of the preparation made or making, what he brought was thought to be only conjecture and such as led to a belief that it would be some days before Proctor would be ready to do anything. . . . Neither night-patrol nor night-pickets were ordered by me, from a belief that both were matters of routine and in constant use. . . . Not to discommode the wounded men, . . . I took quarters for myself and suite in a house on the southern bank, directly fronting the troops and only separated from them by the river, then firmly frozen, and but between eighty and a hundred yards wide."

The only educated officer under Harrison's command was Major E. D. Wood of the Engineers, one of the early graduates of West Point, and an officer of high promise.   He was not with Winchester's division, but with the right wing on the Sandusky, and arrived at the Maumee Rapids some ten days afterward, where he built Fort Meigs, in February. During the campaign he kept a diary, and his criticisms of Winchester, Lewis, Allen, and their command were quoted with approval by the Kentucky historian,[1] as well as by Harrison's biographer : [2] —

" The troops were permitted to select, each for himself, such quarters on the west side of the river as might please him best, whilst the general . . . took his quarters on the east side, — not the least regard being paid to defence, order, regularity, or system, in the posting of the different corps. . . . With only one third or one fourth of the force destined for that service ; destitute of artillery, of engineers, of men who had ever seen or heard the least of an enemy ; and with but a very inadequate supply of ammunition, — how he ever could have entertained the most distant hope of success, or what right he had to presume to claim it, is to me one of the strangest things in the world. . . . Winchester was destitute of every means of supporting his corps long at the river Raisin ; was in the very jaws of the enemy, and beyond the reach of succor. He who fights with such flimsy pretensions to victory will always be beaten, and eternally ought to be."

Defeat under such conditions was disgraceful enough ; but defeat by Colonel Proctor was one of the worst misfortunes that happened to an American general. The Prince Regent took occasion, at the close of the war, to express his official opinion of this officer, then Major-General Proctor, in language

[1] McAffee, p. 233.   [2] Dawson, p. 364.

of unusual severity.[1] Yet Proctor's first movements
at the Raisin River showed no apparent sign of his
being "so extremèly wanting in professional knowledge, and deficient in those active, energetic qualities
which must be required of every officer," as his later
career, in the Prince Regent's opinion, proved him
to be. He had opposed Brock's bold movement on
Detroit ; but he did not hesitate to make a somewhat
similar movement himself. January 21 he marched
with artillery across the river on the ice, to Brownstown opposite Malden, in full view of any American
patrol in the neighborhood. His force consisted of
six hundred whites, all told,[2] besides either four
hundred and fifty, six hundred or eight hundred
Indians, under the chief Round Head, Tecumthe being absent collecting reinforcements on the Wabash.[3]
This large body of more than a thousand men,
without an attempt at concealment, crossed to
Brownstown and marched twelve miles, January 21,
camping at night within five miles of Frenchtown.[4]
If the British historian James was correct, they
numbered eleven hundred and eighty men, of whom
five hundred and thirty were white, and the rest
Indians ;[5] but the official return reported the whites,

[1] Life of Sir George Prevost ; App. xxv. p. 74.   Christie,
ii. 115.

[2] Return of the whole of the troops engaged at Frenchtown,
Jan. 22, 1813 ; MSS. Canadian Archives, c. 678, p. 18.

[3] Christie, ii. 69 ; James, i. 186 ; Richardson, p. 75.

[4] Proctor's Report of Jan. 25, 1813 ; James, i. 418.

[5] James, i. 185, 186.

including every person present, at five hundred and
ninety-seven men. Two hours before dawn, January 22, they again advanced, and before day-break
approached within musket-shot of the picket-fence,
and half-formed their line, before an alarm was
given.

Had Proctor dashed at once on the defenceless
Seventeenth regiment and the fence that covered the
militia, he would probably have captured the whole
without loss ; but he preferred to depend on his
three-pound guns, which gave the Kentuckians opportunity to use their rifles. In such fighting the
Americans had much the advantage, especially as
British regulars were opposite them. Within an
hour the Forty-first regiment lost fifteen killed and
ninety-eight wounded, and of the entire body óf six
hundred British troops not less than twenty-four
were killed and one hundred and sixty-one wounded.[1]
Their three-pound guns were abandoned, so murderous were the Kentucky rifles.[2] Had all the American troops been under cover, the battle would have
been theirs ; but Wells's Seventeenth regiment was
a hundred yards away, on open ground outside the
picket-fence on the right, where it was flanked by
the Canadian militia and Indians and driven back toward the river, until Allen's Rifle regiment went out
to help it. Gradually forced toward the rear, across
the river, this part of the line was at last struck

[1] Return, etc.; MSS. Canadian Archives, c. 648, p. 18.
[2] Richardson, p. 76.

with a panic and fled, carrying with it Winchester
himself, Colonel Allen, and Colonel Lewis; while six
hundred Indians were in hot pursuit, or already in
advance of them.

In the deep snow escape was impossible. Nearly
a hundred Kentuckians fell almost side by side, and
were scalped. Among these was Colonel Allen.
General Winchester and Colonel Lewis were so fortunate as to fall into the hands of the chief Round
Head, who first stripped them and then took them
to Proctor, who had for the time withdrawn his
forces and ceased firing. By Proctor's advice, General Winchester sent an order to the men within
the picket-fence to surrender.

By eight o'clock all resistance had ceased except
from three hundred and eighty-four Kentuckians
who remained within the picket-fence, under the
command of Major Madison of the Rifle regiment.
Surrounded by a thousand enemies, they had no
chance of escape. Their ammunition was nearly
exhausted; retreat was impossible; they could choose
only between surrender and massacre, and they surrendered.[1] The British officers looked at them with
curiosity, as they came within the British line.

"Their appearance," said Major Richardson,[2] "was
miserable to the last degree. They had the air of men
to whom cleanliness was a virtue unknown, and their
squalid bodies were covered by habiliments that had

[1] Statement of Madison, March 13, 1813; Niles, iv. 83.
[2] Richardson's War of 1812, p. 79.

evidently undergone every change of season, and were arrived at the last stage of repair. . . . It was the depth of winter; but scarcely an individual was in possession of a great coat or cloak, and few of them wore garments of wool of any description. They still retained their summer dress, consisting of cotton stuff of various colors shaped into frocks, and descending to the knee. Their trowsers were of the same material. They were covered with slouched hats, worn bare by constant use, beneath which their long hair fell matted and uncombed over their cheeks; and these, together with the dirty blankets wrapped round their loins to protect them against the inclemency of the season, and fastened by broad leathern belts, into which were thrust axes and knives of an enormous length, gave them an air of wildness and savageness which in Italy would have caused them to pass for brigands of the Apennines. The only distinction between the garb of the officer and that of the soldier was that the one, in addition to his sword, carried a short rifle instead of a long one, while a dagger, often curiously worked and of some value, supplied the place of the knife."

This description gave a lifelike idea of what Harrison justly thought the best material in the world for soldiery, had it been properly handled. Men who for four months had suffered every hardship, and were still unclothed, unfed, uncared for, and sacrificed to military incompetence, but hardened to cold, fatigue, and danger, had no reason to be ashamed of their misfortunes or of their squalor. Fortunately about five hundred were saved as pris-

oners, and thirty or forty escaped to the rapids;
the rest, four hundred in number, were killed in
battle, or massacred afterward.

Had Proctor acted with energy, he might have
advanced to the rapids, and there have captured
Harrison with his remaining force of nine hundred
men, his artillery train and stores. Even with the
utmost celerity Harrison could hardly have escaped,
if an active pursuit had been made by Indians through
the swamp which he had with extreme difficulty
crossed two days before,[1] and in the heavy rain which
followed the battle;[2] but Proctor had no wish for
fighting. So far from thinking of attack, he thought
only of escaping it, and hurried back to Malden at
noon the same day, leaving the wounded prisoners
behind without a guard. Nothing excused such conduct, for Proctor knew the fate to which he was
exposing his prisoners. That night the Indians,
drunk with whiskey and mad with their grievances
and losses, returned to Frenchtown and massacred
the wounded. About thirty perished, some apparently burned. Fortunately for the United States the
glamour of Proctor's victory hid his true character,
and he was made a major-general, — the most favorable event of the war for the American armies he
was to meet, and one which cost Great Britain even
more in pride than in power.

---

[1] Dawson, p. 362.   [2] Dawson, p. 356.

CHAPTER V.

IF Proctor was afraid of Harrison, with more
military reason Harrison was afraid of Proctor; and
while the British colonel, deserting his wounded
prisoners, hurried from the field of battle, and felt
himself in danger until the next day he was again
entrenched at Malden, at the same moment Harrison,
burning the post at the Maumee Rapids and destroying such stores as were collected there, hastened back
to the Portage or Carrying River some fifteen miles
in the rear. Within thirty-six hours after the battle,
the two enemies were sixty miles apart. At the Portage River Harrison remained a week, until he had
collected a force of two thousand men. With these
he returned to the rapids February 1, and began to
construct a regularly fortified camp on the south
bank of the river. Fort Meigs, as it was called, did
credit to the skill of Major Wood, the engineer officer who constructed it; but such a fortress seemed
rather intended for defence than for the conquest of
Canada.

In fact, Harrison had succeeded only in making
the most considerable failure that had thus far
marked the progress of the war; but while the

public was still assuming treason and cowardice in
William Hull, who had been sent with fifteen hundred men to hold Detroit and conquer Canada, and
had been left unsupported to face destruction, — the
same public admitted the excuses of Harrison, who
with ten thousand men, unlimited means, and active
support at Niagara, after four months of effort, failed
even to pass the Maumee River except with a detachment so badly managed that only thirty-three
men in a thousand escaped. This was the crowning
misfortune which wrung from Gallatin the complaint
that a " real incapacity " for war existed in the
government itself, and must inevitably exhaust its
resources without good result; but although it drove
Gallatin to Europe, it left Harrison on the Maumee.
Harrison would not take on himself the disgrace of
admitting his inability to recapture Detroit, and the
President would not, without his express admission, order him to desist. As Armstrong afterward explained :[1] " The Cabinet, not inexpert at
deciphering military diplomacy, and peculiarly shy of
incurring any responsibility it could avoid, determined, with perhaps less of patriotism than of prudence, to leave the question of continuing the winter
campaign exclusively with the General." The General, not inclined to sink into obscurity or to admit
failure, set himself to a third campaign as hopeless as
either of its predecessors. Ordering all the troops in
his rear to join him, making a body of four thou-

[1] Armstrong's Notices, i. 85.

sand men, he fixed February 11 as the day for his advance on Malden, not expecting to reduce that place, but merely to raid it.[1] When the day arrived, the roads had again become impassable, the ice was no longer safe ; and Harrison, " with much reluctance and mortification," [2] was reduced to write from the Maumee Rapids to the Secretary of War that the campaign must cease.

Thus the Western movement, likened by Henry Clay to a tenth-century crusade, ended in failure. The Government would have been in a better position had it never sent a man to the Maumee, but merely built a few sloops at Cleveland. The entire result of six months' immense effort was confined to raids into the Indian country ; and even these were costly beyond proportion to their results. When the militia of Kentucky and Ohio, which had been mustered in August for six months' service, returned to their homes in February, 1813, not only had they failed to reoccupy a foot of the ground abandoned by Hull, but they left Harrison almost alone at Fort Meigs, trembling lest the enemy should descend on his rear and destroy his supplies, or force him back to protect them.[3] He had accumulated artillery, ammunition, and stores at the Maumee Rapids, in a fortress which itself required a garrison of two thousand men and from which he could neither fall back, as he thought the wiser course,[4] nor remain with safety

[1] Dawson, p. 370.   [2] McAffee, p. 240.
[3] Dawson, p. 375.   [4] Dawson, p. 373.

exposed to an active enemy. He called for more militia from Kentucky and Ohio, but the people no longer felt enthusiasm for war.

"I am sorry to mention," reported Harrison, March 17,[1] "the dismay and disinclination to the service which appear to prevail in the Western country; numbers must give that confidence which ought to be produced by conscious valor and intrepidity, which never existed in any army in a superior degree than amongst the greater part of the militia who were with me through the winter. The new drafts from this State [Ohio] are entirely of another character, and are not to be depended on."

In short, Harrison, who had in 1812 commanded ten thousand militia, seemed to think double the number necessary for 1813, besides regular troops and a fleet.

President Madison and two successive Secretaries of War had allowed themselves, for fear of displeasing Kentucky, to give Harrison *carte blanche*,[2] which Harrison had used without other limit than that of the entire resources of the West. The time at last came when such management must be stopped, and Secretary Armstrong, naturally impatient under the load of Eustis's and Monroe's failures, quickly decided to stop it. Harrison's letter of February 11, announcing his failure, reached the Department March 1. March 5 the secretary wrote to Harrison ordering him to maintain a threatening attitude, but altering the mode of warfare. Henceforward

[1] Armstrong's Notices, i. 242.   [2] Dawson, p. 337.

the army was to be made subordinate, — the navy
was to take the lead ; and until the middle of May,
when the fleet on Lake Erie should be constructed,
Harrison was to maintain a strict defensive, and to
protect the line of the Maumee with six regular
regiments, only three of which had been yet partly
raised.

Meanwhile, Harrison had but a few hundred regulars and some Pennsylvania and Virginia militia, —
perhaps five hundred men in all, — to hold Fort Meigs,
and mere squads of militia to guard eight other posts
which had cost the government some millions of
dollars.   These five hundred troops, whose service
was mostly near its end, he left at Fort Meigs, and in
the middle of March he set out for Chillicothe and
Cincinnati.   Greatly annoyed at the summary manner
in which Armstrong had put an end to his campaigning, he protested only against the inadequacy of his
force for the defence required of it, and insisted on a
temporary reinforcement of militia to garrison the
fortress that had cost him so much effort to construct
at the Maumee Rapids.

Then the value of General Proctor to his enemy
became immense.   Between January 22, when he
attacked Winchester, and the end of April, when he
moved on Fort Meigs, Proctor molested in no way
the weak and isolated American garrisons.   With
hundreds of scouts and backwoodsmen at his command, he had not the energy or the knowledge to·
profit by his opponents' exposed and defenceless con-

dition. He allowed Major Wood to make Fort Meigs capable of standing a siege; he let Harrison, unmolested, pass a month away from his command; he looked on while the Virginia militia marched home, leaving only a handful of sickly men, under a major of artillery, to defend the unfinished fort; he made no attempt to waylay Harrison, who returned with reinforcements by way of the Auglaize River; and not until Harrison had enjoyed all the time necessary to prepare for attack, did Proctor disturb him.

Harrison, expecting an assault, hurried back from Cincinnati to Fort Meigs with some three hundred men, leaving a brigade of Kentucky militia to follow him. April 12 he reached the fort, but not till April 28 did Proctor appear at the mouth of the Maumee, with about five hundred regulars and nearly as many militia, — nine hundred and eighty-three whites, all told, and twelve hundred Indians under Tecumthe and other chiefs.[1] Besides this large force, he brought two twenty-four pound guns with other artillery from Detroit, and two gunboats supported the land-battery. While the guns were placed in position on the north bank of the river, the Indians crossed and surrounded the fort on the south. May 1 the batteries opened, and during four days kept up a heavy fire. Proctor, like Harrison, moved in the wilderness as though he were conducting a campaign on the Rhine; he liked regu-

[1] Proctor's Report of May 4, 1813; Richardson, p. 94; James, i. 196, 429.

lar modes of warfare, and with a force almost wholly irregular, after allowing Fort Meigs to be built, he besieged it as though he could take it by battering its earthen ramparts. Untaught by his losses at the river Raisin, he gave once more advantage to the Kentucky rifle; and with every opportunity of destroying the reinforcement which he knew to be near, he allowed himself to be surprised by it.

The Kentucky brigade of twelve hundred men, under Brigadier-General Green Clay, had descended the Auglaize River in boats, and arrived at Defiance May 3, where they learned that Fort Meigs was invested. So neglectful of his advantages was Proctor that he not only failed to prevent General Clay from advancing, but failed to prevent communication between the besieged fort and the relief-column, so that Harrison was able to arrange a general attack on the investing lines, and came near driving the British force back to Malden with the loss of all its artillery and baggage. At about nine o'clock on the morning of May 5, Clay's brigade descended the rapids, and eight hundred and sixty-six men under Colonel William Dudley,[1] landing on the north side of the river, surprised and took possession of the British batteries, which were entirely unsupported. Had Clay's whole force been on the ground, and had it been vigorously pushed forward, the small British division which held the north bank must have abandoned all its positions; but Dudley's men were un-

[1] Lossing, p. 486, *note.*

der no discipline, and though ready to advance were in no hurry to retreat, even when ordered. Three companies of the British Forty-first, and some of the Canadian militia soon gathered together; and although these could hardly have been half the number of Dudley's force,[1] yet with Tecumthe and a body of Indians they attacked the batteries, drove the Kentuckians out, dispersed them, and either captured or massacred the whole body, under the eyes of Harrison and Fort Meigs.

This affair, though little less fatal to the Americans than that of the river Raisin, was much less dearly bought by the British. Five hundred prisoners fell into Proctor's hands; two or three hundred more of the Kentucky brigade, including "the weak and obstinate but brave"[2] Dudley himself, must have been either killed in battle or massacred after surrender;[3] only one hundred and seventy escaped; the boats with the baggage were captured; while the whole British loss on the north side of the river hardly exceeded fifty killed and wounded. A bitter feeling against Proctor was caused by the massacre of some forty American prisoners while under a British guard, and also, as was alleged, under the eyes of General Proctor, who did not interpose, although a

[1] Richardson, p. 86; James, i. 198.

[2] Harrison to Armstrong, May 13, 1813; MSS. War Department Archives.

[3] Richardson, pp. 87, 88. Harrison to Armstrong, May 9, 1813; MSS. War Department Archives.

soldier of the Forty-first was murdered in trying to protect them. Probably all the prisoners would have been massacred had Tecumthe not ridden up at full speed, tomahawk in hand, and threatened to kill the first Indian who defied his authority.[1]

On the south side Harrison had better fortune, and Colonel John Miller of the Nineteenth U. S. Infantry by a sortie gallantly captured a battery, with some forty prisoners ; but neither on the north nor on the south did the fighting of May 5 decide any immediate military result. Besides losing on the north bank half the reinforcement brought by General Green Clay, Harrison had lost in the siege and in the sorties on the south bank nearly three hundred men in killed and wounded.[2] If the numbers loosely reported in the American accounts were correct, the siege cost Harrison one thousand men, or fully half his entire force, including his reinforcements. After the fighting of May 5, he withdrew once more into the fort; the British batteries reopened fire, and the siege went on. No further attempt was made to trouble the enemy in open field. Harrison felt himself too weak for further ventures ; yet never had his chance of a great success been so fair.

Proctor's siege of Fort Meigs was already a failure. Not only had the fort proved stronger than he expected, but the weather was bad ; his troops were

[1] Richardson, p. 88.

[2] Harrison to Armstrong, May 13, 1813 ; MSS. War Department Archives.

without shelter ; dysentery and loss in battle rapidly
weakened them ; half his militia went home, and,
what was fatal to further action, his Indians could
not be held together. Within three days after the
battle of May 5, the twelve hundred Indians collected
by Tecumthe's influence and exertions in the northwest territory dispersed, leaving only Tecumthe himself and a score of other warriors in the British camp.[1]
Proctor had no choice but to retire as rapidly as
possible, and May 9 embarked his artillery and left
his encampment without interference from Harrison,
who looked on as a spectator while the movement
was effected.

From that time until the middle of July Proctor
remained quiet. Harrison moved his headquarters to
Upper Sandusky and to Cleveland, and began to prepare for advance under cover of a naval force ; but he
was not allowed to rest, even though Proctor might
have preferred repose. Proctor's position was difficult. Told by Sir George Prevost[2] that he must capture what supplies he needed from the Americans,
and must seek them at Erie and Cleveland, since
Lower Canada could spare neither food nor transport,
he was compelled to look for support to the American
magazines. He was issuing ten thousand rations a
day to the Indian families at Malden, and his re-

[1] Proctor's Report of May 14, 1813 ; James, i. 428 ; Richardson, pp. 93, 94.

[2] Prevost to Proctor, July 11, 1813 ; Armstrong's Notices
i. 228.

sources were near an end.[1] Leaving Malden with
either three hundred and ninety-one regulars, or about
five hundred regulars and militia, and by one British
account nearly a thousand Indians, by another between three and four thousand,[2] Proctor returned
by water to the Maumee Rapids July 20, and tried
to draw the garrison of Fort Meigs into an ambush.
The attempt failed. General Green Clay, who was
in command, had learned caution, and imposed it on
his troops. Proctor then found that his Indians were
leaving him and returning to Detroit and Amherstburg. To occupy them, Proctor took again to his
boats and coasted the Lake shore as far as the
Sandusky River, while the Indians who chose to ac-
company him made their way by land. August 1
the expedition effected a landing at the mouth of
the Sandusky, and scattered panic into the heart
of Ohio.

In truth, nothing could be more alarming than this
movement, which threatened Harrison in all directions, — from Fort Meigs, on the Maumee, to Erie, or
Presqu'isle, where Perry's fleet was building. On
Sandusky River Harrison had collected his chief
magazines. All the supplies for his army were lying
at Upper Sandusky, some thirty miles above the
British landing-place, and he had only eight hundred
raw recruits to defend their unfortified position.[3]

[1] Richardson, p. 111.
[2] James, i. 264, 265 ; Richardson, p. 104 ; Christie, p. 117.
[3] Dawson, p. 408.

Nothing but an untenable stockade, called Fort Stephenson, on the Sandusky River, where the town of Fremont afterward grew, offered an obstacle to the enemy in ascending; and Tecumthe with two thousand Indians was said to be moving from Fort Meigs by the direct road straight for the magazines, thus flanking Fort Stephenson and every intermediate position on the Sandusky.

In just panic for the safety of his magazines, the only result of a year's campaigning, Harrison's first thought was to evacuate Fort Stephenson in order to protect Upper Sandusky. The flank-attack from two thousand Indians, who never showed themselves, impelled him to retire before Proctor, and to leave the river open. July 29, after a council of war, he sent down a hasty order to young Major Croghan who commanded Fort Stephenson, directing him immediately to burn the fort and retreat up the river or along the Lake shore, as he best could, with the utmost haste.[1]   Croghan, a Kentuckian, and an officer of the Seventeenth U. S. regiment, refused to obey. " We have determined to maintain this place, and by Heaven, we will," he wrote back.[2]   Harrison sent Colonel Wells, of the same regiment, to relieve him; but Croghan went to headquarters, and by somewhat lame excuses carried his point, and resumed his command the next day. Harrison gave him only conditional orders to abandon the fort, — orders which Croghan clearly could not regard, and which Harrison

[1] McAffee, p. 322.   [2] McAffee, p. 323.

seemed to feel no confidence in his wishing to follow.[1]
In the face of British troops with cannon he was to
retreat; but " you must be aware that the attempt to
retreat in the face of an Indian force would be vain."
Proctor's main force was believed to be Indian.

Neither evacuating nor defending Fort Stephenson, Harrison remained at Seneca, ten miles behind it
watching for Tecumthe and the flank attack, and
arranging a plan of battle for his eight hundred men
by which he could repel the Indians with dragoons
in the open prairie.[2]   Croghan remained at Fort
Stephenson with one hundred and sixty men, making
every preparation to meet an attack.   August 1 the
woods were already filled with Indians, and retreat
was impossible, when the British boats appeared on
the river, and Proctor sent to demand surrender of
the fort.   Immediately on Croghan's refusal, the
British howitzers opened fire and continued until it
became clear that they were too light to destroy the
stockade.

If experience had been of service to Proctor, he
should have learned to avoid direct attack on Americans in fortified places; but his position was difficult,
and he was as much afraid of Harrison as Harrison
was afraid of him.   Fearing to leave Croghan's little
fort in the rear, and to seek Harrison himself, ten
miles above, on the road to Upper Sandusky; fearing

[1] Governor Duncan's Report, 1834; Armstrong's Notices,
i. 230.

[2] Dawson, p. 408.

delay, which would discontent his Indian allies; fearing to go on to Cleveland or Erie without crippling Harrison; still more afraid to retire to Malden without striking a blow, — Proctor again sacrificed the Forty-first regiment which had suffered at the river Raisin and had been surprised at Fort Meigs. On the afternoon of August 2 the Forty-first regiment and the militia, in three columns of about one hundred and twenty men each,[1] with the utmost gallantry marched to the pickets of Fort Stephenson, and were shot down. After two hours' effort, and losing all its officers, the assaulting column retired, leaving twenty-six dead, forty-one wounded, and about thirty missing, or more than one fifth of their force. The same night the troops re-embarked and returned to Malden.

Proctor's report[2] of this affair was filled with complaints of the Indians, who could not be left idle and who would not fight. At Sandusky, he said, " we could not muster more hundreds of Indians than I might reasonably have expected thousands."

" I could not, therefore, with my very small force remain more than two days, from the probability of being cut off, and of being deserted by the few Indians who had not already done so. . . . On the morning of the 2d inst. the gentlemen of the Indian department who have the direction of it, declared formally their decided opinion that unless the fort was stormed we should never be able to bring an Indian warrior into the field with us, and that they proposed and were ready to storm one face of the

[1] Richardson, p. 105.

[2] Proctor to Prevost, Aug. 9, 1813; MSS. Canadian Archives.

fort if we would attempt another. I have also to observe that in this instance my judgment had not that weight with the troops I hope I might reasonably have expected. . . . The troops, after the artillery had been used for some hours, attacked two faces, and impossibilities being attempted, failed. The fort, from which the severest fire I ever saw was maintained during the attack, was well defended. The troops displayed the greatest bravery, the much greater part of whom reached the fort and made every effort to enter; but the Indians who had proposed the assault, and, had it not been assented to, would have ever stigmatized the British character, scarcely came into fire before they ran out of its reach. A more than adequate sacrifice having been made to Indian opinion, I drew off the brave assailants."

Sir George Prevost seemed to doubt whether Proctor's excuse for the defeat lessened or increased the blame attached to it.[1] The defeat at Sandusky ruined Proctor in the esteem of his men. On the American side, Harrison's conduct roused a storm of indignation. Through the whole day, August 2, he remained at Seneca with eight hundred men, listening to the cannonade at Fort Stephenson till late at night, when he received an express from Croghan to say that the enemy were embarking. The story ran, that as the distant sound of Croghan's guns reached the camp at Seneca, Harrison exclaimed : "The blood be on his own head ; I wash my hands of it.[2]" Whatever else

[1] Life of Prevost, p. 106, *note*.
[2] Governor Duncan's Report, 1834; Armstrong's Notices, i. 230.

might be true, his conduct betrayed an extravagant estimate of his enemy's strength. The only British eye-witness who left an account of the expedition reckoned Proctor's force, on its departure from Malden, at about four hundred troops, and "nearly a thousand Indians." [1] The Indians dispersed until those with Proctor at Fort Stephenson probably numbered two or three hundred,[2] the rest having returned to Detroit and Malden. Harrison reported the British force as five thousand strong, on the authority of General Green Clay.[3]

Whether the British force was large or small, Harrison's arrangements to meet it did not please Secretary Armstrong. "It is worthy of notice," he wrote long afterward,[4] "that of these two commanders, always the terror of each other, one [Proctor] was now actually flying from his supposed pursuer; while the other [Harrison] waited only the arrival of Croghan at Seneca to begin a camp-conflagration and flight to Upper Sandusky."

The well-won honors of the campaign fell to Major George Croghan, with whose name the whole country resounded. Whatever were the faults of the two generals, Major Croghan showed courage and intelligence, not only before and during the attack, but afterward in supporting Harrison against the outcry which for a time threatened to destroy the

[1] Richardson, p. 104.   [2] James, ii. 264.
[3] Dawson, p. 407 ; McAffee, p. 302.
[4] Armstrong's Notices, i. 166, *note*.

General's authority.   Immediately after the siege
of Fort Stephenson every energy of the northwest
turned toward a new offensive movement by water
against Malden, and in the task of organizing the
force required for that purpose, complaints of past
failures were stifled.   Secretary Armstrong did not
forget them, but the moment was not suited for
making a change in so important a command.   Harrison organized, under Armstrong's orders, a force of
seven thousand men to cross the Lake in boats, under
cover of a fleet.

The fleet, not the army, was to bear the brunt
of reconquering the northwest; and in nothing did
Armstrong show his ability so clearly as in the
promptness with which, immediately after taking
office, he stopped Harrison's campaign on the
Maumee, while Perry was set to work at Erie.
Feb. 5, 1813, Armstrong entered on his duties.
March 5 his arrangements for the new movements
were already made.   Harrison did not approve them,[1]
but he obeyed.   The Navy Department had already
begun operations on Lake Erie, immediately after
Hull's surrender ; but though something was accomplished in the winter, great difficulties had
still to be overcome when February 17 Commander
Perry, an energetic young officer on gunboat service
at Newport, received orders from Secretary Jones
to report to Commodore Chauncey on Lake Ontario.
Chauncey ordered him to Presqu'isle, afterward

[1] Harrison to Armstrong, March 17, 1813 ; Notices, i. 242.

called Erie, to take charge of the vessels under construction on Lake Erie.   March 27 he reached the spot, a small village in a remote wilderness, where timber and water alone existed for the supply of the fleets.

When Perry reached Presqu'isle the contractors and carpenters had on the stocks two brigs, a schooner, and three gunboats.   These were to be launched in May, and to be ready for service in June. Besides these vessels building at Erie, a number of other craft, including the prize brig " Caledonia," were at the Black Rock navy-yard in the Niagara River, unable to move on account of the British fort opposite Buffalo and the British fleet on the Lake. Perry's task was to unite the two squadrons, to man them, and to fight the British fleet, without allowing his enemy to interfere at any stage of these difficult operations.

The British squadron under Commander Finnis, an experienced officer, had entire control of the Lake and its shores.   No regular garrison protected the harbor of Presqu'isle ; not two hundred men could be armed to defend it, nor was any military support to be had nearer than Buffalo, eighty miles away. Proctor or Prevost were likely to risk everything in trying to destroy the shipyard at Erie ; for upon that point, far more than on Detroit, Fort Meigs, Sandusky, or Buffalo, their existence depended.   If Perry were allowed to control the Lake, the British must not only evacuate Detroit, but also Malden, must abandon Tecumthe and the military advantages of three or four thousand Indian auxiliaries, and must fall back on a difficult defensive at the Niagara River. That they would make every effort to thwart Perry seemed certain.

Superstition survived in nothing more obstinately than in faith in luck; neither sailors nor soldiers ever doubted the value of this inscrutable quality in the conduct of war. The "Chesapeake" was an unlucky ship to the luckiest commanders, even to the British captain who captured it. The bad luck of the "Chesapeake" was hardly steadier than the good luck of Oliver Perry. Whatever he touched seemed to take the direction he wanted. He began with the advantage of having Proctor for his chief enemy; but Harrison, also a lucky man, had the same advantage and yet suffered constant disasters. Commander Finnis was a good seaman, yet Finnis failed repeatedly, and always by a narrow chance, to injure Perry. Dearborn's incompetence in 1813 was not less than it had been in 1812; but the single success which in two campaigns Dearborn gained on the Niagara obliged the British, May 27, to evacuate Fort Erie opposite Buffalo, and to release Perry's vessels at Black Rock. June 6, at leisure, Perry superintended the removal of the five small craft from the navy-yard at Black Rock; several hundred soldiers, seamen, and oxen warped them up stream into the Lake. Loaded with stores, the little squadron sailed from Buffalo June 13; the

wind was ahead; they were five days making eighty
miles; but June 19 they arrived at Presqu'isle, and
as the last vessel crossed the bar, Finnis and his
squadron came in sight. Finnis alone could explain
how he, a first-rate seaman, with a strong force and
a fair wind, in such narrow seas, could have helped
finding Perry's squadron when he knew where it
must be.

From June 19 to August 1 Perry's combined fleet
lay within the bar at Presqu'isle, while Proctor, with
a sufficient fleet and a military force superior to anything on the Lake, was planning expeditions from
Malden against every place except the one to which
military necessity and the orders of his Government
bade him go. August 4, Perry took out the armaments of his two brigs and floated both over the
bar into deep water. Had the British fleet been at
hand, such a movement would have been impossible
or fatal; but the British fleet appeared just as Perry's
vessels got into deep water, and when for the first
time an attack could not be made with a fair hope
of success.

These extraordinary advantages were not gained
without labor, energy, courage, and wearing anxieties
and disappointments. Of these Perry had his full
share, but no more; and his opponents were no
better off than himself. By great exertions alone
could the British maintain themselves on Lake
Ontario, and to this necessity they were forced to
sacrifice Lake Erie. Sir George Prevost could spare

only a new commander with a few officers and some forty men from the lower Lake to meet the large American reinforcements on the upper. When the commander, R. H. Barclay, arrived at Malden in June, he found as many difficulties there as Perry found at Presqu'isle. Barclay was a captain in the British Royal Navy, thirty-two years old; he had lost an arm in the service, but he was fairly matched as Perry's antagonist, and showed the qualities of an excellent officer.

Perry's squadron, once on the Lake, altogether over-awed the British fleet, and Barclay's only hope lay in completing a vessel called the "Detroit," then on the stocks at Amherstburg. Rough and unfinished, she was launched, and while Perry blockaded the harbor, Barclay, early in September, got masts and rigging into her, and armed her with guns of every calibre, taken from the ramparts.[1] Even the two American twenty-four pound guns, used by Proctor against Fort Meigs, were put on board the "Detroit." Thus equipped, she had still to be manned; but no seamen were near the Lake. Barclay was forced to make up a crew of soldiers from the hardworked Forty-first regiment and Canadians unused to ser-vice. September 6 the "Detroit" was ready to sail, and Barclay had then no choice but to fight at any risk. "So perfectly destitute of provisions was the port that there was not a day's flour in store, and the crews of the squadron under my command were

[1] Richardson, p. 110; James, Naval Occurrences, p. 285.

on half allowance of many things; and when that was done, there was no more." [1]

Early on the morning of September 9 Barclay's fleet weighed and sailed for the enemy, who was then at anchor off the island of Put-in-Bay near the mouth of Sandusky River. The British squadron consisted of six vessels, — the " Detroit," a ship of four hundred and ninety tons, carrying nineteen guns, commanded by Barclay himself; the " Queen Charlotte " of seventeen guns, commanded by Finnis; the " Lady Prevost " of thirteen guns; the " Hunter " of ten; the " Little Belt " carrying three, and the " Chippeway " carrying one gun, — in all, sixty-three guns, and probably about four hundred and fifty men. The American squadron consisted of nine vessels, — the " Lawrence," Perry's own brig, nearly as large as the " Detroit," and carrying twenty guns; the " Niagara," commander Jesse D. Elliott, of the same tonnage, with the same armament; the " Caledonia," a three-gun brig; the schooners " Ariel," " Scorpion," " Somers," " Porcupine," and " Tigress," carrying ten guns ; and the sloop " Trippe," with one gun, — in all, fifty-four guns, with a nominal crew of five hundred and thirty-two men, and an effective crew probably not greatly differing from the British. In other respects Perry's superiority was decided, as it was meant to be. The Americans had thirty-nine thirty-two pound carronades ; the British had not a gun of

[1] Barclay's Report of Sept. 12, 1813 ; James, Naval Occurrences. Appendix, no. 54.

that weight, and only fifteen twenty-four pound car
ronades. The lightest guns on the American fleet
were eight long twelve-pounders, while twenty-four
of the British guns threw only nine-pound shot, or
less. The American broadside threw at close range
about nine hundred pounds of metal; the British
threw about four hundred and sixty. At long range
the Americans threw two hundred and eighty-eight
pounds of metal; the British threw one hundred and
ninety-five pounds. In tonnage the Americans were
superior as eight to seven. In short, the Navy Department had done everything reasonably necessary
to insure success; and if the American crews, like
the British, were partly made up of landsmen, soldiers or volunteers, the reason was in each case the
same. Both governments supplied all the seamen
they had.

Between forces so matched, victory ought not to
have been in doubt; and if it was so, the fault certainly lay not in Perry. When, at daylight September 10, his look-out discovered the British fleet, Perry
got his own squadron under way, and came down
with a light wind from the southeast against Barclay's line, striking it obliquely near the head. Perry
must have been anxious to fight at close range, where
his superiority was as two to one, while at long range
his ship could use only two long twelve-pounders
against the " Detroit's " six twelves, one eighteen, and
two twenty-fours, — an inferiority amounting to helplessness. Both the " Lawrence " and the " Niagara "

were armed for close fighting, and were intended for nothing else. At long range their combined broadside, even if all their twelve-pounders were worked on one side, threw but forty-eight pounds of metal; at short range the two brigs were able to throw six hundred and forty pounds at each broadside.

Perry could not have meant to fight at a distance, nor could Commander Elliott have thought it good seamanship. Yet Perry alone acted on this evident scheme; and though his official account showed that he had himself fought at close range, and that he ordered the other commanders to do the same, it gave no sufficient reasons to explain what prevented the whole fleet from acting together, and made the result doubtful. He did not even mention that he himself led the line in the "Lawrence," with two gunboats, the "Ariel" and the "Scorpion," supporting him, the "Caledonia," "Niagara," and three gunboats following. The "Lawrence" came within range of the British line just at noon, the wind being very light, the Lake calm, and Barclay, in the "Detroit," opposite. Perry's report began at that point: —

"At fifteen minutes before twelve the enemy commenced firing; at five minutes before twelve the action commenced on our part. Finding their fire very destructive, owing to their long guns, and its being mostly directed to the 'Lawrence,' I made sail (at quarter-past twelve) and directed the other vessels to follow, for the purpose of closing with the enemy. Every brace and bowline being shot away, she became unmanageable,

notwithstanding the great exertions of the sailing-master.
In this situation she sustained the action upwards of two
hours, within canister-shot distance, until every gun was
rendered useless, and a greater part of the crew either
killed or wounded. Finding she could no longer annoy
the enemy, I left her in charge of Lieutenant Yarnall,
who, I was convinced from the bravery already displayed
by him, would do what would comport with the honor
of the flag. At half-past two, the wind springing up,
Captain Elliott was enabled to bring his vessel, the
' Niagara,' gallantly into close action. I immediately
went on board of her, when he anticipated my wish by
volunteering to bring the schooners, which had been kept
astern by the lightness of the wind, into close action.
. . . At forty-five minutes past two the signal was made
for ' close action.' The ' Niagara ' being very little injured, I determined to pass through the enemy's line ;
bore up, and passed ahead of their two ships and a brig,
giving a raking fire to them from the starboard guns, and
to a large schooner and sloop, from the larboard side,
at half pistol-shot distance. The smaller vessels at this
time having got within grape and canister distance, under
the direction of Captain Elliott, and keeping up a well-
directed fire, the two ships, a brig, and a schooner surrendered, a schooner and sloop making a vain attempt
to escape."

From this reticent report, any careful reader could
see that for some reason, not so distinctly given as
would have been the case if the wind alone were at
fault, the action had been very badly fought on the
American side. The British official account confirmed the impression given by Perry. Barclay's

story was as well told as his action was well
fought : —

" At a quarter before twelve I commenced the action
by a few long guns ; about a quarter-past, the American
commodore, also supported by two schooners, . . . came
to close action with the ' Detroit.' The other brig [the
' Niagara '] of the enemy, apparently destined to engage
the ' Queen Charlotte,' kept so far to windward as to
render the ' Queen Charlotte's ' twenty-four pounder carronades useless, while she was, with the ' Lady Prevost,'
exposed to the heavy and destructive fire of the ' Caledonia ' and four other schooners, armed with heavy and
long guns. . . . The action continued with great fury
until half-past two, when I perceived my opponent [the
' Lawrence '] drop astern, and a boat passing from him
to the ' Niagara,' which vessel was at this time perfectly
fresh. The American commodore, seeing that as yet the
day was against him, . . . made a noble and, alas ! too
successful an effort to regain it ; for he bore up, and supported by his small vessels, passed within pistol-shot and
took a raking position on our bow. . . . The weather-
gage gave the enemy a prodigious advantage, as it enabled them not only to choose their position, but their
distance also, which they [the ' Caledonia,' ' Niagara,'
and the gunboats] did in such a manner as to prevent
the carronades of the ' Queen Charlotte ' and ' Lady
Prevost ' from having much effect, while their long ones
did great execution, particularly against the ' Queen
Charlotte.' "

Barclay's report, agreeing with Perry's, made it
clear that while Perry and the head of the American line fought at close quarters, the " Caledonia,"

"Niagara," and the four gunboats supporting them preferred fighting at long range, — not because they wanted wind, but because the "Caledonia" and gunboats were armed with long thirty-two and twenty-four pounders, while the British vessels opposed to them had only one or two long twelve-pounders. Certainly the advantage in this respect on the side of the American brig and gunboats was enormous; but these tactics threw the "Niagara," which had not the same excuse, out of the battle, leaving her, from twelve o'clock till half-past two, firing only two twelve-pound guns, while her heavy armament was useless, and might as well have been left ashore. Worse than this, the persistence of the "Caledonia," "Niagara," and their gunboats in keeping beyond range of their enemies' carronades nearly lost the battle, by allowing the British to concentrate on the "Lawrence" all their heavy guns, and in the end compelling the "Lawrence" to strike. On all these points no reasonable doubt could exist. The two reports were the only official sources of information on which an opinion as to the merits of the action could properly be founded. No other account, contemporaneous and authoritative, threw light on the subject, except a letter by Lieutenant Yarnall, second in command to Perry on the "Lawrence," written September 15, and published in the Ohio newspapers about September 29, — in which Yarnall said that if Elliott had brought his ship into action when the signal was given, the battle would have ended in much less time, and with less loss to the "Law-rence." This statement agreed with the tenor of the two official reports.

Furious as the battle was, a more furious dispute raged over it when in the year 1834 the friends of Perry and of Elliott wrangled over the action. With their dispute history need not concern itself. The official reports left no reasonable doubt that Perry's plan of battle was correct; that want of wind was not the reason it failed; but that the "Niagara" was badly managed by Elliott, and that the victory, when actually forfeited by this mismanagement, was saved by the personal energy of Perry, who, abandoning his own ship, brought the "Niagara" through the ene-my's line, and regained the advantage of her heavy battery. The luck which attended Perry's career on the Lake saved him from injury, when every other officer on the two opposing flagships and four-fifths of his crew were killed or wounded, and enabled him to perform a feat almost without parallel in naval warfare, giving him a well-won immortality by means of the disaster unnecessarily incurred. No process of argument or ingenuity of seamanship could de-prive Perry of the fame justly given him by the pub-lic, or detract from the splendor of his reputation as the hero of the war. More than any other battle of the time, the victory on Lake Erie was won by the courage and obstinacy of a single man.

Between two opponents such as Perry and Barclay, no one doubted that the ships were fought to their utmost. Of the "Lawrence" not much was left; ship, officers, and crew were shot to pieces. Such carnage was not known on the ocean, for even the cockpit where the sick and wounded lay, being above water, was riddled by shot, and the wounded were wounded again on the surgeon's board. Of one hundred and three effectives on the "Lawrence," twenty-two were killed and sixty-one wounded. The brig herself when she struck was a wreck, unmanageable, her starboard bulwarks beaten in, guns dismounted, and rigging cut to pieces. The British ships were in hardly better condition. The long guns of the gunboats had raked them with destructive effect. Barclay was desperately wounded; Finnis was killed; Barclay's first lieutenant was mortally wounded; not one commander or second in command could keep the deck; the squadron had forty-one men killed and ninety-four wounded, or nearly one man in three; the "Detroit" and "Queen Charlotte" were unmanageable and fell foul; the "Lady Prevost" was crippled, and drifted out of the fight. Perry could console himself with the thought that if his ship had struck her flag, she had at least struck to brave men.

CHAPTER VI.

GENERAL HARRISON, waiting at Seneca on the Sandusky River, received, September 12, Perry's famous despatch of September 10 : " We have met the enemy, and they are ours." The navy having done its work, the army was next to act.

The force under Harrison's command was ample for the required purpose, although it contained fewer regular troops than Armstrong had intended. The seven regular regiments assigned to Harrison fell short in numbers of the most moderate expectations. Instead of providing seven thousand rank-and-file, the recruiting service ended in producing rather more than twenty-five hundred.[1] Divided into two brigades under Brigadier-Generals McArthur and Lewis Cass, with a light corps under Lieutenant-Colonel Ball of the Light Dragoons, they formed only one wing of Harrison's army.

To supply his main force, Harrison had still to depend on Kentucky; and once more that State made a great effort. Governor Shelby took the field in person, leading three thousand volunteers,[2]

[1] McAffee, p. 334.
[2] Harrison to Meigs, Oct. 11, 1813; Official Letters, p. 239.

organized in eleven regiments, five brigades, and two divisions. Besides the militia, who volunteered for this special purpose, Harrison obtained the services of another Kentucky corps, which had already proved its efficiency.

One of Armstrong's happiest acts, at the beginning of his service as War Secretary,[1] was to accept the aid of Richard M. Johnson in organizing for frontier defence a mounted regiment of a thousand men, armed with muskets or rifles, tomahawks, and knives.[2] Johnson and his regiment took the field about June 1, and from that time anxiety on account of Indians ceased. The regiment patrolled the district from Fort Wayne to the river Raisin, and whether in marching or fighting proved to be the most efficient corps in the Western country. Harrison obtained the assistance of Johnson's regiment for the movement into Canada, and thereby increased the efficiency of his army beyond the proportion of Johnson's numbers.

While the mounted regiment moved by the road to Detroit, Harrison's main force was embarked in boats September 20, and in the course of a few days some forty-five hundred infantry were safely conveyed by way of Bass Island and Put-in-Bay to Middle Sister Island, about twelve miles from

[1] Armstrong, i. 171, *note ;* McAffee, p. 286.
[2] R. M. Johnson to Armstrong, Dec. 22, 1834 ; Armstrong, i. 232.

the Canadian shore.[1]   Harrison and Perry then
selected a landing place, and the whole force was
successfully set ashore, September 27, about three
miles below Malden.

Although Proctor could not hope to maintain
himself at Malden or Detroit without control of the
Lake, he had still the means of rendering Harrison's
possession insecure.   According to the British account, he commanded at Detroit and Malden a force
of nine hundred and eighty-six regulars, giving about
eight hundred effectives.[2]   Not less than thirty-five
hundred Indian warriors had flocked to Amherstburg, and although they greatly increased the British
general's difficulties by bringing their families with
them, they might be formidable opponents to Harrison's advance.   Every motive dictated to Proctor
the necessity of resisting Harrison's approach.   To
Tecumthe and his Indians the evacuation of Malden
and Detroit without a struggle meant not only the
sacrifice of their cause, but also cowardice; and when
Proctor announced to them, September 18, that he
meant to retreat, Tecumthe rose in the council and
protested against the flight, likening Proctor to a
fat dog that had carried its tail erect, and now that
it was frightened dropped its tail between its legs
and ran.[3]   He told Proctor to go if he liked, but the
Indians would remain.

[1] Perry to Secretary Jones, Sept. 24, 1813; Official Letters,
p. 215.

[2] James, i. 269.   [3] Richardson, p. 119.

Proctor insisted upon retiring at least toward the Moravian town, seventy miles on the road to Lake Ontario, and the Indians yielded. The troops immediately began to burn or destroy the public property at Detroit and Malden, or to load on wagons or boats what could not be carried away. September 24, three days before Harrison's army landed, the British evacuated Malden and withdrew to Sandwich, allowing Harrison to establish himself at Malden without a skirmish, and neglecting to destroy the bridge over the Canards River.

Harrison was surprised at Proctor's tame retreat.

" Nothing but infatuation," he reported,[1] " could have governed General Proctor's conduct. The day that I landed below Malden he had at his disposal upward of three thousand Indian warriors; his regular force reinforced by the militia of the district would have made his number nearly equal to my aggregate, which on the day of landing did not exceed forty-five hundred. . . His inferior officers say that his conduct has been a series of continued blunders."

This crowning proof of Proctor's incapacity disorganized his force. Tecumthe expressed a general sentiment of the British army in his public denunciation of Proctor's cowardice. One of the inferior British officers afterward declared that Proctor's " marked inefficiency " and " wanton sacrifice " of the troops raised more than a doubt not only of his capacity but even of his personal courage, and

[1] Harrison to Meigs, Oct. 11, 1813 ; Official Letters, p. 239.

led to serious thoughts of taking away his authority.[1] The British at Sandwich went through the
same experience that marked the retreat of Hull
and his army from the same spot, only the year
before.

Harrison on his side made no extreme haste to
pursue. His army marched into Malden at four
o'clock on the afternoon of September 27,[2] and he
wrote to Secretary Armstrong that evening : " I
will pursue the enemy to-morrow, although there is
no probability of my overtaking him, as he has upwards of a thousand horses, and we have not one
in the army." [3] The pursuit was not rapid. Sandwich, opposite Detroit, was only thirteen miles above
Malden, but Harrison required two days to reach
it, arriving at two o'clock on the afternoon of September 29. From there, September 30, he wrote
again to Secretary Armstrong that he was preparing
to pursue the enemy on the following day ; [4] but he
waited for R. M. Johnson's mounted regiment, which
arrived at Detroit September 30, and was obliged
to consume a day in crossing the river. Then the
pursuit began with energy, but on the morning of
October 2 Proctor had already a week's advance
and should have been safe.

[1] Richardson, pp. 126, 133, 134.

[2] Perry to Secretary Jones, Sept. 27, 1813 ; Official Letters,
p. 220.

[3] Harrison to Armstrong, Sept. 27, 1813 ; Dawson, p. 421.

[4] Harrison to Armstrong, Oct. 9, 1813 ; Official Letters, p. 233.

Proctor seemed to imagine that the Americans would not venture to pursue him. Moving, according to his own report,[1] "by easy marches," neither obstructing the road in his rear nor leaving detachments to delay the enemy, he reached Dolson's October 1, and there halted his army, fifty miles from Sandwich, while he went to the Moravian town some twenty-six miles beyond. He then intended to make a stand at Chatham, three miles behind Dolson's.

"I had assured the Indians," said Proctor's report of October 23, "that we would not desert them, and it was my full determination to have made a stand at the Forks (Chatham), by which our vessels and stores would be protected; but after my arrival at Dover [Dolson's] three miles lower down the river, I was induced to take post there first, where ovens had been constructed, and where there was some shelter for the troops, and had accordingly directed that it should be put into the best possible state of defence that time and circumstances would admit of; indeed it had been my intention to have opposed the enemy nearer the mouth of the river, had not the troops contrary to my intention been moved, during my absence of a few hours for the purpose of acquiring some knowledge of the country in my rear."

The British army, left at Dolson's October 1, without a general or orders,[2] saw the American army arrive in its front, October 3, and retired three

[1] Report of Oct. 23, 1813; MSS. British Archives. Lower Canada, vol. cxxiii.

[2] Richardson, pp. 133, 134.

miles to Chatham, where the Indians insisted upon
fighting ; but when, the next morning, October 4,
the Americans advanced in order of battle,[1] the
Indians after a skirmish changed their minds and
retreated. The British were compelled to sacrifice
the supplies they had brought by water to Chatham
for establishing their new base, and their retreat
precipitated on the Moravian town the confusion of
flight already resembling rout.

Six miles on their way they met General Proctor
returning from the Moravian town, and as much
dissatisfied with them as they with him. Pressed
closely by the American advance, the British troops
made what haste they could over excessively bad
roads until eight o'clock in the evening, when they
halted within six miles of the Moravian town.[2] The
next morning, October 5, the enemy was again reported to be close at hand, and the British force
again retreated. About a mile and a half from the
Moravian town it was halted. Proctor had then
retired as far as he could, and there he must either
fight, or abandon women and children, sick and
wounded, baggage, stores, and wagons, desert his
Indian allies, and fly to Lake Ontario. Probably
flight would not have saved his troops. More than
a hundred miles of unsettled country lay between
them and their next base. The Americans had in

---

[1] Harrison's Report, Oct. 9, 1813 ; Official Letters, p. 234.

[2] Narrative of Lieutenant Bullock, Dec. 6, 1813 ; Richardson,
p. 137.

their advance the mounted regiment of R. M. Johnson, and could outmarch the most lightly equipped British regulars. Already, according to Proctor's report, the rapidity of the Americans had destroyed the efficiency of the British organization : [1] —

"In the attempt to save provisions we became encumbered with boats not suited to the state of navigation. The Indians and the troops retreated on different sides of the river, and the boats to which sufficient attention had not been given became particularly exposed to the fire of the enemy who were advancing on the side the Indians were retiring, and most unfortunately fell into possession of the enemy, and with them several of the men, provisions, and all the ammunition that had not been issued to the troops and Indians. This disastrous circumstance afforded the enemy the means of crossing and advancing on both sides of the river. Finding the enemy were advancing too near I resolved to meet him, being strong in cavalry, in a wood below the Moravian town, which last was not cleared of Indian women and children, or of those of the troops, nor of the sick."

The whole British force was then on the north bank of the river Thames, retreating eastward by a road near the river bank. Proctor could hardly claim to have exercised choice in the selection of a battle-ground, unless he preferred placing his little force under every disadvantage. "The troops were formed with their left to the river," his report continued, "with a reserve and a six-pounder on the road, near

[1] Proctor's Report of Oct. 23, 1813 ; MSS. British Archives.

the river; the Indians on the right." According to
the report of officers of the Forty-first regiment, two
lines of troops were formed in a thick forest, two
hundred yards apart. The first line began where
the six-pound field-piece stood, with a range of some
fifty yards along the road. A few Canadian Light
Dragoons were stationed near the gun. To the left
of the road was the river; to the right a forest, free
from underbrush that could stop horsemen, but offering cover to an approaching enemy within twenty
paces of the British line.[1] In the wood about two
hundred men of the British Forty-first took position
as well as they could, behind trees, and there as
a first line they waited some two hours for their
enemy to appear.

The second line, somewhat less numerous, two
hundred yards behind the first, and not within sight,
was also formed in the wood; and on the road, in
rear of the second line, Proctor and his staff stationed
themselves. The Indians were collected behind a
swamp on the right, touching and covering effectually the British right flank, while the river covered
the left.

Such a formation was best fitted for Harrison's
purposes, but the mere arrangement gave little idea
of Proctor's weakness. The six-pound field-piece,
which as he afterward reported " certainly should
have produced-the best effect if properly managed,"
had not a round of ammunition, and could not be

[1] Richardson, pp. 122, 139.

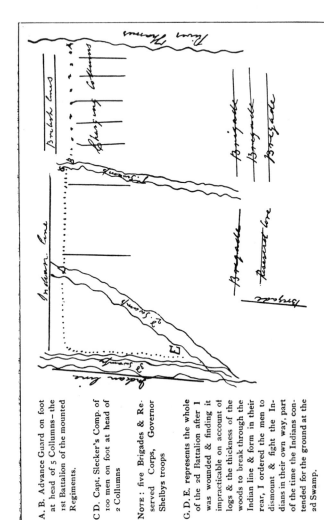

A. B. Advance Guard on foot at head of 5 Collumns—the 1st Battalion of the mounted Regiments.

C. D. Capt. Slecker's Comp. of 100 men on foot at head of 2 Collumns

NOTE: five Brigades & Reserved Corps, Governor Shelbys troops

G. D. E. represents the whole of the 2d Battalion after I was wounded & finding it impracticable on account of logs & the thickness of the woods to break through the Indian line & form in their rear, I ordered the men to dismount & fight the Indians in their own way, part of the time the Indians contended for the ground at the 2d Swamp.

ACCOMPANYING COL. R. M. JOHNSON'S LETTER OF NOV. 21st 1813, DETAILING THE AFFAIR OF THE 5th AT THE RIVER THAMES, ETC—WAR DEPARTMENT ARCHIVES, MSS.

fired.[1] The Forty-first regiment was almost mutinous, but had it been in the best condition it could
not have held against serious attack. The whole
strength of the Forty-first was only three hundred
and fifty-six rank-and-file, or four hundred and eight
men all told.[2] The numbers of the regiment actually in the field were reported as three hundred and
fifteen rank-and-file, or three hundred and sixty-seven
men all told.[3] The dragoons were supposed not to
exceed twenty. This petty force was unable to see
either the advancing enemy or its own members.
The only efficient corps in the field was the Indians,
who were estimated by the British sometimes at five
hundred, at eight hundred, and twelve hundred in
number, and who were in some degree covered by
the swamp.

Harrison came upon the British line soon after two
o'clock in the afternoon, and at once formed his army
in regular order of battle. As the order was disregarded, and the battle was fought, as he reported, in
a manner " not sanctioned by anything that I had
seen or heard of," [4] the intended arrangement mattered little. In truth, the battle was planned as well
as fought by Richard M. Johnson, whose energy impressed on the army a new character from the moment he joined it. While Harrison drew up his

---

[1] Richardson, p. 136.   [2] James, i. 278.
[3] Report of Lieutenant Bullock, Dec. 6, 1813 ; Richardson,
p. 140.
[4] Harrison's Report of Oct. 9, 1813 ; Official Letters, p. 233.

infantry in order of battle, Johnson, whose mounted
regiment was close to the British line, asked leave to
charge,[1] and Harrison gave him the order, although he
knew no rule of war that sanctioned it.

Johnson's tactics were hazardous, though effective.
Giving to his brother, James Johnson, half the regiment to lead up the road against the six-pound gun
and the British Forty-first regiment, R. M. Johnson
with the other half of his regiment wheeled to the
left, at an angle with the road, and crossed the
swamp to attack twice his number of Indians posted
in a thick wood.

James Johnson, with his five hundred men, galloped
directly through the British first line,[2] receiving a
confused fire, and passing immediately to the rear
of the British second line, so rapidly as almost to
capture Proctor himself, who fled at full speed.[3]   As
the British soldiers straggled in bands or singly
toward the rear, they found themselves among the
American mounted riflemen, and had no choice but
to surrender.   About fifty men, with a single lieutenant, contrived to escape through the woods ; all the
rest became prisoners.

R. M. Johnson was less fortunate.   Crossing the
swamp to his left, he was received by the Indians in

[1] R. M. Johnson to Armstrong, Dec. 22, 1834 ; Armstrong's
Notices, i. 232.

[2] Report of Lieutenant Bullock, Dec. 6, 1813 ; Richardson,
p. 140.

[3] Richardson, p. 136.

underbrush which the horses could not penetrate. Under a sharp fire his men were obliged to dismount and fight at close quarters. At an early moment of the battle, Johnson was wounded by the rifle of an Indian warrior who sprang forward to despatch him, but was killed by a ball from Johnson's pistol. The fighting at that point was severe, but Johnson's men broke or turned the Indian line, which was uncovered after the British defeat, and driving the Indians toward the American left, brought them under fire of Shelby's infantry, when they fled.

In this contest Johnson maintained that his regiment was alone engaged. In a letter to Secretary Armstrong, dated six weeks after the battle, he said : [1] —

" I send you an imperfect sketch of the late battle on the river Thames, fought solely by the mounted regiment ; at least, so much so that not fifty men from any other corps assisted. . . . Fought the Indians, twelve hundred or fifteen hundred men, one hour and twenty minutes, driving them from the extreme right to the extreme left of my line, at which last point we came near Governor Shelby, who ordered Colonel Simrall to reinforce me ; but the battle was over, and although the Indians were pursued half a mile, there was no fighting."

Harrison's official report gave another idea of the relative share taken by the Kentucky infantry in the action ; but the difference in dispute was trifling.

[1] R. M. Johnson to Armstrong, Nov. 21, 1813 ; MSS. War Department Archives.

The entire American loss was supposed to be only about fifteen killed and thirty wounded. The battle lasted, with sharpness, not more than twenty minutes; and none but the men under Johnson's command enjoyed opportunity to share in the first and most perilous assault.

The British loss was only twelve men killed and thirty-six wounded. The total number of British prisoners taken on the field and in the Moravian town, or elsewhere on the day of battle, was four hundred and seventy-seven; in the whole campaign, six hundred. All Proctor's baggage, artillery, small arms, stores, and hospital were captured in the Moravian town. The Indians left thirty-three dead on the field, among them one reported to be Tecumthe. After the battle several officers of the British Forty-first, well acquainted with the Shawnee warrior, visited the spot, and identified his body. The Kentuckians had first recognized it, and had cut long strips of skin from the thighs, to keep, as was said, for razor-straps, in memory of the river Raisin.[1]

After Perry's victory on Lake Erie, Tecumthe's life was of no value to himself or his people, and his death was no subject for regret; but the manner chosen for producing this result was an expensive mode of acquiring territory for the United States. The Shawnee warrior compelled the government to pay for once something like the value of the lands

[1] Richardson, p. 125. Lewis Cass to Armstrong, Oct. 28, 1813 ; MSS. War Department Archives.

it took. The precise cost of the Indian war could not be estimated, being combined in many ways with that of the war with England; but the British counted for little, within the northwestern territory, except so far as Tecumthe used them for his purposes. Not more than seven or eight hundred British soldiers ever crossed the Detroit River ; but the United States raised fully twenty thousand men, and spent at least five million dollars and many lives in expelling them. The Indians alone made this outlay necessary. The campaign of Tippecanoe, the surrender of Detroit and Mackinaw, the massacres at Fort Dearborn, the river Raisin, and Fort Meigs, the murders along the frontier, and the campaign of 1813 were the price paid for the Indian lands in the Wabash Valley.

No part of the war more injured British credit on the American continent than the result of the Indian alliance. Except the capture of Detroit and Mackinaw at the outset, without fighting, and the qualified success at the river Raisin, the British suffered only mortifications, ending with the total loss of their fleet, the abandonment of their fortress, the flight of their army, and the shameful scene before the Moravian town, where four hundred British regulars allowed themselves to be ridden over and captured by five hundred Kentucky horsemen, with hardly the loss of a man to the assailants. After such a disgrace the British ceased to be formidable in the northwest. The Indians recognized the hopelessness of their course, and from that moment abandoned their dependence on England.

The battle of the Thames annihilated the right division of the British army in Upper Canada. When the remnants of Proctor's force were mustered, October 17, at Ancaster, a hundred miles from the battlefield, about two hundred rank-and-file were assembled.[1] Proctor made a report of the battle blaming his troops, and Prevost issued a severe reprimand to the unfortunate Forty-first regiment on the strength of Proctor's representations. In the end the Prince Regent disgraced both officers, recognizing by these public acts the loss of credit the government had suffered ; but its recovery was impossible.

So little anxiety did General Harrison thenceforward feel about the Eighth Military District which he commanded, that he returned to Detroit October 7 ; his army followed him, and arrived at Sandwich, October 10, without seeing an enemy. Promptly discharged, the Kentucky Volunteers marched homeward October 14 ; the mounted regiment and its wounded colonel followed a few days later, and within a fortnight only two brigades of the regular army remained north of the Maumee.

At Detroit the war was closed, and except for two or three distant expeditions was not again a subject of interest. The Indians were for the most part obliged to remain within the United States jurisdiction. The great number of Indian families that

[1] Return of Right Division, Richardson, p. 129.

had been collected about Detroit and Malden were rather a cause for confidence than fear, since they were in effect hostages, and any violence committed by the warriors would have caused them, their women and children, to be deprived of food and to perish of starvation. Detroit was full of savages dependent on army supplies, and living on the refuse and offal of the slaughter-yard; but their military strength was gone. Some hundreds of the best warriors followed Proctor to Lake Ontario, but Tecumthe's north-western confederacy was broken up, and most of the tribes made submission.

CHAPTER VII.

THE new Secretaries of War and Navy who took office in January, 1813, were able in the following October to show Detroit recovered. Nine months solved the problem of Lake Erie. The problem of Lake Ontario remained insoluble.

In theory nothing was simpler than the conquest of Upper Canada. Six months before war was declared, Jan. 2, 1812, John Armstrong, then a private citizen, wrote, to Secretary Eustis a letter containing the remark, —

" In invading a neighboring and independent territory like Canada, having a frontier of immense extent ; destitute of means strictly its own for the purposes of defence ; separated from the rest of the empire by an ocean, and having to this but one outlet, — this outlet forms your true object or point of attack."

The river St. Lawrence was the true object of attack, and the Canadians hardly dared hope to defend it.

" From St. Regis to opposite Kingston," said the Quebec " Gazette " in 1814, " the southern bank of the river belongs to the United States. It is well known that this river is the only communication between Upper and Lower Canada. It is rapid and narrow in many places. A few cannon judiciously posted, or even musketry, could render the communication impracticable without powerful escorts, wasting and parcelling the force applicable to the defence of the provinces. It is needless to say that no British force can remain in safety or maintain itself in Upper Canada without a ready communication with the lower province."

Closure of the river anywhere must compel the submission of the whole country above, which could not provide its supplies. The American, who saw his own difficulties of transport between New York and the Lakes, thought well of his energy in surmounting them ; but as the war took larger proportions, and great fleets were built on Lake Ontario, the difficulties of Canadian transport became insuperable. Toward the close of the war, Sir George Prevost wrote to Lord Bathurst [1] that six thirty-two-pound guns for the fleet, hauled in winter four hundred miles from Quebec to Kingston, would cost at least £2000 for transport. Forty twenty-four-pounders hauled on the snow had cost £4,800 ; a cable of the largest size hauled from Sorel to Kingston, two hundred and fifty-five miles, cost £1000 for transport. In summer, when the river was open, the difficulties were hardly less. The commissary-general reported that the impediments of navigation were incalculable, and the scarcity of workmen, laborers, and voyageurs not to be described.[2]

[1] Prevost to Bathurst, Feb. 14, 1815 ; MSS. British Archives.
[2] W. H. Robinson to Prevost, Aug. 27, 1814 ; MSS. British Archives.

If these reasons for attacking and closing the river St. Lawrence had not been decisive with the United States government, other reasons were sufficient. The political motive was as strong as the military. Americans, especially in New England, denied that treasonable intercourse existed with Canada ; but intercourse needed not to be technically treasonable in order to have the effects of treason. Sir George Prevost wrote to Lord Bathurst, Aug. 27, 1814,[1] when the war had lasted two years, —

" Two thirds of the army in Canada are at this moment eating beef provided by American contractors, drawn principally from the States of Vermont and New York. This circumstance, as well as that of the introduction of large sums of specie into this province, being notorious in the United States, it is to be expected Congress will take steps to deprive us of those resources, and under that apprehension large droves are daily crossing the lines coming into Lower Canada."

This state of things had then lasted during three campaigns, from the beginning of the war.   The Indians at Malden, the British army at Niagara, the naval station at Kingston were largely fed by the United States. If these supplies could be stopped, Upper Canada must probably fall ; and they could be easily stopped by interrupting the British line of transport anywhere on the St. Lawrence.

The task was not difficult. Indeed, early in the

[1] Prevost to Bathurst, Aug. 27, 1814; MSS. British Archives, Lower Canada, vol. cxxviii. no. 190.

war an enterprising officer of irregulars, Major Benjamin Forsyth, carried on a troublesome system of annoyance from Ogdensburg, which Sir George Prevost treated with extreme timidity.[1] The British commandant at Prescott, Major Macdonnell, was not so cautious as the governor-general, but crossed the river on the ice with about five hundred men, drove Forsyth from the town, destroyed the public property, and retired in safety with a loss of eight killed and fifty-two wounded.[2] This affair, Feb. 23, 1813, closed hostilities in that region, and Major Forsyth was soon ordered to Sackett's Harbor. His experience, and that of Major Macdonnell, proved how easy the closure of such a river must be, exposed as it was for two hundred miles to the fire of cannon and musketry.

The St. Lawrence was therefore the proper point of approach and attack against Upper Canada. Armstrong came to the Department of War with that idea fixed in his mind. The next subject for his consideration was the means at his disposal.

During Monroe's control of the War Department for two months, between Dec. 3, 1812, and Feb. 5, 1813, much effort had been made to increase the army. Monroe wrote to the chairman of the Military Committee Dec. 22, 1812, a sketch of his ideas.[3]

---

[1] James, i. 140.

[2] Report of Major Macdonnell, Feb. 23, 1813 ; James, i. Appendix no. 16.

[3] State Papers, Military Affairs, i. 608.

He proposed to provide for the general defence by dividing the United States into military districts, and apportioning ninety-three hundred and fifty men among them as garrisons. For offensive operations he required a force competent to overpower the British defence, and in estimating his wants, he assumed that Canada contained about twelve thousand British regulars, besides militia, and three thousand men at Halifax.

"To demolish the British force from Niagara to Quebec," said Monroe, "would require, to make the thing secure, an efficient regular army of twenty thousand men, with an army of reserve of ten thousand. . . . If the government could raise and keep in the field thirty-five thousand regular troops, . . . the deficiency to be supplied even to authorize an expedition against Halifax would be inconsiderable. Ten thousand men would be amply sufficient; but there is danger of not being able to raise that force, and to keep it at that standard. . . . My idea is that provision ought to be made for raising twenty thousand men in addition to the present establishment."

Congress voted about fifty-eight thousand men, and after deducting ten thousand for garrisons, counted on forty-eight thousand for service in Canada. When Armstrong took control, Feb. 5, 1813, he began at once to devise a plan of operation for the army which by law numbered fifty-eight thousand men, and in fact numbered, including the staff and regimental officers, eighteen thousand nine hundred and forty-five men, according to the returns in the adjutant-general's office February 16, 1813. Before he had been a week in the War Department, he wrote, February 10, to Major-General Dearborn announcing that four thousand men were to be immediately collected at Sackett's Harbor, and three thousand at Buffalo. April 1, or as soon as navigation opened, the four thousand troops at Sackett's Harbor were to be embarked and transported in boats under convoy of the fleet across the Lake at the mouth of the St. Lawrence, thirty-five miles, to Kingston. After capturing Kingston, with its magazines, navy-yards, and ships, the expedition was to proceed up the Lake to York (Toronto) and capture two vessels building there. Thence it was to join the corps of three thousand men at Buffalo, and attack the British on the Niagara River.[1]

In explaining his plan to the Cabinet, Armstrong pointed out that the attack from Lake Champlain on Montreal could not begin before May 1 ; that Kingston, between April 1 and May 15, was shut from support by ice ; that not more than two thousand men could be gathered to defend it ; and that by beginning the campaign against Kingston rather than against Montreal, six weeks' time would be gained before reinforcements could arrive from England.[2]

[1] Armstrong to Dearborn, Feb. 10, 1813 ; Armstrong's Notices, i. 221.

[2] Note presented to Cabinet, Feb. 8, 1813 ; Wilkinson's Memoirs, iii. Appendix xxvi.; State Papers, Military Affairs, i. 439.

Whatever defects the plan might have, Kingston, and Kingston alone, possessed so much military importance as warranted the movement. Evidently Armstrong had in mind no result short of the capture of Kingston.

Dearborn received these instructions at Albany, and replied, February 18, that nothing should be omitted on his part in endeavoring to carry into effect the expedition proposed.[1] Orders were given for concentrating the intended force at Sackett's Harbor. During the month of March the preparations were stimulated by a panic due to the appearance of Sir George Prevost at Prescott and Kingston. Dearborn hurried to Sackett's Harbor in person, under the belief that the governor-general was about to attack it.

Armstrong estimated the British force at Kingston as nine hundred regulars, or two thousand men all told; and his estimate was probably correct. The usual garrison at Kingston and Prescott was about eight hundred rank-and-file. In both the British and American services, the returns of rank-and-file were the ordinary gauge of numerical force. Rank-and-file included corporals, but not sergeants or commissioned officers; and an allowance of at least ten sergeants and officers was always to be made for every hundred rank-and-file, in order to estimate the true numerical strength of an army or garrison. Unless otherwise mentioned, the return excluded also

[1] State Papers; Military Affairs, i. 440.

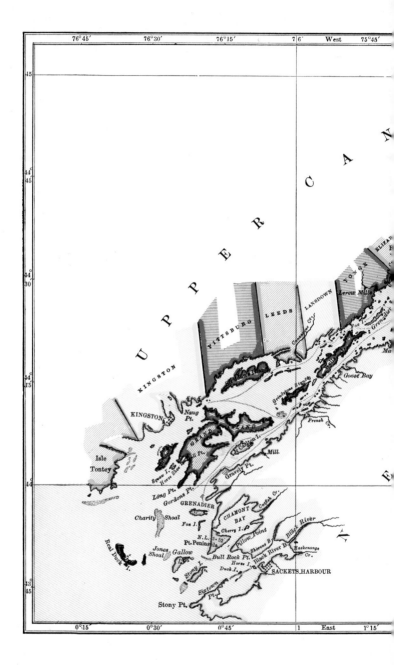

EAST END OF

LAKE ONTARIO

AND

RIVER ST. LAWRENCE

FROM

Kingston to French Mills

REDUCED FROM AN

ORIGINAL DRAWING IN THE
NAVAL DEPARTMENT

BY JOHN MELISH.

SCALE

1 2 3 4 5   10   15   20 Miles

STRUTHERS & CO., ENGR'S, N.Y.

the sick and disabled.   The relative force of every
army was given in effectives, or rank-and-file actually
present for duty.

In the distribution of British forces in Canada for
1812–1813, the garrison at Prescott was allowed three
hundred and seventy-six rank-and-file, with fifty-two
officers including sergeants.   To Kingston three
hundred and eighty-four rank-and-file were allotted,
with sixty officers including sergeants.   To Montreal
and the positions between Prescott and the St. John's
River about five thousand rank-and-file were allotted.[1]
At Prescott and Kingston, besides the regular troops,
the men employed in ship-building or other labor, the
sailors, and the local militia were to be reckoned as
part of the garrison, and Armstrong included them all
in his estimate of two thousand men.

The British force should have been known to
Dearborn nearly as well as his own.   No consid-
erable movement of troops between Lower and Upper
Canada could occur without his knowledge.   Yet
Dearborn wrote to Armstrong, March 9, 1813, from
Sackett's Harbor,[2] —

"I have not yet had the honor of a visit from Sir
George Prevost.   His whole force is concentrated at
Kingston, probably amounting to six or seven thousand,
— about three thousand of them regular troops.   The ice

[1] Distribution of Forces in Canada; Canadian Archives, Freer
Papers, 1812–1813, p. 47.

[2] Dearborn to Armstrong, March 9, 1813; State Papers, Military Affairs, i. 441.

is good, and we expect him every day. . . . As soon as the fall [fate?] of this place [Sackett's Harbor] shall be decided, we shall be able to determine on other measures. If we hold this place, we will command the Lake, and be able to act in concert with the troops at Niagara."

A few days later, March 14, Dearborn wrote again.[1]

"Sir George," he said, had "concluded that it is too late to attack this place. . . . We are probably just strong enough on each side to defend, but not in sufficient force to hazard an offensive movement. The difference of attacking and being attacked, as it regards the contiguous posts of Kingston and Sackett's Harbor, cannot be estimated at less than three or four thousand men, arising from the circumstance of militia acting merely on the defensive."

Clearly Dearborn did not approve Armstrong's plan, and wished to change it. In this idea he was supported, or instigated, by the naval commander on the Lake, Isaac Chauncey, a native of Connecticut, forty years of age, who entered the service in 1798 and became captain in 1806. Chauncey and Dearborn consulted together, and devised a new scheme, which Dearborn explained to Armstrong about March 20 :[2] —

"To take or destroy the armed vessels at York will give us the complete command of the Lake. Commodore Chauncey can take with him ten or twelve hundred troops to be commanded by Pike ; take York ; from thence pro-

[1] Dearborn to Armstrong, March 9, 1813; State Papers, Military Affairs, i. 442.

[2] State Papers, Military Affairs, i. 442.

ceed to Niagara and attack Fort George by land and water, while the troops at Buffalo cross over and carry Forts Erie and Chippewa, and join those at Fort George; and then collect our whole force for an attack on Kingston. After the most mature deliberation the above was considered by Commodore Chauncey and myself as the most certain of ultimate success."

Thus Dearborn and Chauncey inverted Armstrong's plan. Instead of attacking on the St. Lawrence, they proposed to attack on the Niagara. Armstrong acquiesced. "Taking for granted," as he did [1] on Dearborn's assertion, "that General Prevost . . . has assembled at Kingston a force of six or eight thousand men, as stated by you," he could not require that his own plan should be pursued. "The alteration in the plan of campaign so as to make Kingston the last object instead of making it the first, would appear to be necessary, or at least proper," he wrote to Dearborn, March 29.[2]

The scheme proposed by Dearborn and Chauncey was carried into effect by them. The contractors furnished new vessels, which gave to Chauncey for a time the control of the Lake. April 22 the troops, numbering sixteen hundred men, embarked. Armstrong insisted on only one change in the expedition, which betrayed perhaps a shade of malice, for he required Dearborn himself to command it,

[1] Armstrong to Dearborn, April 19, 1813; State Papers, Military Affairs, i. 442.

[2] State Papers, Military Affairs, i. 442.

and Dearborn was suspected of shunning service in
the field.

From the moment Dearborn turned away from
the St. Lawrence and carried the war westward,
the naval and military movements on Lake Ontario
became valuable chiefly as a record of failure.   The
fleet and army arrived at York early in the morning
of April 27.   York, a village numbering in 1806, according to British account, more than three thousand inhabitants, was the capital of Upper Canada,
and contained the residence of the lieutenant-gov-
ernor and the two brick buildings where the Legislature met.   For military purposes the place was
valueless, but it had been used for the construction
of a few war-vessels, and Chauncey represented,
through Dearborn, that "to take or destroy the
armed vessels at York will give us the complete
command of the Lake."   The military force at York,
according to British account, did not exceed six hundred men, regulars and militia; and of these, one
hundred and eighty men, or two companies of the
Eighth or King's regiment, happened to be there
only in passing.[1]

Under the fire of the fleet and riflemen, Pike's
brigade was set ashore; the British garrison, after
a sharp resistance, was driven away, and the town
capitulated.   The ship on the stocks was burned;
the ten-gun brig "Gloucester" was made prize; the
stores were destroyed or shipped; some three hun-

[1] James, i. 143, 149.

dred prisoners were taken; and the public buildings, including the houses of Assembly, were burned.
The destruction of the Assembly houses, afterward
alleged as ground for retaliation against the capitol at Washington, was probably the unauthorized
act of private soldiers. Dearborn protested that it
was done without his knowledge and against his
orders.[1]

The success cost far more than it was worth. The
explosion of a powder magazine, near which the
American advance halted, injured a large number
of men on both sides. Not less than three hundred
and twenty Americans were killed or wounded in the
battle or explosion,[2] or about one fifth of the entire
force. General Pike, the best brigadier then in the
service, was killed. Only two or three battles in
the entire war were equally bloody.[3] "Unfortunately the enemy's armed ship the ' Prince Regent,' "
reported Dearborn,[4] " left this place for Kingston four
days before we arrived."

Chauncey and Dearborn crossed to Niagara, while
the troops remained some ten days at York, and were
then disembarked at Niagara, May 8, according to
Dearborn's report, " in a very sickly and depressed
state; a large proportion of the officers and men

---

[1] Letter of Dearborn, Oct. 17, 1814; Niles, viii. 36.

[2] Niles, iv. 238.

[3] Table of Land Battles; Niles, x. 154.

[4] Dearborn to Armstrong, April 28, 1813; State Papers, Military Affairs, i. 443.

were sickly and debilitated." [1]   Nothing was ready
for the movement which was to drive the British
from Fort George, and before active operations could
begin, Dearborn fell ill.   The details of command fell
to his chief-of-staff, Colonel Winfield Scott.

The military organization at Niagara was at best
unfortunate.   One of Secretary Armstrong's earliest
measures was to issue the military order previously
arranged by Monroe, dividing the Union into military
districts.   Vermont and the State of New York north
of the highlands formed the Ninth Military District,
under Major-General Dearborn.   In the Ninth District
were three points of activity, — Plattsburg on Lake
Champlain, Sackett's Harbor on Lake Ontario, and
the Niagara River.   Each point required a large force
and a commander of the highest ability ; but in May,
1813, Plattsburg and Sackett's Harbor were denuded
of troops and officers, who were all drawn to Niagara,
where they formed three brigades, commanded by
Brigadier-Generals John P. Boyd, who succeeded Pike,
John Chandler, and W. H. Winder.   Niagara and the
troops in its neighborhood were under the command
of Major-General Morgan Lewis, a man of ability, but
possessing neither the youth nor the energy to lead
an army in the field, while Boyd, Chandler, and
Winder were competent only to command regiments.

Winfield Scott in effect assumed control of the
army, and undertook to carry out Van Rensselaer's

[1] Dearborn to Armstrong, May 13, 1813; State Papers, Military Affairs, i. 444.

plan of the year before for attacking Fort George
in the rear, from the Lake. The task was not very
difficult. Chauncey controlled the Lake, and his fleet
was at hand to transfer the troops. Dearborn's force
numbered certainly not less than four thousand rank-
and-file present for duty. The entire British regular
force on the Niagara River did not exceed eighteen
hundred rank-and-file, and about five hundred militia.[1] At Fort George about one thousand regulars
and three hundred militia were stationed, and the
military object to be gained by the Americans was
not so much the capture of Fort George, which was
then not defensible, as that of its garrison.

Early on the morning of May 27, when the mist
cleared away, the British General Vincent saw Chauncey's fleet, " in an extended line of more than two
miles," standing toward the shore. When the ships
took position, " the fire from the shipping so completely enfiladed and scoured the plains, that it became impossible to approach the beach," and Vincent
could only concentrate his force between the Fort and
the enemy, waiting attack. Winfield Scott at the
head of an advance division first landed, followed by
the brigades of Boyd, Winder, and Chandler, and after
a sharp skirmish drove the British back along the
Lake shore, advancing under cover of the fleet. Vincent's report continued : [2] —

[1] James, i. p. 151.
[2] Vincent to Sir George Prevost, May 28, 1813; James, i. 407 ;
Appendix no. 21.

" After awaiting the approach of the enemy for about half an hour I received authentic information that his force, consisting of from four to five thousand men, had reformed his columns and was making an effort to turn my right flank. Having given orders for the fort to be evacuated, the guns to be spiked, and the ammunition destroyed, the troops under my command were put in motion, and marched across the country in a line parallel to the Niagara River, toward the position near the Beaver Dam beyond Queenston mountain. . . . Having assembled my whole force the following morning, which did not exceed sixteen hundred men, I continued my march toward the head of the Lake."

Vincent lost severely in proportion to his numbers, for fifty-one men were killed, and three hundred and five were wounded or missing, chiefly in the Eighth or King's regiment.[1] Several hundred militia were captured in his retreat. The American loss was about forty killed and one hundred and twenty wounded. According to General Morgan Lewis, Col. Winfield Scott " fought nine-tenths of the battle." [2] Dearborn watched the movements from the fleet.

For a time this success made a deep impression on the military administration of Canada, and the abandonment of the whole country west of Kingston was thought inevitable.[3] The opportunity for achieving a decided advantage was the best that occurred for

---

[1] Return of killed, etc.; James, i. 410.

[2] Morgan Lewis to Armstrong, July 5, 1813 ; MSS. War Department Archives.

[3] James, i. 203.

the Americans during the entire war; but whatever might be said in public, the battle of Fort George was a disappointment to the War Department[1] as well as to the officers in command of the American army, who had hoped to destroy the British force. The chief advantage gained was the liberation of Perry's vessels at Black Rock above the Falls, which enabled Perry to complete his fleet on Lake Erie.

On Lake Ontario, May 31, Chauncey insisted, not without cause, on returning to Sackett's Harbor. Dearborn, instead of moving with his whole force, ordered Brigadier-General Winder, June 1, to pursue Vincent. Winder, with eight hundred or a thousand men marched twenty miles, and then sent for reinforcements. He was joined, June 5, by General Chandler with another brigade. Chandler then took command, and advanced with a force supposed to number in the aggregate two thousand men[2] to Stony Creek, within ten miles of Vincent's position at Hamilton, where sixteen hundred British regulars were encamped. There Chandler and Winder posted themselves for the night, much as Winchester and his Kentuckians had camped at the river Raisin four months earlier.[3]

Vincent was not to be treated with such freedom.

[1] Armstrong to Dearborn, June 19, 1813; State Papers, Military Affairs, i. 449.

[2] Table of land battles; Niles, x. 154.

[3] Morgan Lewis to Armstrong, June 14, 1813; Official Letters, p. 165. Chandler to Dearborn, June 18, 1813; Official Letters, p. 169.

Taking only seven hundred rank-and-file,[1] he led
them himself against Chandler's camp. The attack
began, in intense darkness, at two o'clock in the
morning of June 6. The British quickly broke the
American centre and carried the guns. The lines
became mixed, and extreme confusion lasted till
dawn. In the darkness both American generals,
Chandler and Winder, walked into the British force
in the centre, and were captured.[2] With difficulty
the two armies succeeded in recovering their order,
and then retired in opposite directions. The British
suffered severely, reporting twenty-three killed, one
hundred and thirty-four wounded, and fifty-five missing, or two hundred and twelve men in all; but they
safely regained Burlington Heights at dawn.[3] The
American loss was less in casualties, for it amounted
only to fifty-five killed and wounded, and one hundred
missing; but in results the battle at Stony Creek
was equally disgraceful and decisive. The whole
American force, leaving the dead unburied, fell back
ten miles, where Major-General Lewis took command
in the afternoon of June 7. An hour later the British fleet under Sir James Yeo made its appearance,
threatening to cut off Lewis's retreat. Indians hov-
ered about. Boats and baggage were lost. Dearborn

[1] Vincent to Prevost, June 6, 1813; James, i. p. 431.

[2] Chandler's Report of June 18, 1813; State Papers, Military Affairs, i. p. 448.

[3] Report of Colonel Harvey, June 6, 1813; Canadiana,
April, 1889. Report of General Vincent, June 6, 1813; James,
i. p. 431.

sent pressing orders to Lewis directing him to return, and on the morning of June 8 the division reached Fort George.[1]

These mortifications prostrated Dearborn, whose strength had been steadily failing. June 8 he wrote to Armstrong: "My ill state of health renders it extremely painful to attend to the current duties; and unless my health improves soon, I fear I shall be compelled to retire to some place where my mind may be more at ease for a short time."[2] June 10, his adjutant-general, Winfield Scott, issued orders devolving on Major-General Morgan Lewis the temporary command not only of the Niagara army but also of the Ninth Military district.[3] "In addition to the debility and fever he has been afflicted with," wrote Dearborn's aid, S. S. Connor, to Secretary Armstrong, June 12,[4] "he has, within the last twenty-four hours, experienced a violent spasmodic attack on his breast, which has obliged him to relinquish business altogether." "I have doubts whether he will ever again be fit for service," wrote Morgan Lewis to Armstrong, June 14;[5] "he has been repeatedly in a state of convalescence, but relapses on the least agitation of mind." June 20 Dearborn himself wrote in a very despondent spirit both in regard to his health and

[1] Morgan Lewis to Armstrong, June 14 (8?), 1813; Official Letters, p. 165.
[2] State Papers; Military Affairs, i. 445.
[3] State Papers; Military Affairs, i. 447.
[4] State Papers; Military Affairs, i. 448.
[5] State Papers; Military Affairs, i. 446.

to the military situation : " I have been so reduced in strength as to be incapable of any command. Brigadier-General Boyd is the only general officer present." [1]

The sudden departure of Morgan Lewis, ordered to Sackett's Harbor, left General Boyd for a few days to act as the general in command at Niagara. Boyd, though well known for his success at Tippecanoe, was not a favorite in the army. " A compound of ignorance, vanity, and petulance," wrote his late superior, Morgan Lewis,[2] " with nothing to recommend him but that species of bravery in the field which is vaporing, boisterous, stifling reflection, blinding observation, and better adapted to the bully than the soldier."

Galled by complaints of the imbecility of the army, Boyd, with Dearborn's approval,[3] June 23, detached Colonel Boerstler of the Fourteenth Infantry with some four hundred men and two field-pieces, to batter a stone house at Beaver Dam, some seventeen miles from Fort George.[4] Early in the morning of June 24 Boerstler marched to Beaver Dam. There he found himself surrounded in the woods by hostile Indians, numbering according to British authority about two hundred. The Indians, annoying both front and rear, caused Boerstler to attempt retreat,

[1] State Papers ; Military Affairs, i. 449.

[2] Morgan Lewis to Armstrong, July 5, 1813 ; MSS. War Department Archives.

[3] Memoir of Dearborn, etc., compiled by Charles Coffin, p. 139.

[4] Court of Inquiry on Colonel Boerstler, Feb. 17, 1815; Niles x. 19.

but his retreat was stopped by a few militia-men, said to number fifteen.[1] A small detachment of one hundred and fifty men came to reinforce Boerstler, and Lieutenant Fitzgibbon of the British Forty-ninth regiment, with forty-seven men, reinforced the Indians. Unable to extricate himself, and dreading dispersion and massacre, Boerstler decided to surrender; and his five hundred and forty men accordingly capitulated to a British lieutenant with two hundred and sixty Indians, militia, and regulars.

Dearborn reported the disaster as " an unfortunate and unaccountable event; "[2] but of such events the list seemed endless. A worse disaster, equally due to Dearborn and Chauncey, occurred at the other end of the Lake. Had they attacked Kingston, as Armstrong intended, their movement would have covered Sackett's Harbor; but when they placed themselves a hundred and fifty miles to the westward of Sackett's Harbor, they could do nothing to protect it. Sackett's Harbor was an easy morning's sail from Kingston, and the capture of the American naval station was an object of infinite desire on the part of Sir George Prevost, since it would probably decide the result of the war.

Prevost, though not remarkable for audacity, could not throw away such an opportunity without ruining his reputation. He came to Kingston, and while

[1] James, i. 216.

[2] Dearborn to Armstrong, June 25, 1813 ; State Papers, Military Affairs, i. 449.

Dearborn was preparing to capture Fort George in the night of May 26–27, Prevost embarked his whole regular force, eight hundred men all told,[1] on Yeo's fleet at Kingston, set sail in the night, and at dawn of May 27 was in sight of Sackett's Harbor.[2]

Had Yeo and Prevost acted with energy, they must have captured the Harbor without serious resistance. According to Sir George's official report, "light and adverse winds" prevented the ships from nearing the Fort until evening.[3] Probably constitutional vacillation on the part of Sir James Yeo caused delay, for Prevost left the control wholly to him and Colonel Baynes.[4]

At Sackett's Harbor about four hundred men of different regular regiments, and about two hundred and fifty Albany volunteers were in garrison; and a general alarm, given on appearance of the British fleet in the distance, brought some hundreds of militia into the place; but the most important reinforcement was Jacob Brown, a brigadier-general of State militia who lived in the neighborhood, and had been requested by Dearborn to take command in case of an emergency   Brown arrived at the

---

[1] James, i. 165; Colonel Baynes to Prevost, May 30, 1813; James, i. 413.

[2] Report of Sir George Prevost, June 1, 1813; MSS. British Archives.

[3] Prevost to Bathurst, June 1, 1813; MSS. British Archives. Prevost's Life, p. 82, 83.

[4] James, i. 165, 166.   Brenton to Freer, May 30, 1813; MSS. Canadian Archives, Freer Papers, 1812–1813, p. 183.

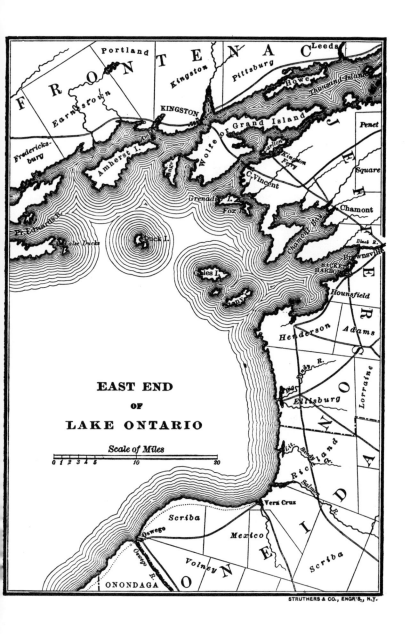

EAST END
OF
LAKE ONTARIO

Scale of Miles

0 1 2 3 4 5   10   20

STRUTHERS & CO., ENGR'S., N.Y.

Harbor in time to post the men in order of battle. Five hundred militia were placed at the point where the British were expected to land; the regulars were arranged in a second line; the forts were in the rear.

At dawn of May 28, under command of Colonel Baynes, the British grenadiers of the One Hundredth regiment landed gallantly under " so heavy and galling a fire from a numerous but almost invisible foe, as to render it impossible to halt for the artillery to come up." [1] Pressing rapidly forward, without stopping to fire, the British regulars routed the militia and forced the second line back until they reached a block-house at the edge of the village, where a thirty-two pound gun was in position, flanked by log barracks and fallen timber. While Brown with difficulty held his own at the military barracks, the naval lieutenant in charge of the ship-yard, being told that the battle was lost, set fire to the naval barracks, shipping, and store-houses. Brown's indignation at this act was intense.

" The burning of the marine barracks was as infamous a transaction as ever occurred among military men," he wrote to Dearborn. [2] " The fire was set as our regulars met the enemy upon the main line; and if anything could have appalled these gallant men it would have been the flames in their rear.   We have all, I presume, suffered in the public estimation in consequence of this disgraceful

---

[1] Report of Colonel Baynes, May 30, 1813 ; James, i. 413.
[2] Brown to Dearborn, July 25, 1813; Dearborn MSS.

burning. The fact is, however, that the army is entitled to much higher praise than though it had not occurred. The navy are alone responsible for what happened on Navy Point, and it is fortunate for them that they have reputations sufficient to sustain the shock."

Brown's second line stood firm at the barracks, and the British attack found advance impossible. Sir George Prevost's report admitted his inability to go farther : [1] —

" A heavier fire than that of musketry having become necessary in order to force their last position, I had the mortification to learn that the continuation of light and adverse winds had prevented the co-operation of the ships, and that the gunboats were unequal to silence the enemy's elevated batteries, or to produce any effect on their block houses. Considering it therefore impracticable without such assistance to carry the strong works by which the post was defended, I reluctantly ordered the troops to leave a beaten enemy whom they had driven before them for upwards of three hours, and who did not venture to offer the slightest opposition to the re-embarkation, which was effected with proper deliberation and in perfect order."

If Sir George was correct in regarding the Americans as " a beaten enemy," his order of retreat to his own troops seemed improper ; but his language showed that he used the words in a sense of his own, and Colonel Baynes's report gave no warrant for the British claim of a victory.[2]

[1] Prevost's Report of June 1, 1813; MSS. British Archives.
[2] James, i. 175.

" At this point," said Baynes,[1] " the further energies
of the troops became unavailing. Their [American]
block-houses and stockaded battery could not be carried
by assault, nor reduced by field-pieces had we been provided with them. . . . Seeing no object within our reach
to attain that could compensate for the loss we were mo-
mentarily sustaining from the heavy fire of the enemy's
cannon, I directed the troops to take up the position we
had charged from. From this position we were ordered
to re-embark, which was performed at our leisure and in
perfect order, the enemy not presuming to show a single
soldier without the limits of his fortress."

Another and confidential report was written by
E. B. Brenton of Prevost's staff to the governor's
military secretary, Noah Freer.[2] After describing
the progress of the battle until the British advance
was stopped, Brenton said that Colonel Baynes came
to Sir George to tell him that the men could not
approach nearer the works with any prospect of
success : —

" It was however determined to collect all the troops
at a point, to form the line, and to make an attack immediately upon the battery and barracks in front. For
this purpose the men in advance were called in, the line
formed a little without the reach of the enemy's musketry, and though evidently much fagged, was, after being supplied with fresh ammunition, again led in line.
At this time I do not think the whole force collected in
the lines exceeded five hundred men."

[1] Report of Colonel Baynes, May 30, 1813; James, i. 413.
[2] Brenton to Freer, May 30, 1813; MSS. Canadian Archives.
Freer Papers, 1812–1813.

The attack was made, and part of the Hundred-
and-fourth regiment succeeded in getting shelter behind one of the American barracks, preparing for a
farther advance. Sir George Prevost, under a fire
which his aid described as tremendous, — "I do
not exaggerate when I tell you that the shot, both
of musketry and grape, was falling about us like
hail," — watched the American position through a
glass, when, "at this time those who were left of
the troops behind the barracks made a dash out to
charge the enemy; but the fire was so destructive
that they were instantly turned by it, and the retreat was sounded. Sir George, fearless of danger
and disdaining to run or to suffer his men to run,
repeatedly called out to them to retire in order;
many however made off as fast as they could."

These reports agreed that the British attack was
totally defeated, with severe loss, before the retreat
was sounded. Such authorities should have silenced
dispute; but Prevost had many enemies in Canada,
and at that period of the war the British troops
were unused to defeat. Both Canadians and English attacked the governor-general privately and publicly, freely charging him with having disgraced the
service, and offering evidence of his want of courage
in the action.[1] Americans, though not interested
in the defence of Prevost, could not fail to remark
that the British and Canadian authorities who condemned him, assumed a condition of affairs alto-

[1] Quarterly Review, xxvii. 419; Christie, ii. 81; James, i. 177.

gether different from that accepted by American authorities. The official American reports not only supported the views taken by Prevost and Baynes of the hopelessness of the British attack, but added particulars which made Prevost's retreat necessary. General Brown's opinion was emphatic : " Had not General Prevost retired *most rapidly* under the guns of his vessels, he would never have returned to Kingston." [1] These words were a part of Brown's official report. Writing to Dearborn he spoke with the same confidence : [2] —

" The militia were all rallied before the enemy gave way, and were marching perfectly in his view towards the rear of his right flank; and I am confident that even then, if Sir George had not retired with the utmost pre-cipitation to his boats, he would have been cut off."

Unlike the Canadians, Brown thought Prevost's conduct correct and necessary, but was by no means equally complimentary to Sir James Yeo, whom he blamed greatly for failing to join in the battle. The want of wind which Yeo alleged in excuse, Brown flatly denied. From that time Brown entertained and freely expressed contempt for Yeo, as he seemed also to feel little respect for Chauncey. His expe-rience with naval administration on both sides led him to expect nothing but inefficiency from either.

Whatever were the true causes of Prevost's failure, Americans could not admit that an expedition which

[1] Brown's Report of June 1, 1813; Niles, iv. 260.
[2] Brown to Dearborn, July 25, 1813; Dearborn MSS.

cost the United States so much, and which so nearly succeeded, was discreditable to the British governor-general, or was abandoned without sufficient reason. The British return of killed and wounded proved the correctness of Prevost, Baynes, and Brown in their opinion of the necessity of retreat. According to the report of Prevost's severest critics, he carried less than seven hundred and fifty rank-and-file to Sackett's Harbor.[1] The returns showed forty-four rank-and-file killed; one hundred and seventy-two wounded, and thirteen missing, — in all, two hundred and twenty-nine men, or nearly one man in three. The loss in officers was relatively even more severe; and the total loss in an aggregate which could hardly have numbered much more than eight hundred and fifty men all told, amounted to two hundred and fifty-nine killed, wounded, and missing, leaving Prevost less than six hundred men to escape,[2] in the face of twice their numbers and under the fire of heavy guns.[3]

The British attack was repulsed, and Jacob Brown received much credit as well as a commission of brigadier-general in the United States army for his success; but the injury inflicted by the premature destruction at the navy-yard was very great, and was sensibly felt. Such a succession of ill news could not but affect the Government. The repeated failures to destroy the British force at Niagara; the

[1] James, i. 165.   [2] Return, etc.; James, i. 417.
[3] Baynes's Report of May 30, 1813; James, i. 413.

disasters of Chandler, Winder, and Boerstler; the narrow and partial escape of Sackett's Harbor; the total incapacity of Dearborn caused by fever and mortification, — all these evils were not the only or the greatest subjects for complaint. The two commanders, Dearborn and Chauncey, had set aside the secretary's plan of campaign, and had substituted one of their own, on the express ground of their superior information. While affirming that the garrison at Kingston had been reinforced to a strength three or four times as great as was humanly possible, they had asserted that the capture of York would answer their purpose as well as the capture of Kingston, to "give us the complete command of the Lake." They captured York, April 27, but the British fleet appeared June 6, and took from them the command of the Lake. These miscalculations or misstatements, and the disasters resulting from them, warranted the removal of Chauncey as well as Dearborn from command; but the brunt of dissatisfaction fell on Dearborn alone. Both Cabinet and Congress agreed in insisting on Dearborn's retirement, and the President was obliged to consent. July 6, Secretary Armstrong wrote, —

"I have the President's orders to express to you the decision that you retire from the command of District No. 9, and of the troops within the same, until your health be re-established and until further orders."

CHAPTER VIII.

ARMSTRONG'S embarrassment was great in getting rid of the generals whom Madison and Eustis left on his hands. Dearborn was one example of what he was obliged to endure, but Wilkinson was a worse. According to Armstrong's account,[1] New Orleans was not believed to be safe in Wilkinson's keeping. The senators from Louisiana, Tennessee, and Kentucky remonstrated to the President, and the President ordered his removal. Armstrong and Wilkinson had been companions in arms, and had served with Gates at Saratoga. For many reasons Armstrong wished not unnecessarily to mortify Wilkinson, and in conveying to him, March 10, the abrupt order [2] to proceed with the least possible delay to the headquarters of Major-General Dearborn at Sackett's Harbor, the Secretary of War added, March 12, a friendly letter of advice : [3] —

[1] Strictures on General Wilkinson's Defence ; from the Albany " Argus." Niles, ix. 425.

[2] Armstrong to Wilkinson, March 10, 1813 ; Wilkinson's Memoirs, iii. 341.

[3] Armstrong to Wilkinson, March 12, 1813 ; Wilkinson's Memoirs, iii. 342.

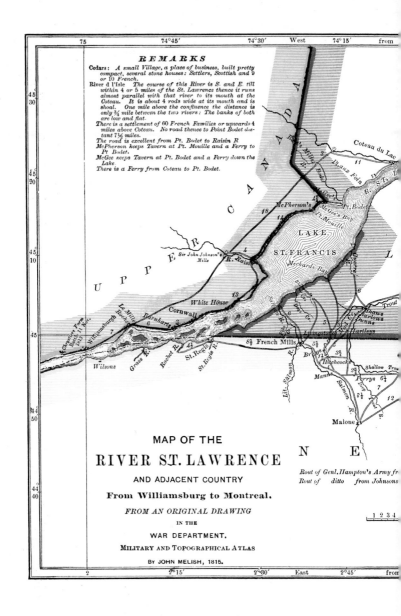

REMARKS

Cedars: *A small Village, a place of business, built pretty compact, several stone houses: Settlers, Scottish and 9 or 10 French.*

River d l'Isle: *The course of this River is S. and E. till within 4 or 5 miles of the St. Lawrence thence it runs almost parallel with that river to its mouth at the Coteau. It is about 4 rods wide at its mouth and is shoal. One mile above the confluence the distance is only ¾ mile between the two rivers: The banks of both are low and flat.*

There is a settlement of 60 French Families or upwards 4 miles above Coteau. No road thence to Point Bodet distant 7½ miles.

The road is excellent from Pt. Bodet to Raisin R.

McPherson keeps Tavern at Pt. Mouille and a Ferry to Pt. Bodet.

McGee keeps Tavern at Pt. Bodet and a Ferry down the Lake.

There is a Ferry from Coteau to Pt. Bodet.

MAP OF THE

RIVER ST. LAWRENCE

AND ADJACENT COUNTRY

From Williamsburg to Montreal.

FROM AN ORIGINAL DRAWING

IN THE

WAR DEPARTMENT.

MILITARY AND TOPOGRAPHICAL ATLAS

By JOHN MELISH, 1815.

Rout of Genl. Hampton's Army fr...
Rout of ditto from Johnsons

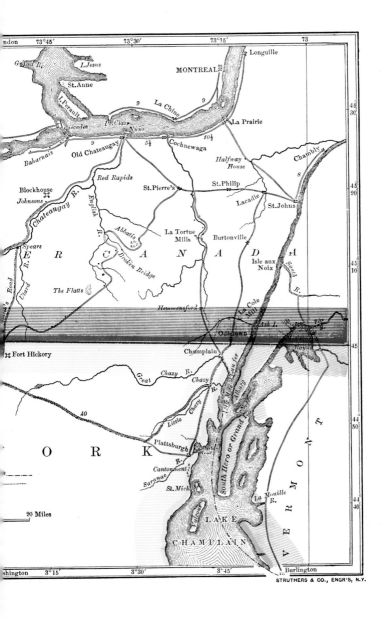

" Why should you remain in your land of cypress when patriotism and ambition equally invite to one where grows the laurel?   Again, the men of the North and East want you; those of the South and West are less sensible of your merits and less anxious to have you among them. I speak to you with a frankness due to you and to myself, and again advise, Come to the North, and come quickly!   If our cards be well played, we may renew the scene of Saratoga."

The phrase was curious.   Saratoga suggested defeated invasion rather than conquest; the surrender of a British army in the heart of New York rather than the capture of Montreal.   The request for Wilkinson's aid was disheartening.   No one knew better than Armstrong the feebleness of Wilkinson's true character.   "The selection of this unprincipled imbecile was not the blunder of Secretary Armstrong," said Winfield Scott long afterward;[1] but the idea that Wilkinson could be chief-of-staff to Dearborn, — that one weak man could give strength to another, — was almost as surprising as the selection of Wilkinson to chief command would have been.   Armstrong did not intend that Wilkinson should command more than a division under Dearborn;[2] but he must have foreseen that in the event of Dearborn's illness or incapacity, Wilkinson would become by seniority general-in-chief.

Wilkinson at New Orleans received Armstrong's

[1] Autobiography, p. 94, *note.*
[2] Strictures ; Niles, ix. 425.

letter of March 10 only May 19,[1] and started, June 10, for Washington, where he arrived July 31, having consumed the greater part of the summer in the journey. On arriving at Washington, he found that Dearborn had been removed, and that he was himself by seniority in command of the Ninth Military District.[2] This result of Dearborn's removal was incalculably mischievous, for if its effect on Wilkinson's vanity was unfortunate, its influence on the army was fatal. Almost every respectable officer of the old service regarded Wilkinson with antipathy or contempt.

Armstrong's ill-fortune obliged him also to place in the position of next importance Wilkinson's pronounced enemy, Wade Hampton. A major-general was required to take command on Lake Champlain, and but one officer of that rank claimed employment or could be employed; and Wade Hampton was accordingly ordered to Plattsburg.[3] Of all the major-generals Hampton was probably the best; but his faults were serious. Proud and sensitive even for a South Carolinian; irritable, often harsh, sometimes unjust, but the soul of honor,[4] Hampton was rendered wholly intractable wherever Wilkinson was concerned, by the long-standing feud which had made the two generals for years the heads of hostile sec-

---

[1] Wilkinson to Armstrong, May 23, 1813; Wilkinson's Memoirs, iii. 341.

[2] Armstrong's Notices, ii. 23.

[3] Armstrong's Notices, ii. 23.

[4] Scott's Autobiography, p. 50.

tions in the army.[1] Hampton loathed Wilkinson. At the time of his appointment to command on Lake Champlain he had no reason to expect that Wilkinson would be his superior; but though willing and even wishing to serve under Dearborn, he accepted only on the express understanding that his was a distinct and separate command,[2] and that his orders were to come directly from the War Department. Only in case of a combined movement uniting different armies, was he to yield to the rule of seniority. With that agreement he left Washington, June 15, and assumed command, July 3, on Lake Champlain.

Nearly a month afterward Wilkinson arrived in Washington, and reported at the War Department. By that time Armstrong had lost whatever chance he previously possessed of drawing the army at Niagara back to a position on the enemy's line of supply. Three insuperable difficulties stood in his way, — the season was too late ; the army was too weak; and the generals were incompetent. Armstrong found his generals the chief immediate obstacle, and struggled perseveringly and good-humoredly to overcome it. Wilkinson began, on arriving at Washington, by showing a fancy for continuing the campaign at Niagara.[3] Armstrong was obliged to give an em-

[1] Scott's Autobiography, p. 36.

[2] Hampton to Armstrong, Aug. 23, 1813 ; Wilkinson's Memoirs, iii. Appendix xxxvi.

[3] Memorandum by Armstrong, July 23, 1813; Wilkinson to Armstrong, Aug. 6, 1813 ; State Papers, Military Affairs, i. 463 ; Armstrong's Notices, ii. 31.

phatic order, dated August 8, that Kingston should be the primary object of the campaign, but he left Wilkinson at liberty to go there by almost any route, even by way of Montreal.[1] Disappointed at the outset by finding Wilkinson slow to accept responsibility or decided views,[2] he was not better pleased when the new general began his duties in Military District No. 9.

Wilkinson left Washington August 11, and no sooner did he reach Albany than he hastened to write, August 16, two letters to General Hampton, assuming that every movement of that general was directly dependent on Wilkinson's orders.[3] Considering the relations between the two men, these letters warranted the inference that Wilkinson intended to drive Hampton out of his Military District, and if possible from the service. Hampton instantly leaped to that conclusion, and wrote to Armstrong, August 23, offering his resignation in case Wilkinson's course was authorized by government.[4] Wilkinson also wrote to the secretary August 30, substantially avowing his object to be what Hampton supposed : [5] —

" You have copies of my letters to Major-General Hampton, which I know he has received, yet I have no

[1] Armstrong to Wilkinson, Aug. 8, 1813 ; State Papers, Military Affairs, i. 464.

[2] Armstrong's Notices, ii. 32.

[3] Wilkinson's Memoirs, iii. Appendix xxxv.

[4] Hampton to Armstrong, Aug. 23, 1813 ; Memoirs, iii. Appendix xxxvi.

[5] Wilkinson's Memoirs, iii. 358.

answer. The reflection which naturally occurs is that
if I am authorized to command he is bound to obey;
and if he will not respect the obligation, he should be
turned out of the service."

Armstrong pacified Hampton by promising once
more that all his orders and reports should pass
through the Department Hampton promised to serve
cordially and vigorously through the campaign, but
he believed himself intended for a sacrifice, and declared his intention of resigning as soon as the
campaign was ended.[1] Wilkinson, after having at
Albany provoked this outburst, started for Sackett's
Harbor, where he arrived August 20.

At Sackett's Harbor Wilkinson found several general officers. Morgan Lewis was there in command,
Commodore Chauncey was there with his fleet. Jacob
Brown was also present by virtue of his recent appointment as brigadier-general. The quartermaster-
general, Robert Swartwout, a brother of Burr's friend
who went to New Orleans, was posted there. Wilkinson summoned these officers to a council of
war August 26, which deliberated on the different plans of campaign proposed to it, and unanimously decided in favor of one called by Armstrong
"No. 3 of the plans proposed by the government."[2]

[1] Hampton to Armstrong, Aug. 31, 1813 ; MSS. War Department Archives.   Armstrong to Wilkinson, Sept. 6, 1813; Wilkinson's Memoirs, iii. Appendix xxxvii.

[2] Armstrong's Notices, ii. 33; Memorandum of July 23, 1813;
State Papers, Military Affairs, i. 463.

As defined in Wilkinson's language [1] the scheme was —

" To rendezvous the whole of the troops on the Lake in this vicinity, and in co-operation with our squadron to make a bold feint upon Kingston, slip down the St. Lawrence, lock up the enemy in our rear to starve or surrender, or oblige him to follow us without artillery, baggage, or provisions, or eventually to lay down his arms ; to sweep the St. Lawrence of armed craft, and in concert with the division under Major-General Hampton to take Montreal."

Orders were given, August 25, for providing river transport for seven thousand men, forty field-pieces, and twenty heavy guns, to be in readiness by September 15. [2]

The proposed expedition closely imitated General Amherst's expedition against Montreal in 1760, with serious differences of relative situation. After Wolfe had captured Quebec and hardly twenty-five hundred French troops remained to defend Montreal, in the month of July Amherst descended the river from Lake Ontario with more than ten thousand men, chiefly British veterans, capturing every fortified position as he went. Wilkinson's council of war proposed to descend the river in October or November with seven thousand men, leaving a hostile fleet and fortresses in their rear, and running past every for-

[1] Minutes, etc. ; Wilkinson's Memoirs, iii. Appendix no. 1.

[2] Wilkinson to Swartwout, Aug. 25, 1813; Wilkinson's Memoirs, iii. 51.

tified position to arrive in the heart of a comparatively well populated country, held by a force greater than their own, with Quebec to support it, while Wilkinson would have no certain base of supplies, reinforcements, or path of escape. Knowledge of Wilkinson's favorite Quintus Curtius or of Armstrong's familiar Jomini was not required to satisfy any intelligent private, however newly recruited, that under such circumstances the army would be fortunate to escape destruction.[1]

Wilkinson next went to Niagara, where he arrived September 4, and where he found the army in a bad condition, with Boyd still in command, but restrained by the President's orders within a strict defensive. Wilkinson remained nearly a month at Fort George making the necessary preparations for a movement. He fell ill of fever, but returned October 2 to Sackett's Harbor, taking with him all the regular troops at Niagara. At that time Chauncey again controlled the Lake.

Secretary Armstrong also came to Sackett's Harbor, September 5, and established the War Department at that remote point for nearly two months.[2] When Wilkinson arrived, October 2, Armstrong's difficulties began. Wilkinson, then fifty-six years old, was broken by the Lake fever. "He was so

[1] Cf. Wilkinson to Armstrong, Oct. 19, 1813; State Papers, Military Affairs, i. 472.

[2] Armstrong to Wilkinson, Sept. 6, 1813 ; Wilkinson's Memoirs, iii. Appendix xxxvii.

much indisposed in mind and body," according to
Brigadier-General Boyd,[1] " that in any other service
he would have perhaps been superseded in his command."　According to Wilkinson's story, he told
Secretary Armstrong that he was incapable of commanding the army, and offered to retire from it;
but the secretary said there was no one to take his
place, and he could not be spared.　In private
Armstrong was believed to express himself more
bluntly, and Wilkinson was told that the secretary said: " I would feed the old man with pap
sooner than leave him behind." [2]　Wilkinson's debility did not prevent him from giving orders, or
from becoming jealous and suspicious of every one,
but chiefly of Armstrong.[3]　Whatever was suggested by Armstrong was opposed by Wilkinson.
Before returning to Sackett's Harbor, October 4,
Wilkinson favored an attack on Kingston.[4]　On
reaching Sackett's Harbor, finding that Armstrong
also favored attacking Kingston, Wilkinson argued
" against my own judgment " in favor of passing
Kingston and descending upon Montreal.[5]　Ten days
afterward Armstrong changed his mind.　Yeo had
succeeded in returning to Kingston, bringing reinforcements.

[1] Testimony of Brigadier-General Boyd; Wilkinson's Memoirs,
iii. 80.

[2] Wilkinson's Memoirs, iii. 354.

[3] Wilkinson's Memoirs, iii. 357.

[4] Wilkinson's Memoirs, iii. 353.

[5] Wilkinson's Memoirs, iii. 190 ; Paper A, *note.*

" He will bring with him about fifteen hundred effectives," wrote Armstrong;[1] " and thanks to the storm and our snail-like movements down the Lake, they will be there before we can reach it. The manœuvre intended is lost, so far as regards Kingston. What we now do against that place must be done by hard blows, at some risk."

Accordingly, October 19, Armstrong wrote to Wilkinson a letter advising abandonment of the attack on Kingston, and an effort at " grasping the safer and the greater object below."[2]

" I call it the safer and greater object, because at Montreal you find the weaker place and the smaller force to encounter ; at Montreal you meet a fresh, unexhausted, efficient reinforcement of four thousand men ; at Montreal you approach your own resources, and establish between you and them an easy and an expeditious intercourse ; at Montreal you occupy a point which must be gained in carrying your attacks home to the purposes of the war, and which, if seized now, will save one campaign ; at Montreal you hold a position which completely severs the enemy's line of operations, which shuts up the Ottawa as well as the St. Lawrence against him, and which while it restrains all below, withers and perishes all above itself."

As Armstrong veered toward Montreal Wilkinson turned decidedly toward Kingston, and wrote the

[1] Armstrong to Hampton, Oct. 16, 1813 ; Wilkinson's Memoirs, iii. 361.

[2] Armstrong to Wilkinson, Oct. 19, 1813 ; State Papers, Military Affairs, i. 472.

same day to the secretary a letter [1] of remonstrance, closing by a significant remark : —

" Personal considerations would make me prefer a visit to Montreal to the attack of Kingston ; but before I abandon this attack, which by my instructions I am ordered to make, it is necessary to my justification that you should by the authority of the President direct the operations of the army under my command particularly against Montreal."

The hint was strong that Wilkinson believed Armstrong to be trying to evade responsibility, as Armstrong believed Wilkinson to be trying to shirk it. Both insinuations were probably well-founded ; neither Armstrong nor Wilkinson expected to capture Kingston, and still less Montreal. Wilkinson plainly said as much at the time. " I speak conjecturally," he wrote ; " but should we surmount every obstacle in descending the river we shall advance upon Montreal ignorant of the force arrayed against us, and in case of misfortune, having no retreat, the army must surrender at discretion." Armstrong's conduct was more extraordinary than Wilkinson's, and could not be believed except on his own evidence. He not only looked for no capture of Montreal, but before writing his letter of October 19 to Wilkinson, he had given orders for preparing winter quarters for the army sixty or eighty miles above Montreal, and did this

[1] Wilkinson to Armstrong, Oct. 19, 1813 ; State Papers, Military Affairs, i. 472.

without informing Wilkinson. In later years he
wrote : [1] —

" Suspecting early in October, from the lateness of the
season, the inclemency of the weather, and the continued
indisposition of the commanding general, that the campaign then in progress would terminate as it did, — ' with
the disgrace of doing nothing, but without any material
diminution of physical power,' — the Secretary of War,
then at Sackett's Harbor, hastened to direct Major-
General Hampton to employ a brigade of militia attached to his command, in constructing as many huts
as would be sufficient to cover an army of ten thousand
men during the winter."

The order dated October 16 and addressed to the
quartermaster-general,[2] prescribed the cantonment
of ten thousand men within the limits of Canada,
and plainly indicated the secretary's expectation
that the army could not reach Montreal. In other
ways Armstrong showed the same belief more
openly.

All the available troops on or near Lake Ontario
were concentrated at Sackett's Harbor about the
middle of October, and did not exceed seven thousand effectives, or eight thousand men.[3] "I calculate
on six thousand combatants," wrote Wilkinson after

[1] Armstrong's Notices, ii. 63.
[2] Armstrong to Swartwout, Oct. 16, 1813; Wilkinson's Memoirs, iii. 70.
[3] Council of War, Nov. 8, 1813; Wilkinson's Memoirs, iii.
Appendix xxiv. Report of Adjutant-General, Dec. 1, 1813, Appendix vii.

starting,[1] " exclusive of Scott and Randolph, neither
of whom will, I fear, be up in season." The army
was divided into four brigades under Generals Boyd,
Swartwout, Jacob Brown, and Covington, — the latter
a Maryland man, forty-five years old, who entered
the service in 1809 as lieutenant-colonel of dragoons.
The brigades of Boyd and Covington formed a division commanded by Major-General Morgan Lewis.
The second division was intended for Major-General
Hampton ; a reserve under Colonel Macomb, and
a park of artillery under Brigadier-General Moses
Porter, completed the organization.[2]

The men were embarked in bateaux, October 17,
at Henderson's Bay, to the westward of Sackett's
Harbor. The weather had been excessively stormy,
and continued so. The first resting-point to be
reached was Grenadier Island at the entrance of the
St. Lawrence, only sixteen or eighteen miles from
the starting-point; but the bateaux were dispersed
by heavy gales of wind, October 18, 19, and 20, and
the last detachments did not reach Grenadier Island
until November 3. " All our hopes have been nearly
blasted," wrote Wilkinson October 24 ; but at length,
November 5, the expedition, numbering nearly three
hundred boats, having safely entered the river, began
the descent from French Creek. That day they

[1] Wilkinson to Armstrong, Oct. 28, 1813 ; MSS. War Department Archives.

[2] General Order of Encampment ; Wilkinson's Memoirs, iii.
126 ; Order of October 9, Appendix iii.

moved forty miles, and halted about midnight six miles above Ogdensburg. The next day was consumed in running the flotilla past Ogdensburg under the fire of the British guns at Prescott. The boats floated down by night and the troops marched by land. November 7 the army halted at the White House, about twenty miles below Ogdensburg. There Wilkinson called a council of war, November 8, to consider whether the expedition should proceed. Lewis, Boyd, Brown, and Swartwout voted simply in favor of attacking Montreal. Covington and Porter were of the opinion " that we proceed from this place under great danger, . . . but . . . we know of no other alternative." [1]

More than any other cause, Armstrong's conduct warranted Wilkinson in considering the campaign at an end. If the attack on Montreal was seriously intended, every motive required Armstrong to join Hampton at once in advance of Wilkinson's expedition. No one knew so well as he the necessity of some authority to interpose between the tempers and pretensions of these two men in case a joint campaign were to be attempted, or to enforce co-operation on either side. Good faith toward Hampton, even more than toward Wilkinson, required that the secretary who had led them into such a situation should not desert them. Yet Armstrong, after waiting till Wilkinson was fairly at Grenadier Island, began to prepare for return to Washington. From

[1] Minutes etc.; Wilkinson's Memoirs, iii. Appendix xxiv.

the village of Antwerp, half way between Sackett's Harbor and Ogdensburg, the secretary wrote to Wilkinson, October 27, " Should my fever continue I shall not be able to approach you as I intended." [1] Three days later he wrote again from Denmark on the road to Albany, —

" I rejoice that your difficulties are so far surmounted as to enable you to say with assurance when you will pass Prescott. I should have met you there ; but bad roads, worse weather, and a considerable degree of illness admonished me against receding farther from a point where my engagements call me about the 1st proximo. The resolution of treading back my steps was taken at Antwerp." [2]

From Albany Armstrong wrote, November 12, for the last time, " in the fulness of my faith that you are in Montreal," [3] that he had sent orders to Hampton to effect a junction with the river expedition. Such letters and orders, whatever Armstrong meant by them, were certain to impress both Wilkinson and Hampton with a conviction that the secretary intended to throw upon them the whole responsibility for the failure of an expedition which he as well as they knew to be hopeless.

Doubtless a vigorous general might still have found

[1] Armstrong to Wilkinson, Oct. 27, 1813 ; Wilkinson's Memoirs, iii. Appendix xli.

[2] Armstrong to Wilkinson, Oct. 30, 1813 ; State Papers, Military Affairs, i. 474.

[3] Armstrong to Wilkinson, Nov. 12, 1813; State Papers, Military Affairs, i. 474.

means if not to take Montreal, at least to compel the British to evacuate Upper Canada; but Wilkinson was naturally a weak man, and during the descent of the river he was excessively ill, never able to make a great exertion. Every day his difficulties increased. Hardly had his flotilla begun its descent, when a number of British gunboats commanded by Captain Mulcaster, the most energetic officer in the British naval service on the Lake, slipping through Chauncey's blockade, appeared in Wilkinson's rear, and caused him much annoyance. Eight hundred British rank-and-file from Kingston and Prescott were with Mulcaster, and at every narrow pass of the river, musketry and artillery began to open on Wilkinson from the British bank. Progress became slow. November 7, Macomb was landed on the north bank with twelve hundred men to clear away these obstructions.[1] The day and night of November 8 were consumed at the White House in passing troops across the river. Brown's brigade was landed on the north shore to reinforce Macomb. The boats were delayed to keep pace with Brown's march on shore, and made but eleven miles November 9, and the next day, November 10, fell down only to the Long Saut, a continuous rapid eight miles in length. The enemy pressed close, and while Brown marched in advance to clear the bank along the rapid, Boyd was ordered to take all the other troops and protect the rear.

[1] Journal etc.; State Papers, Military Affairs, i. 477.

The flotilla stopped on the night of November 10 near a farm called Chrystler's on the British bank; and the next morning, November 11, at half-past ten o'clock Brown having announced that all was clear below, Wilkinson was about to order the flotilla to run the rapids when General Boyd sent word that the enemy in the rear were advancing in column. Wilkinson was on his boat, unable to leave his bed;[1] Morgan Lewis was in no better condition; and Boyd was left to fight a battle as he best could. Boyd never had the confidence of the army; Brown was said to have threatened to resign rather than serve under him,[2] and Winfield Scott, who was that day with Macomb and Brown in the advance, described[3] Boyd as amiable and respectable in a subordinate position, but "vacillating and imbecile beyond all endurance as a chief under high responsibilities."

The opportunity to capture or destroy Mulcaster and his eight hundred men was brilliant, and warranted Wilkinson in turning back his whole force to accomplish it. Boyd actually employed three brigades, and made an obstinate but not united or well-supported attempt to crush the enemy. Colonel Ripley with the Twenty-first regiment drove in the British skirmishers, and at half-past two o'clock the battle became general. At half-past four, after a

---

[1] Evidence of General Boyd; Wilkinson's Memoirs, iii. 84; Evidence of Doctor Bull; Wilkinson's Memoirs, iii. 214.

[2] Wilkinson's Memoirs, iii. 364.

[3] Autobiography, pp. 93, 94.

stubborn engagement, General Covington was killed ; his brigade gave way, and the whole American line fell back, beaten and almost routed.

This defeat was the least creditable of the disasters suffered by American arms during the war. No excuse or palliation was ever offered for it.[1] The American army consisted wholly of regulars, and all the generals belonged to the regular service. Wilkinson could hardly have had less than three thousand men with him, after allowing for his detachments, and was alone to blame if he had not more. Boyd, according to his own account, had more than twelve hundred men and two field-pieces under his immediate command on shore.[2] The reserve, under Colonel Upham of the Eleventh regiment, contained six hundred rank-and-file,[3] with four field-pieces. Wilkinson's official report admitted that eighteen hundred rank-and-file were engaged ; Colonel Walbach, his adjutant-general, admitted two thousand,[4] while Swartwout thought that twenty-one hundred were in action. The American force was certainly not less than two thousand, with six field-pieces.

The British force officially reported by Lieutenant-Colonel Morrison of the Eighty-ninth regiment, who was in command, consisted of eight hundred rank-

---

[1] Wilkinson's Defence, Memoirs, iii. 451; Ripley's Evidence, Wilkinson's Memoirs, iii. 139.

[2] Evidence of General Boyd; Wilkinson's Memoirs, iii. 85.

[3] Wilkinson to Armstrong, Nov. 18, 1813; Niles, v. 235.

[4] Evidence of Colonel Walbach; Wilkinson's Memoirs, iii. 151.

and-file, and thirty Indians. The rank-and-file consisted of three hundred and forty-two men of the
Forty-ninth regiment, about as many more of the
Eighty-ninth, and some Canadian troops. They had
three six-pound field-pieces, and were supported on
their right flank by gunboats.[1]

On the American side the battle was ill fought
both by the generals and by the men. Wilkinson
and Morgan Lewis, the two major-generals, who were
ill on their boats, never gave an order. Boyd, who
commanded, brought his troops into action by detachments, and the men, on meeting unexpected
resistance, broke and fled. The defeat was bloody
as well as mortifying. Wilkinson reported one hundred and two killed, and two hundred and thirty-
seven wounded, but strangely reported no missing,[2] although the British occupied the field of battle, and claimed upward of one hundred prisoners.[3]
Morrison reported twenty-two killed, one hundred
and forty-eight wounded, and twelve missing. The
American loss was twice that of the British, and
Wilkinson's reports were so little to be trusted
that the loss might well have been greater than
he represented it. The story had no redeeming
incident.

If three brigades, numbering two thousand men,
were beaten at Chrystler's farm by eight hundred

[1] James, i. 323–325, 467.

[2] Return, etc., State Papers, Military Affairs, i. 476.

[3] Morrison's Report of Nov. 12, 1813; James, i. 451.

British and Canadians, the chance that Wilkinson
could capture Montreal, even with ten thousand men,
was small.   The conduct of the army showed its
want of self-confidence.   Late as it was, in the dusk
of the evening Boyd hastened to escape across the
river.   "The troops being much exhausted," reported
Wilkinson,[1] "it was considered most convenient that
they should embark, and that the dragoons with the
artillery should proceed by land.   The embarkation
took place without the smallest molestation from the
enemy, and the flotilla made a harbor near the head
of the Saut on the opposite shore."   In truth, neither
Wilkinson nor his adjutant gave the order of embarkation,[2] nor was Boyd willing to admit it as his.[3]
Apparently the army by common consent embarked
without orders.

Early the next morning, November 12, the flotilla
ran the rapids and rejoined Brown and Macomb near
Cornwall, where Wilkinson learned that General
Hampton had taken the responsibility of putting an
end to an undertaking which had not yet entered
upon its serious difficulties.

Four months had passed since Hampton took command on Lake Champlain.   When he first reached

[1] Journal, Nov. 11, 1813; State Papers, Military Affairs, i. 478.
[2] Evidence of Colonel Walbach ; Wilkinson's Memoirs, iii.
145 ; Evidence of Colonel Pinkney, iii. 311.
[3] Evidence of Brigadier-General Boyd; Wilkinson's Memoirs,
iii. 91.

Burlington, July 3, neither men nor material were ready, nor was even a naval force present to cover his weakness. While he was camped at Burlington, a British fleet, with about a thousand regulars, entered the Lake from the Isle aux Noix and the Richelieu River, and plundered the American magazines at Plattsburg, July 31, sweeping the Lake clear of American shipping.[1]   Neither Hampton's army nor McDonough's small fleet ventured to offer resistance.   Six weeks afterward, in the middle of September, Hampton had but about four thousand men, in bad condition and poor discipline.

Wilkinson, though unable to begin his own movement, was earnest that Hampton should advance on Montreal.[2]   Apparently in order to assist Wilkinson's plans, Hampton moved his force, September 19, to the Canada line.   Finding that a drought had caused want of water on the direct road to Montreal, Hampton decided to march his army westward to the Chateaugay River, forty or fifty miles, and established himself there, September 26, in a position equally threatening to Montreal and to the British line of communication up the St. Lawrence.   Armstrong approved the movement,[3] and Hampton remained three weeks at Chateaugay, building roads

[1] James, i. 242; Christie, ii. 94.

[2] Wilkinson to Armstrong, Aug. 30, 1813; State Papers, Military Affairs, i. 466.

[3] Armstrong to Hampton, Sept. 28, 1813; State Papers, Military Affairs, i. 460.   Cf. Armstrong's Notices, ii. 25.

and opening lines of communication while waiting for Wilkinson to move.

October 16 Armstrong ordered Hampton, in view of Wilkinson's probable descent of the river, to " approach the mouth of the Chateaugay, or other point which shall better favor our junction, and hold the enemy in check." [1]   Hampton instantly obeyed, and moved down the Chateaugay to a point about fifteen miles from its mouth. There he established his army, October 22, and employed the next two days in completing his road, and getting up his artillery and stores.

Hampton's movements annoyed the British authorities at Montreal. Even while he was still within American territory, before he advanced from Chateaugay Four Corners, Sir George Prevost reported, October 8, to his government,[2] —

" The position of Major-General Hampton at the Four Corners on the Chateaugay River, and which he continued to occupy, either with the whole or a part of his force, from the latest information I have been able to obtain from thence, is highly judicious, — as at the same time that he threatens Montreal and obliges me to concentrate a considerable body of troops in this vicinity to protect it, he has it in his power to molest the communication with the Upper Province, and impede the progress of the supplies required there for the Navy and Army."

[1] State Papers, Military Affairs, i. 461.
[2] Prevost to Bathurst, Oct. 8, 1813; MSS. British Archives.

If this was the case, October 8, when Hampton was still at Chateaugay, fifty miles from its mouth, the annoyance must have been much greater when he advanced, October 21, to Spear's, within ten miles of the St. Lawrence on his left, and fifteen from the mouth of the Chateaugay. Hampton accomplished more than was expected. He held a position equally well adapted to threaten Montreal, to disturb British communication with Upper Canada, and to succor Wilkinson.

That Hampton, with only four thousand men, should do more than this, could not fairly be required. The defences of Montreal were such as required ten times his force to overcome. The regular troops defending Montreal were not stationed in the town itself, which was sufficiently protected by a broad river and rapids. They were chiefly at Chambly, St. John's, Isle aux Noix, or other points on the Richelieu River, guarding the most dangerous line of approach from Lake Champlain; or they were at Coteau du Lac on the St. Lawrence about twenty miles northwest of Hampton's position. According to the general weekly return of British forces serving in the Montreal District under command of Major-General Sir R. H. Sheaffe, Sept. 15, 1813, the aggregate rank-and-file present for duty was five thousand seven hundred and fifty-two. At Montreal were none but sick, with the general staff. At Chambly were nearly thirteen hundred effectives; at St. John's nearly eight hundred; at Isle aux Noix about nine hundred. Ex-

cluding the garrison at Prescott, and including the
force at Coteau du Lac, Major-General Sheaffe commanded just five thousand effectives.[1]

Besides the enrolled troops, Prevost could muster a
considerable number of sailors and marines for the
defence of Montreal; and his resources in artillery,
boats, fortifications, and supplies of all sorts were
ample. In addition to the embodied troops, Prevost
could count upon the militia, a force almost as good
as regulars for the defence of a forest-clad country
where axes were as effective as musketry in stopping
an invading army. In Prevost's letter to Bathurst
of October 8, announcing Hampton's invasion, the
governor-general said : —

" Measures had been in the mean time taken by Major-
General Sir Roger Sheaffe commanding in this district,
to resist the advance of the enemy by moving the whole
of the troops under his command nearer to the frontier
line, and by calling out about three thousand of the
sedentary militia. I thought it necessary to increase
this latter force to nearly eight thousand by embodying
the whole of the sedentary militia upon the frontier,
this being in addition to the six battalions of incor-
porated militia amounting to five thousand men ; and
it is with peculiar satisfaction I have to report to your
Lordship that his Majesty's Canadian subjects have
a second time answered the call to arms in defence
of their country with a zeal and alacrity beyond all
praise "

[1] Weekly General Return, Sept. 15, 1813 ; MSS. Canadian
Archives, Freer Papers, 1813, p. 35.

Thus the most moderate estimate of the British force about Montreal gave at least fifteen thousand rank-and-file under arms.[1] Besides this large array of men, Prevost was amply protected by natural defences. If Hampton had reached the St. Lawrence at Caughnawaga, he would still have been obliged to cross the St. Lawrence, more than two miles wide, under the fire of British batteries and gunboats. Hampton had no transports. Prevost had bateaux and vessels of every description, armed and unarmed, above and below the rapids, besides two river steamers constantly plying to Quebec.

Hampton's command consisted of four thousand infantry new to service, two hundred dragoons, and artillery.[2] With such a force, his chance of suffering a fatal reverse was much greater than that of his reaching the St. Lawrence. His position at the Chateaugay was not less perilous than that of Harrison on the Maumee, and far more so than that which cost Dearborn so many disasters at Niagara.

The British force in Hampton's immediate front consisted at first of only three hundred militia, who could make no resistance, and retired as Hampton advanced. When Hampton made his movement to Spear's, Lieutenant-Colonel de Salaberry in his front commanded about eight hundred men, and immedi-

[1] Cf. Wilkinson's Memoirs, iii. Appendix xxiv.; Council of War, Nov. 8, 1813; Wilkinson's Defence, Memoirs, iii. 449.

[2] Hampton to Armstrong, Oct. 12, 1813; State Papers, Military Affairs, i. 460.

ately entrenched himself and obstructed the road with abattis.[1] Hampton felt the necessity of dislodging Salaberry, who might at any moment be rein-forced; and accordingly, in the night of October 25, sent a strong force to flank Salaberry's position, while he should himself attack it in front.

The flanking party failed to find its way, and the attack in front was not pressed.[2] The American loss did not exceed fifty men. The British loss was reported as twenty-five. Sir George Prevost and his officers were greatly pleased by their success;[3] but Prevost did not attempt to molest Hampton, who fell back by slow marches to Chateaugay, where he waited to hear from the Government. The British generals at Montreal showed little energy in thus allowing Hampton to escape; and the timidity of their attitude before Hampton's little army was the best proof of the incompetence alleged against Prevost by many of his contemporaries.

Hampton's retreat was due more to the conduct of Armstrong than to the check at Spear's or to the movements of Prevost. At the moment when he moved against Salaberry, October 25, a messenger arrived from Sackett's Harbor, bringing instructions from the quartermaster-general for building huts for ten thousand men for winter quarters. These orders

[1] James, i. 307.

[2] Hampton to Armstrong, Nov. 1, 1813; State Papers, Military Affairs, i. 461.

[3] Prevost to Bathurst, Oct. 30, 1813 ; James, i. 462.

naturally roused Hampton's suspicions that no serious movement against Montreal was intended.

" The papers sunk my hopes," he wrote to Armstrong, November 1,[1] " and raised serious doubts of receiving that efficacious support that had been anticipated. I would have recalled the column, but it was in motion, and the darkness of the night rendered it impracticable."

In a separate letter of the same date [2] which Hampton sent to Armstrong by Colonel King, assuming that the campaign was at an end, he carried out his declared purpose of resigning. " Events," he said, " have had no tendency to change my opinion of the destiny intended for me, nor my determination to retire from a service where I can neither feel security nor expect honor. The campaign I consider substantially at an end." The implication that Armstrong meant to sacrifice him was certainly disrespectful, and deserved punishment ; but when Colonel King, bearing these letters, arrived in the neighborhood of Ogdensburg, he found that Armstrong had already done what Hampton reproached him for intending to do. He had retired to Albany, "suspecting . . . that the campaign . . . would terminate as it did."

A week afterward, November 8, Hampton received a letter from Wilkinson, written from Ogdensburg, asking him to forward supplies and march his troops

[1] Hampton to Armstrong, Nov. 1, 1813; State Papers, Military Affairs, i. 461.

[2] Hampton to Armstrong, Nov. 1, 1813 ; Wilkinson's Memoirs iii. Appendix lxix.

to some point of junction on the river below St. Regis.[1] Hampton replied from Chateaugay that he had no supplies to forward; and as, under such circumstances, his army could not throw itself on Wilkinson's scanty means, he should fall back on Plattsburg, and attempt to act against the enemy on some other road to be indicated.[2] Wilkinson received the letter on his arrival at Cornwall, November 12, the day after his defeat at Chrystler's farm; and with extraordinary energy moved the whole expedition the next day to French Mills, six or seven miles up the Salmon River, within the United States lines, where it went into winter quarters.

Armstrong and Wilkinson made common cause in throwing upon Hampton the blame of failure. Wilkinson at first ordered Hampton under arrest, but after reflection decided to throw the responsibility upon Armstrong.[3] The secretary declined to accept it, but consented after some delay to accept Hampton's resignation when renewed in March, 1814. Wilkinson declared that Hampton's conduct had blasted his dawning hopes and the honor of the army.[4] Armstrong sneered at Wilkinson for seizing

[1] Wilkinson to Hampton, Nov. 6, 1813; State Papers, Military Affairs, i. 462.

[2] Hampton to Wilkinson, Nov. 8, 1813; State Papers, Military Affairs, 462.

[3] Wilkinson to Hampton; Wilkinson's Memoirs, iii. Appendix v. Wilkinson to Armstrong, Nov. 24, 1813; State Papers, Military Affairs, i. 480.

[4] Wilkinson to Armstrong, Nov. 17, 1813; State Papers, Military Affairs, i. 478.

the pretext for abandoning his campaign.[1]   Both the generals believed that Armstrong had deliberately led them into an impossible undertaking, and deserted them, in order to shift the blame of failure from himself.[2]   Hampton behaved with dignity, and allowed his opinion to be seen only in his contemptuous silence; nor did Armstrong publicly blame Hampton's conduct until Hampton was dead.   The only happy result of the campaign was to remove all the older generals — Wilkinson, Hampton, and Morgan Lewis — from active service.

The bloodless failure of an enterprise which might have ended in extreme disaster was not the whole cost of Armstrong's and Wilkinson's friendship and quarrels.   In November nearly all the regular forces, both British and American, had been drawn toward the St. Lawrence.   Even Harrison and his troops, who reached Buffalo October 24, were sent to Sackett's Harbor, November 16, to protect the navy.   Not a regiment of the United States army was to be seen between Sackett's Harbor and Detroit.   The village of Niagara and Fort George on the British side were held by a few hundred volunteers commanded by Brigadier-General McClure of the New York militia.   As long as Wilkinson and Hampton threatened Montreal, Niagara was safe, and needed no further attention.

After November 13, when Wilkinson and Hampton

---

[1] Armstrong's Notices, ii. 43.
[2] Wilkinson's Memoirs, iii. 362, *note*.

withdrew from Canada, while the American army forgot its enemy in the bitterness of its own personal feuds, the British generals naturally thought of recovering their lost posts on the Niagara River. McClure, who occupied Fort George and the small town of Newark under its guns, saw his garrison constantly diminishing. Volunteers refused to serve longer on any conditions.[1] The War Department ordered no reinforcements, although ten or twelve thousand soldiers were lying idle at French Mills and Plattsburg. December 10 McClure had about sixty men of the Twenty-fourth infantry, and some forty volunteers, at Fort George, while the number of United States troops present for duty at Fort George, Fort Niagara, Niagara village, Black Rock, and Buffalo, to protect the people and the magazines, amounted to four companies, or three hundred and twenty-four men.

As early as October 4, Armstrong authorized McClure to warn the inhabitants of Newark that their town might suffer destruction in case the defence of Fort George should render such a measure proper.[2] No other orders were given, but Wilkinson repeatedly advised that Fort George should be evacuated,[3]

---

[1] McClure to Armstrong, Dec. 10, 1813; State Papers, Military Affairs, i. 486.

[2] Armstrong to McClure, Oct. 4, 1813 ; State Papers, Military Affairs, i. 484.

[3] Wilkinson to Armstrong, Sept. 16, 1813 ; Sept. 20, 1813; State Papers, Military Affairs, i. 467, 469.

and Armstrong did nothing to protect it, further than to issue a requisition from Albany, November 25, upon the Governor of New York for one thousand militia.[1]

The British, though not rapid in their movements, were not so slow as the Americans. Early in December Lieutenant-General Gordon Drummond came from Kingston to York, and from York to the head of the Lake where the British had maintained themselves since losing the Niagara posts in May. Meanwhile General Vincent had sent Colonel Murray with five hundred men to retake Fort George. McClure at Fort George, December 10, hearing that Murray had approached within ten miles, evacuated the post and crossed the river to Fort Niagara; but before doing so he burned the town of Newark and as much as he could of Queenston, turning the inhabitants, in extreme cold, into the open air. He alleged as his motive the wish to deprive the enemy of winter quarters;[2] yet he did not destroy the tents or military barracks,[3] and he acted without authority, for Armstrong had authorized him to burn Newark only in case he meant to defend Fort George.

"The enemy is much exasperated, and will make a descent on this frontier if possible," wrote McClure from

---

[1] Armstrong to McClure, Nov. 25, 1813; State Papers, Military Affairs, i. 485.

[2] McClure to Armstrong, Dec. 10 and 13, 1813; State Papers, Military Affairs, i. 486.

[3] James, ii. 77.

the village of Niagara, December 13 ; " but I shall watch
them close with my handful of men until a reinforcement
of militia and volunteers arrives. . . . I am not a little
apprehensive that the enemy will take advantage of the
exposed condition of Buffalo and our shipping there.
My whole effective force on this extensive frontier does
not exceed two hundred and fifty men."

Five days passed, and still no reinforcements arrived, and no regular troops were even ordered to
start for Niagara. " I apprehended an attack," wrote
McClure ;[1] and he retired thirty miles to Buffalo,
" with a view of providing for the defence." On the
night of December 18 Colonel Murray, with five
hundred and fifty regular rank-and-file, crossed the
river from Fort George unperceived ; surprised the
sentinels on the glacis and at the gates of Fort
Niagara ; rushed through the main gate ; and,
with a loss of eight men killed and wounded, captured the fortress with some three hundred and fifty
prisoners.

Nothing could be said on the American side in
defence or excuse of this disgrace. From Armstrong
at the War Department to Captain Leonard who
commanded the fort, every one concerned in the
transaction deserved whatever punishment the law or
army regulations could inflict. The unfortunate people of Niagara and Buffalo were victims to official
misconduct. The British, thinking themselves re-

[1] McClure to Armstrong, Dec. 22, 1813 ; State Papers, Military Affairs, i. 487.

leased from ordinary rules of war by the burning of Newark and Queenston, showed unusual ferocity. In the assault on Fort Niagara they killed sixty-seven Americans, all by the bayonet, while they wounded only eleven. Immediately afterward they "let loose"[1] their auxiliary Indians on Lewiston and the country around. On the night of December 29, Lieutenant-General Drummond sent a force of fifteen hundred men including Indians[2] across the river above the falls, and driving away the militia, burned Black Rock and Buffalo with all their public stores and three small war-schooners.[3]

These acts of retaliation were justified by Sir George Prevost in a long proclamation[4] dated Jan. 12, 1814, which promised that he would not "pursue further a system of warfare so revolting to his own feelings and so little congenial to the British character unless the future measures of the enemy should compel him again to resort to it." The Americans themselves bore Drummond's excessive severity with less complaint than usual. They partly suspected that the destruction effected on the Thames, at York and at Newark, by American troops, though unauthorized by orders, had warranted some retaliation; but they felt more strongly that their anger should properly be vented on their own government and themselves, who had allowed a handful of British troops to cap-

[1] Christie, ii. 140.   [2] James, ii. 20, 21.
[3] James, ii. 23.
[4] Christie, ii. 143; Niles, v. 382.

ture a strong fortress and to ravage thirty miles of frontier, after repeated warning, without losing two hundred men on either side, while thousands of regular troops were idle elsewhere, and the neighborhood ought without an effort to have supplied five thousand militia.

Fort Niagara, which thus fell into British hands, remained, like Mackinaw, in the enemy's possession until the peace.

CHAPTER IX.

MILITARY movements in the Southern department attracted little notice, but were not the less important. The Southern people entered into the war in the hope of obtaining the Floridas. President Madison, like President Jefferson, gave all the support in his power to the scheme. Throughout the year 1812 United States troops still occupied Amelia Island and the St. Mary's River, notwithstanding the refusal of Congress to authorize the occupation. The President expected Congress at the session of 1812–1813 to approve the seizure of both Floridas, and took measures in advance for that purpose.

October 12, 1812, Secretary Eustis wrote to the Governor of Tennessee calling out fifteen hundred militia for the defence of the "lower country." The force was not intended for defence but for conquest; it was to support the seizure of Mobile, Pensacola, and St. Augustine by the regular troops. For that object every man in Tennessee was ready to serve; and of all Tennesseeans, Andrew Jackson was the most ardent. Governor Blount immediately authorized Jackson, as major-general of the State militia, to call out two thousand volunteers. The call was

issued November 14; the volunteers collected at
Nashville December 10; and Jan. 7, 1813, the infantry embarked in boats to descend the river, while
the mounted men rode through the Indian country
to Natchez.

"I have the pleasure to inform you," wrote Jackson
to Eustis in departing,[1] "that I am now at the head of
two thousand and seventy volunteers, the choicest of our
citizens, who go at the call of their country to execute
the will of the Government; who have no Constitutional
scruples, and if the Government orders, will rejoice at
the opportunity of placing the American eagle on the ramparts of Mobile, Pensacola, and Fort St. Augustine."

The Tennessee army reached Natchez, February 15,
and went into camp to wait orders from Washington,
which were expected to direct an advance on Mobile
and Pensacola.

While Jackson descended the Mississippi, Monroe,
then acting Secretary of War, wrote, January 13, to
Major-General Pinckney,[2] whose military department
included Georgia: "It is intended to place under
your command an adequate force for the reduction
of St. Augustine should it be decided on by Congress,
before whom the subject will be in a few days." A
fortnight later, January 30, Monroe wrote also to
Wilkinson,[3] then commanding at New Orleans: "The

[1] Parton's Jackson, i. 372.

[2] Monroe to Pinckney, Jan. 13, 1813; MSS. War Department Records.

[3] Monroe to Wilkinson, Jan. 30, 1813; MSS. War Department Records.

subject of taking possession of West Florida is now
before Congress, and will probably pass. You will
be prepared to carry into effect this measure should
it be decided on."

Neither Madison nor Monroe raised objection to
the seizure of territory belonging to a friendly power ;
but Congress showed no such readiness to act. Senator Anderson of Tennessee, as early as Dec. 10,
1812, moved,[1] in secret session of the Senate, that
a committee be appointed to consider the expediency
of authorizing the President " to occupy and hold the
whole or any part of East Florida, including Amelia
Island, and also those parts of West Florida which
are not now in the possession and under the jurisdiction of the United States." After much debate
the Senate, December 22, adopted the resolution by
eighteen votes to twelve, and the committee, consisting of Anderson, Samuel Smith, Tait of Georgia,
Varnum of Massachusetts, and Goodrich of Connecticut, reported a bill,[2] January 19, authorizing the
President to occupy both Floridas, and to exercise
government there, " provided . . . that the section
of country herein designated that is situated to the
eastward of the river Perdido may be the subject of
future negotiation."

The bill met opposition from the President's personal enemies, Giles, Leib, and Samuel Smith, as well
as from the Federalists and some of the Northern

[1] Annals of Congress, 1812–1813, p. 124.
[2] Annals of Congress, 1812--1813, p. 127.

Democrats. January 26, Samuel Smith moved to strike out the second section, which authorized the seizure of Florida east of the Perdido; and the Senate, February 2, by a vote of nineteen to sixteen, adopted Smith's motion. The vote was sectional. North and South Carolina, Georgia, Tennessee, and Louisiana supported the bill; Maryland, Delaware, Pennsylvania, New York, Connecticut, and Rhode Island opposed it; Virginia, Kentucky, Ohio, Massachusetts, New Hampshire, and Vermont were divided; New Jersey threw one vote in its favor, the second senator being absent. Had Leib not changed sides the next day, the whole bill would have been indefinitely postponed; but the majority rallied, February 5, and by a vote of twenty-one to eleven authorized the President to seize Florida west of the Perdido, or, in other words, to occupy Mobile. The House passed the bill in secret session February 9, and the President signed it February 12.[1]

In refusing to seize East Florida, the Senate greatly disarranged Madison's plans. Three days afterward, February 5, Armstrong took charge of the War Department, and his first orders were sent to Andrew Jackson directing him to dismiss his force, "the causes of embodying and marching to New Orleans the corps under your command having ceased to exist."[2] Jackson, ignorant that the Administration was not to blame, and indignant at his curt dismissal,

---

[1] Act of Feb. 12, 1813; Wilkinson's Memoirs, iii. 339.
[2] Parton's Jackson, i. 377.

marched his men back to Tennessee, making himself responsible for their pay and rations. On learning these circumstances, Armstrong wrote, March 22, a friendly letter thanking him for the important services his corps would have rendered " had the Executive policy of occupying the two Floridas been adopted by the national legislature." [1]

After the Senate had so persistently refused to support Madison's occupation of East Florida, he could hardly maintain longer the illegal possession he had held during the past year of Amelia Island. February 15, Armstrong wrote to Major-General Pinckney,[2] "The late private proceedings of Congress have resulted in a decision not to invade East Florida at present;" but not until March 7, did the secretary order Pinckney to withdraw the troops from Amelia Island and Spanish territory.[3]

The troops were accordingly withdrawn from Amelia Island, May 16; but nothing could restore East Florida to its former repose, and the anarchy which had been introduced from the United States could never be mastered except by the power that created it. Perhaps Madison would have retained possession, as the least of evils, in spite of the Senate's vote of February 3, had not another cause,

[1] Armstrong to Jackson, March 22, 1813   MSS. War Department Records.

[2] Armstrong to Pinckney, Feb. 15, 1813 ; MSS. War Department Records.

[3] Armstrong to Pinckney, March 7, 1813 ; MSS. War Department Records.

independent of legislative will, overcome his repugnance to the evacuation. The Russian offer of mediation arrived while the President was still in doubt. The occupation of Florida, being an act of war against Spain, could not fail to excite the anger of England, and in that feeling of displeasure the Czar must inevitably share. From the moment their cause against Napoleon was common, Russia, England, and Spain were more than likely to act together in resistance to any territorial aggression upon any member of their alliance. The evacuation of East Florida by the United States evaded a serious diplomatic difficulty; and probably not by mere coincidence, Armstrong's order to evacuate Amelia Island was dated March 7, while Daschkoff's letter offering the Czar's mediation was dated March 8.

The Cabinet was so little united in support of the Executive policy that Madison and Monroe ordered the seizure of Mobile without consulting Gallatin, whose persistent hostility to the Florida intrigues was notorious. When Monroe in April gave to Gallatin and Bayard the President's instructions [1] for the peace negotiations, among the rest he directed them to assert "a right to West Florida by cession from France, and a claim to East Florida as an indemnity for spoliations." On receiving these instructions, Gallatin wrote to Monroe, May 2, asking,[2] —

[1] Gallatin's Works, i. 539, *note*.
[2] Gallatin to Monroe, May 2, 1813; Gallatin's Writings, i. 539.

"Where is the importance of taking possession of Mobile this summer? We may do this whenever we please, and is it not better to delay every operation of minor importance which may have a tendency to impede our negotiations with Great Britain and Russia? You know that to take by force any place in possession of another nation, whatever our claim to that place may be, is war; and you must be aware that both Russia and Great Britain will feel disposed, if not to support the pretensions of Spain against us, at least to take part against the aggressor."

Monroe quickly replied:[1] "With respect to West Florida, possession will be taken of it before you get far on your voyage. That is a question settled." In fact, possession had been taken of it three weeks before he wrote, in pursuance of orders sent in February, apparently without Gallatin's knowledge. Monroe added views of his own, singularly opposed to Gallatin's convictions.

"On the subject of East Florida," wrote Monroe to Gallatin, May 6,[2] "I think I intimated to you in my last that Colonel Lear was under the most perfect conviction, on the authority of information from respectable sources at Cadiz, that the Spanish regency had sold that and the other province to the British government, and that it had done so under a belief that we had, or should soon get, possession of it. My firm belief is that if we were possessed of both, it would facilitate your negotiations in favor of impressment and every other object, especially if

[1] Monroe to Gallatin, May 5, 1813; Gallatin's Writings, i. 540.
[2] Monroe to Gallatin, May 6, 1813; Gallatin's Writings, i. 542.

it was distinctly seen by the British ministers or minister that, instead of yielding them or any part of either, we would push our fortunes in that direction, and in Canada, if they did not hasten to accommodate."

Gallatin, on the eve of sailing for Russia, replied with good temper, expressing opinions contrary to those of the President and Secretary of State.

" On the subject of Florida," Gallatin said,[1] " I have always differed in opinion with you, and am rejoiced to have it in our power to announce the evacuation of the province.   Let it alone until you shall, by the introduction of British troops, have a proof of the supposed cession.   In this I do not believe.   It can be nothing more than a permission to occupy it in order to defend it for Spain.   By withdrawing our troops, we withdraw the pretence ; but the impolitic occupancy of Mobile will, I fear, renew our difficulties.   The object is at present of very minor importance, swelled into consequence by the representations from that quarter, and which I would not at this moment have attempted, among other reasons, because it was a Southern one, and will, should it involve us in a war with Spain, disgust every man north of Washington.   You will pardon the freedom with which, on the eve of parting with you, I speak on this subject. It is intended as a general caution, which I think important, because I know and see every day the extent of geographical feeling, and the necessity of prudence if we mean to preserve and invigorate the Union."

No sooner did the Act of Feburary 12 become law than Armstrong wrote, February 16, to Wilkinson at

[1] Gallatin to Monroe, May 8, 1813; Gallatin's Writings, i. 544.

New Orleans, enclosing a copy of the Act, and ordering him immediately to take possession of Mobile and
the country as far as the Perdido.[1] Wilkinson, who
had for years looked forward to that step, hastened
to obey the instruction. When Gallatin remonstrated,
the measure had been already taken and could not be
recalled.

Since July 9, 1812, Wilkinson had again commanded at New Orleans. No immediate attack was
to be feared, nor could a competent British force be
collected there without warning; but in case such an
attack should be made, Wilkinson had reason to fear
the result, for his regular force consisted of only sixteen hundred effectives, ill equipped and without defences.[2] The War Department ordered him to depend
on movable ordnance and temporary works rather
than on permanent fortifications ;[3] but with his usual
disregard of orders he began the construction or the
completion of extensive works at various points on
the river and coast, at a cost which the government
could ill afford.

While engaged in this task Wilkinson received,
March 14, Armstrong's order of February 16 for the
invasion of West Florida. When the government's
orders were agreeable to Wilkinson, they reached him

[1] Armstrong to Wilkinson, Feb. 16, 1813; Wilkinson's Memoirs, iii. 339.

[2] Minutes of a Council of War, Aug. 4, 1813; Wilkinson's
Memoirs, i. 498–503.

[3] Eustis to Wilkinson, April 15, 1812 ; Wilkinson's Memoirs,
i. 495.

promptly and were executed with rapidity. Within three weeks he collected at Pass Christian a force of about six hundred men, supported by gunboats, and entered the Bay of Mobile on the night of April 10, while at the same time the garrison at Fort Stoddert descended the Tensaw River, and cut the communication by land between Mobile and Pensacola. At that time Mobile Point was undefended. The only Spanish fortress was Fort Charlotte at Mobile, garrisoned by one hundred and fifty combatants. Wilkinson summoned the fort to surrender, and the commandant had no choice but to obey, for the place was untenable and without supplies. The surrender took place April 15. Wilkinson then took possession of the country as far as the Perdido, and began the construction of a fort, to be called Fort Bowyer, on Mobile Point at the entrance of the Bay, some sixty miles below the town.[1]

This conquest, the only permanent gain of territory made during the war, being effected without bloodshed, attracted less attention than it deserved. Wilkinson committed no errors, and won the President's warm approval.[2] Wilkinson was greatly pleased by his own success, and wished to remain at New Orleans to carry out his projected defences; but Armstrong had written as early as March 10, ordering him to the Lakes. As so often happened with orders that

[1] Wilkinson's Memoirs, i. 507–522.

[2] Armstrong to Wilkinson, May 22, 1813; Wilkinson's Memoirs, i. 521.

displeased the general, Armstrong's letter, though dated March 10, and doubtless arriving in New Orleans before April 10, was received by Wilkinson only on his return, May 19. After another delay of three weeks, he started northward, and travelled by way of Mobile through the Creek country to Washington.

Wilkinson's departure, June 10, and the evacuation of Amelia Island by General Pinckney May 16, closed the first chapter of the war in the South. Armstrong wrote to Wilkinson, May 27 : [1] " The mission to Petersburg and the instructions to our envoys will put a barrier between you and Pensacola for some time to come at least, and permanently in case of peace." The sudden stop thus put by the Senate and the Russian mediation to the campaign against Pensacola and St. Augustine deranged the plans of Georgia and Tennessee, arrested the career of Andrew Jackson, and caused the transfer of Wilkinson from New Orleans to the Lakes. The government expected no other difficulties in the Southern country, and had no reason to fear them. If new perils suddenly arose, they were due less to England, Spain, or the United States than to the chance that gave energy and influence to Tecumthe.

The Southern Indians were more docile and less warlike than the Indians of the Lakes. The Chickasaws and Choctaws, who occupied the whole extent of

[1] Armstrong to Wilkinson, May 27, 1813; MSS. War Department Records.

country on the east bank of the Mississippi River from the Ohio to the Gulf, gave little trouble or anxiety ; and even the great confederacy of Muskogees, or Creeks, who occupied the territory afterward called the State of Alabama and part of Georgia, fell in some degree into a mode of life which seemed likely to make them tillers of the soil. In 1800 the Creeks held, or claimed, about three hundred miles square from the Tennessee River to the Gulf, and from the middle of Georgia nearly to the line which afterward marked the State of Mississippi. The Seminoles, or wild men, of Florida were a branch of the Muskogees, and the Creek warriors themselves were in the habit of visiting Pensacola and Mobile, where they expected to receive presents from the Spanish governor.

Two thirds of the Creek towns were on the Coosa and Tallapoosa rivers in the heart of Alabama. Their inhabitants were called Upper Creeks. The Lower Creeks lived in towns on the Chattahooche River, the modern boundary between Alabama and Georgia. The United States government, following a different policy in 1799 from that of Jefferson toward the Northwestern Indians, induced the Creeks to adopt a national organization for police purposes ; it also helped them to introduce ploughs, to learn cotton-spinning, and to raise crops. The success of these experiments was not at first great, for the larger number of Indians saw no advantage in becoming laborers, and preferred sitting in the squares of the towns, or hunting; but here and there chiefs or half-breeds had farms, slaves, stock, orchards, and spinning-wheels.

Large as the Creek country was, and wild as it had ever been, it did not abound in game. A good hunter, passing in any direction through the three hundred miles of Alabama and Georgia, found difficulty in obtaining game enough for his support.[1] For that reason the Seminoles left their old towns and became wild people, as their name implied, making irregular settlements in Florida, where game and food were more plenty. The mass of the Creek nation, fixed in the villages in the interior, clung to their habits of hunting even when obliged to cultivate the soil, and their semi-civilization rendered them a more perplexing obstacle to the whites than though they had obstinately resisted white influence.

Had the Indian problem been left to the people of Georgia and Tennessee, the Indians would soon have disappeared; but the national government established under President Washington in 1789 put a sharp curb on Georgia, and interposed decisively between the Georgians and the Creeks.[2] President Washington in 1796 appointed Benjamin Hawkins of North Carolina as Indian agent among the Creeks, and Hawkins protected and governed them with devotion; but the result of his friendliness was the

[1] Hawkins's Sketch, p. 24.

[2] U. S. Commissioners to Governor Irwin, July 1, 1796; State Papers, Indian Affairs, i. 611.

same as that of others' greed. The Indians slowly
lost ground.

The Creeks complained of grievances similar to
those of the Northwestern Indians, and their position was even more helpless. They had no other
outlet than Pensacola and Mobile. Except from the
Spaniards they could expect no aid in case of trouble,
and the Spanish governors of Florida, after the ab-
dication of Carlos IV. in 1807, could scarcely maintain their own position, much less supply the Creeks
with arms or gunpowder. While the Northwestern
Indians could buy at Malden all the weapons and
ammunition they wanted, the Creeks possessed few
firearms, and these in bad condition; nor were they
skilful in using guns.

The United States government prevented the Georgians from compelling the Indians to sell their lands,
but nothing could prevent them from trespass; and
the Indian woods along the frontier were filled with
cattle, horses, and hogs belonging to the whites, while
white men destroyed the game, hunting the deer by
firelight, and scaring the Indian hunters from their
hunting-grounds. " Every cane-swamp where they
go to look for a bear — which is part of their support — is near eat out by the stocks put over by
the citizens of Georgia." [1] This complaint was made
in 1796, and as time went on the Indian hunting-
grounds were more rapidly narrowed. Not only from

[1] Talk of the Creek Indians, June 24, 1796; State Papers,
Indian Affairs, i. 604.

Georgia but also from Fort Stoddert, along the course
of the Tombigbee River, above Mobile, intruders
pressed into the Creek country. The Indians had
no choice but to sell their lands for annuities, and
under this pressure the Creeks, in 1802 and 1803,
were induced to part with the district between the
Oconee and Ocmulgee in the centre of Georgia.
They retained their towns on the Chattahoochee,
where Hawkins's agency was established in the town
of Coweta, on the edge of the Creek country.

Hawkins was satisfied with their behavior, and
believed the chiefs to be well disposed. They showed
none of the restlessness which characterized the
Northwestern Indians, until Tecumthe conceived the
idea of bringing them into his general league to
check the encroachments of the whites. After Tecumthe's interview with Governor Harrison at Vincennes, in July, 1811, he made a long journey
through the Chickasaw and Choctaw country, and
arrived among the Creeks in October, bringing with
him a score of Indian warriors. The annual council of the Creeks was held in that month at the
village of Tuckaubatchee, — an ancient town of the
Upper Creeks on the Tallapoosa. The rumor that
Tecumthe would be present brought great numbers
of Indians, even Cherokees and Choctaws, to the
place, while Hawkins attended the council in his
character as agent.

Tecumthe and his warriors marched into the centre
of the square and took their places in silence. That

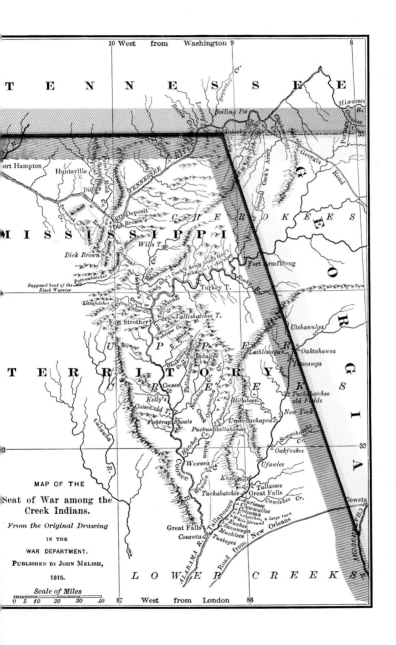

MAP OF THE
Seat of War among the Creek Indians.
From the Original Drawing
IN THE
WAR DEPARTMENT.
PUBLISHED BY JOHN MELISH,
1815.

Scale of Miles
0 5 10   20   30   40

night " they danced the dance of the Indians of the
Lakes," which became thenceforward a political sym-
bol of their party among the Creeks. Some nights
afterward Tecumthe addressed the council. Ver-
sions more or less untrustworthy have been given of
the speech; [1] but the only official allusion to it by a
person entitled to credit seemed to show that it was
in substance the address made by Tecumthe at Vincennes. Hawkins, recalling to the Creek chiefs in
1814 the course of events which had caused their
troubles, reminded them how "Tecumseh, in the
square of Tuckaubatchee, . . . told the Creeks not
to do any injury to the Americans; to be in peace
and friendship with them; not to steal even a bell
from any one of any color. Let the white people
on this continent manage their affairs their own
way. Let the red people manage their affairs their
own way." [2] Hawkins and the old chiefs would
have certainly interfered had Tecumthe incited
the Creeks to war or violence; but according to
Hawkins the speech was a pacific "talk," delivered
by Tecumthe in the name of the British. Indian
tradition preserved another form of Tecumthe's
rhetoric, which seemed to complete the identity with
the Vincennes address. Unable to express himself
in the Muskogee language, Tecumthe used panto-
mime familiar to Indians. Holding his war-club

[1] Life of Sam Dale, p. 59.
[2] Hawkins to the Creek Chiefs, June 16, 1814; State Papers,
Indian Affairs, i. 845.

with outstretched arm, he opened first the little finger, then the next and the next, till the club fell from his hand.

Indian union was unquestionably the chief theme of all Tecumthe's public addresses. Whether in private he taught other doctrines must be matter of surmise ; but he certainly brought into the Creek nation a religious fanaticism of a peculiar and dangerous kind. Prophets soon appeared, chiefly among the Alabamas, a remnant of an ancient race, not of Creek blood, but members of the Creek confederacy.[1] The prophets, with the usual phenomena of hysteria, claimed powers of magic, and promised to bring earthquakes to destroy an invading army. They preached the total destruction of everything, animate and inanimate, that pertained to civilization. As the nation generally was badly armed, and relied chiefly on their bows, arrows, and war-clubs for battle,[2] the moral support of magic was needed to give them confidence.

So secret was the influence of Tecumthe's friends that no suspicion of the excitement reached Hawkins even when the war with England began ; and the old chiefs of the nation — known to be devoted to peace and to the white alliance — were kept in ignorance of all that was done among the young warriors. The

[1] Report of Alexander Cornells, June 22, 1813; State Papers, Indian Affairs, i. 845, 846.

[2] Hawkins to General Pinckney, July 9, 1813; State Papers, Indian Affairs, i. 848.

Alabamas, or Coosadas, lived below the junction of the Coosa and Tallapoosa, on the west bank of the Alabama River, about eight miles above the modern town of Montgomery; they were considered by Hawkins the most industrious and best behaved of all the Creeks, whose fields were the granaries of the upper towns and furnished supplies even to Mobile. Their town was the last place in which Hawkins expected to see conspiracy, violence, or fanaticism. The young men "sang the song of the Indians of the Lakes, and danced the dance" in secret for eighteen months after Tecumthe's visit, without public alarm, and probably would have continued to do so except for an outbreak committed by some of their nation three hundred miles away.

In 1812 a band of six Indians led by the Little Warrior of Wewocau, a Creek town on the Coosa, was sent by the nation on a public mission to the Chickasaws.[1] Instead of delivering their "talks" and returning, they continued their journey to the northern Lakes and joined Tecumthe at Malden. They took part in the massacre at the river Raisin, Jan. 22, 1813, and soon afterward began their return, bringing talks from the Shawanese and British and also a letter from some British officer at Malden to the Spanish officials at Pensacola, from whom they hoped to obtain weapons and powder. According to common report, Tecumthe told the Little Warrior

[1] Hawkins to the Creek Chiefs, March 29, 1813; State Papers, Indian Affairs, i. 839.

that he was about to aid the British in capturing Fort Meigs, and as soon as the fort was taken he would come to join the Creeks.[1] Until then his friends were to increase their party by the secret means and magic that had proved so successful, but were not to begin open war.[2]

The Little Warrior and his party, including a warrior from Tuskegee, a Creek town at the fork of the Coosa and Tallapoosa, after crossing Indiana in the month of February reached the north bank of the Ohio River about seven miles above its mouth, where were two cabins occupied by white families.[3] Unable to resist the temptation to spill blood, the band murdered the two families with the usual Indian horrors. This outrage was committed February 9; and the band, crossing the Ohio, passed southward through the Chickasaw country, avowing the deed and its motive.[4]

The Little Warrior arrived at home about the middle of March, and reported that he brought talks from the Shawanese and British. The old chiefs of the Upper Creeks immediately held a council March 25, and after listening to the talks, reprimanded the Little Warrior and ordered him to leave the Council

[1] Hawkins to Armstrong, Aug. 23, 1813; State Papers, Indian Affairs, i 851.

[2] Report of Alexander Cornells, June 23, 1813; State Papers, Indian Affairs, i. 846.

[3] Letter from Kaskaskias, Feb. 27, 1813; Niles, iv. 135.

[4] Hawkins to the Creek Chiefs, March 29, 1813; State Papers, Indian Affairs, i. 839.

House.[1] On the same day Hawkins wrote to them
from Coweta, demanding delivery of the Little Warrior and his six companions to answer for the murders they had committed. On hearing this demand,
the old chiefs at Tuckaubatchee under the lead of
the Big Warrior held another council, while the
Little Warrior, the Tuskegee Warrior, and the murderers took to the woods. The old chiefs in council
decided to execute the murderers, and sent out parties to do it. The Little Warrior was found in the
swamp, well armed, but was decoyed out and killed
by treachery ; " the first and second man's gun
snapped at him, but the third man's gun fired and
killed ; . . . four men that had on pouches kept
them shaking following after him, so that he could
not hear the gun snap; if he had found out that,
he would have wounded a good many with his
arrows." [2]

The Tuskegee warrior and four others were found
in a house on the Hickory Ground at the fork of the
rivers. As long as they had ammunition, they held
the attack at a distance, but at last the house was
fired. The Tuskegee Warrior being wounded, was
burned in the house, while his two young brothers
were taken out and tomahawked. One warrior broke
away, but was caught and killed ; two more were

[1] Hawkins to Armstrong, March 25, 1813 ; State Papers,
Indian Affairs, i. 840.
[2] Report of the Big Warrior, April 26, 1813 ; State Papers,
Indian Affairs, i. 843.

killed elsewhere.   One escaped, and " set out the
morning after to kill white people."   Warriors were
sent after him.

" He made battle, firing at the warriors, and was near
killing one; the bullet passed near his ear.   He then
drew his knife and tomahawk, defended himself, and
the warriors shot three balls through him.   He fell,
retained the power of speech till next day, and died.
He said he had been to the Shawanese helping of them,
and had got fat eating white people's flesh.   Every one
to the very last called on the Shawanese general,
Tecumseh." [1]

Such political executions, in the stifled excitement
of the moment, could not but rouse violent emotion
throughout the Creek nation.   The old chiefs, having
given life for life, felt the stronger for their assertion
of authority; but they knew nothing of the true situation.   For several weeks no open outbreak occurred,
but the prophets were more active than ever.   About
June 4 the old chiefs at Tuckaubatchee, hearing that
the prophets " kept as usual their fooleries," sent a
runner to the Alabamas with a message : [2] —

" You are but a few Alabama people.   You say that
the Great Spirit visits you frequently; that he comes in
the sun and speaks to you; that the sun comes down
just above your heads.   Now we want to see and hear
what you say you have seen and heard.   Let us have

[1] Report of Nimrod Doyell, May 3, 1813; State Papers,
Indian Affairs, i. 843.

[2] Report of Alexander Cornells, June 22, 1813; State Papers,
Indian Affairs, i. 845.

the same proof you have had, and we will believe what
we see and hear. You have nothing to fear; the people
who committed murders have suffered for their crimes,
and there is an end of it."

The runner who carried this message was one of
the warriors who had aided in killing the seven
murderers.   The Alabamas instantly put him to
death, and sent his scalp to their friends at the forks
of the river. Then began a general uprising, and
every warrior who had aided in killing the murderers was himself killed or hunted from the Upper
Creek country. The chiefs of Tuckaubatchee with
difficulty escaped to the agency at Coweta, where
they were under the protection of Georgia.

The Lower Creek towns did not join the outbreak;
but of the Upper Creek towns twenty-nine declared
for war, and only five for peace. At least two thousand warriors were believed to have taken the war-
club by August 1, and got the name of Red Clubs,
or Red Sticks, for that reason. Everywhere they
destroyed farms, stock, and all objects of white civilization, and killed or drove away their opponents.[1]

With all this the Spaniards had nothing to do.
The outbreak was caused by the Indian War in the
Northwest, and immediately by the incompetence of
General Winchester and by the massacre at the
river Raisin. The Creeks were totally unprepared
for war, except so far as they trusted to magic;

[1] Talosee Fixico to Hawkins, July 5, 1813; State Papers,
Indian Affairs, i. 847.

they had neither guns, powder, nor balls. For that reason they turned to the Spaniards, who could alone supply them. When the Little Warrior was put to death, the British letter which he carried from Malden for the Spanish officials at Pensacola came into the charge of another Creek warrior, Peter McQueen, a half-breed. In July, McQueen, with a large party of warriors started for Pensacola, with the letter and four hundred dollars, to get powder.[1] On arriving there they saw the Spanish governor, who treated them civilly, and in fear of violence gave them, according to McQueen's account,[2] " a small bag of powder each for ten towns, and five bullets to each man." With this supply, which the governor represented as a friendly present for hunting purposes, they were obliged to content themselves, and started on their return journey.

News that McQueen's party was at Pensacola instantly reached the American settlements above Mobile, where the inhabitants were already taking refuge in stockades.[3] A large number of Americans, without military organization, under several leaders, one of whom was a half-breed named Dixon Bailey, started July 26 to intercept McQueen, and succeeded in surprising the Indians July 27 at a place called

[1] Hawkins to Armstrong, July 20, 1813; State Papers, Indian Affairs, i. 849.

[2] Hawkins to Armstrong, Aug. 23, 1813 ; State Papers, Indian Affairs, i. 851.

[3] Carson to Claiborne, July 29, 1813; Life of Dale, p. 78.

Burnt Corn, about eighty miles north of Pensacola. The whites at first routed the Indians, and captured the pack-mules with the ammunition; but the Indians quickly rallied, and in their turn routed the whites, with a loss of two killed and fifteen wounded, — although they failed to recover the greater part of the pack-animals. With the small amount of powder left to him, McQueen then returned to his people.

Angry at the attack and eager to revenge the death of his warriors, McQueen summoned the warriors of thirteen towns, some eight hundred in number, and about August 20 started in search of his enemies. The Creek war differed from that on the Lakes in being partly a war of half-breeds. McQueen's strongest ally was William Weatherford, a half-breed, well known throughout the country as a man of property and ability, as nearly civilized as Indian blood permitted, and equally at home among Indians and whites. McQueen and Weatherford were bitterly hostile to the half-breeds Bailey and Beasley, who were engaged in the affair of Burnt Corn.[1] Both Beasley and Bailey were at a stockade called Fort Mims, some thirty-five miles above Mobile, on the eastern side of the Alabama River, where about five hundred and fifty persons were collected, — a motley crowd of whites, half-breeds, Indians, and negroes, old and young, women and children, protected only by a

[1] Hawkins to Floyd, Sept. 30, 1813; State Papers, Indian Affairs, i. 854.

picket wall, pierced by five hundred loop-holes three and a half feet from the ground, and two rude gates.[1] Beasley commanded, and wrote, August 30, that he could " maintain the post against any number of Indians." [2] To Fort Mims the Creek warriors turned, for the reason that Beasley and Bailey were there, and they arrived in the neighborhood, August 29, without giving alarm. Twice, negroes tending cattle outside rushed back to the fort reporting that painted warriors were hovering about; but the horsemen when sent out discovered no sign of an enemy, and Beasley tied up and flogged the second negro for giving a false alarm.

At noon, August 30, when the drum beat for dinner no patrols were out, the gates were open, and sand had drifted against that on the eastern side so that it could not quickly be closed. Suddenly a swarm of Indians raising the warwhoop rushed toward the fort. Beasley had time to reach the gate, but could not close it, and was tomahawked on the spot. The Indians got possession of the loopholes outside, and of one inclosure. The whites, under Dixon Bailey, held the inner inclosure and fought with desperation ; but at last the Indians succeeded in setting fire to the house in the centre, and the fire spread to the whole stockade. The Indians then effected an entrance, and massacred most of the inmates. Fifteen persons escaped, and

---

[1] Pickett's Alabama, ii. 264.
[2] Life of Dale, 106.

among these was Dixon Bailey mortally wounded. Most of the negroes were spared to be slaves. Two hundred and fifty scalps became trophies of the Creek warriors, — a number such as had been seldom taken by Indians from the white people on a single day.

CHAPTER X.

THE battle at Burnt Corn was regarded by the Indians as a declaration of war by the whites. Till then they seemed to consider themselves engaged in a domestic quarrel, or civil war ; [1] but after the massacre at Fort Mims they could not retreat, and yet knew that they must perish except for supernatural aid. Their destiny was controlled by that of Tecumthe. Ten days after the massacre at Fort Mims, Perry won his victory on Lake Erie, which settled the result of the Indian wars both in the North and in the South. Tecumthe had expected to capture Fort Meigs, and with it Fort Wayne and the line of the Maumee and Wabash. On the impulse of this success he probably hoped to raise the war-spirit among the Chickasaws and Choctaws, and then in person to call the Creeks into the field. Proctor's successive defeats blasted Indian hopes, and the Creeks had hardly struck their first blow in his support when Tecumthe himself fell, and the Indians of the Lakes submitted or fled to Canada.

[1] Hawkins to Armstrong, July 20, 1813 ; State Papers, Indian Affairs, i. 849.

At best, the Creek outbreak would have been hopeless. Although the number of hostile Creek warriors was matter of conjecture, nothing showed that they could exceed four thousand. At Pensacola, Peter McQueen was said to have claimed forty-eight hundred " gun-men " on his side.[1] At such a moment he probably exaggerated his numbers. The Big Warrior, who led the peace party, estimated the hostile Creeks, early in August, as numbering at least twenty-five hundred warriors.[2] If the number of gun-men was four thousand, the number of guns in their possession could scarcely be more than one thousand. Not only had the Creeks few guns, and those in poor condition, but they had little powder or lead, and no means of repairing their weapons. Their guns commonly missed fire, and even after discharging them, the Creeks seldom reloaded, but resorted to the bow-and-arrows which they always carried. As warriors they felt their inferiority to the Shawanese and Indians of the Lakes, while their position was more desperate, for the Choctaws and Cherokees behind them refused to join in their war.

Four thousand warriors who had never seen a serious war even with their Indian neighbors, and armed for the most part with clubs, or bows-and-arrows, were not able to resist long the impact of

[1] Hawkins to Floyd, Sept. 30, 1813 ; State Papers, Indian Affairs, i. 854.

[2] Big Warrior to Hawkins, Aug. 4, 1813 ; State Papers, Indian Affairs, i. 851.

three or four armies, each nearly equal to their whole
force, coming from every quarter of the compass.
On the other hand, the military difficulties of conquering the Creeks were not trifling.   The same obstacles
that stopped Harrison in Ohio, stopped Pinckney in
Georgia.   Pinckney, like Harrison, could set in motion three columns of troops on three converging
lines, but he could not feed them or make roads
for them.   The focus of Indian fanaticism was the
Hickory Ground at the fork of the Coosa and Tallapoosa, about one hundred and fifty miles distant from
the nearest point that would furnish supplies for
an American army coming from Georgia, Tennessee, or Mobile.   Pinckney's natural line of attack
was through Georgia to the Lower Creek towns and
the American forts on the Chattahoochee, whence he
could move along a good road about eighty miles to
the Upper Creek towns, near the Hickory Ground.
The next convenient line was from Mobile up the
Alabama River about one hundred and fifty miles to
the same point.   The least convenient was the path-
less, mountainous, and barren region of Upper Alabama and Georgia, through which an army from
Tennessee must toil for at least a hundred miles in
order to reach an enemy.

The State of Georgia was most interested in the
Creek war, and was chiefly to profit by it.   Georgia
in 1813 had a white population of about one hundred and twenty-five thousand, and a militia probably
numbering thirty thousand.   Military District No. 6,

embracing the two Carolinas and Georgia, was supposed to contain two thousand regular troops, and
was commanded by Major-General Pinckney.   Under
Pinckney's command, a thousand regulars and three
thousand militia, advancing from Georgia by a good
road eighty miles into the Indian country, should have
been able to end the Creek war within six months
from the massacre at Fort Mims; but for some
reason the attempts on that side were not so successful as they should have been, and were neither rapid
nor vigorous.   Tennessee took the lead.

In respect of white population, the State of Tennessee was more than double the size of Georgia; but
it possessed a greater advantage in Andrew Jackson,
whose extreme energy was equivalent to the addition
of an army.   When news of the Mims massacre
reached Nashville about the middle of September,
Jackson was confined to his bed by a pistol-shot,
which had broken his arm and nearly cost his life
ten days before in a street brawl with Thomas H.
Benton.   From his bed he issued an order calling
back into service his two thousand volunteers of 1812;
and as early as October 12, little more than a month
after the affair at Fort Mims, he and his army of
twenty-five hundred men were already camped on the
Tennessee River south of Huntsville in Alabama.
There was his necessary base of operations, but one
hundred and sixty miles of wilderness lay between
him and the Hickory Ground.

On the Tennessee River Jackson's position bore

some resemblance to that of Harrison on the Maumee
a year before.   Energy could not save him from failure.   Indeed, the greater his energy the more serious
were his difficulties.   He depended on supplies from
east Tennessee descending the river ; but the river
was low, and the supplies could not be moved.   He
had taken no measures to procure supplies from
Nashville.   Without food and forage he could not
safely advance, or even remain where he was.   Under
such conditions, twenty-five hundred men with half
as many horses could not be kept together.   Harrison under the same difficulties held back his main
force near its magazines till it disbanded, without
approaching within a hundred miles of its object.
Jackson suffered nearly the same fate.   He sent
away his mounted men under General Coffee to
forage on the banks of the Black Warrior River,
fifty miles to the southwest, where no Creeks were
to be feared.   He forced his infantry forward through
rough country some twenty miles, to a point where
the river made its most southern bend, and there,
in the mountainous defile, he established, October 23,
a camp which he called Deposit, where his supplies
were to be brought when the river should permit.

Coffee's mounted men returned October 24.   Then,
October 25, in the hope of finding food as he went,
Jackson plunged into the mountains beyond the river,
intending to make a raid, as far as he could, into the
Creek country.   Except fatigue and famine, he had
nothing to fear.   The larger Creek towns were a

hundred miles to the southward, and were busy with threatened attacks nearer home. After a week's march Jackson reached the upper waters of the Coosa. Within a short distance were two or three small Creek villages. Against one of these Jackson sent his mounted force, numbering nine hundred men, under General Coffee. Early in the morning of November 3, Coffee surrounded and destroyed Talishatchee. His report represented that the Indians made an obstinate resistance.[1] "Not one of the warriors escaped to tell the news, — a circumstance unknown heretofore." According to Coffee's estimate, Talishatchee contained two hundred and eighty-four Indians of both sexes and all ages. If one in three could be reckoned as capable of bearing arms, the number of warriors was less than one hundred. Coffee's men after the battle counted one hundred and eighty-six dead Indians, and estimated the total loss at two hundred. In every attack on an Indian village a certain number of women and children were necessarily victims, but the proportion at Talishatchee seemed large.

"I lost five men killed, and forty-one wounded," reported Coffee, — "none mortally, the greater part slightly, a number with arrows. Two of the men killed was with arrows; this appears to form a very principal part of the enemy's arms for warfare, every man having a bow with a bundle of arrows, which is used after the first fire with the gun until a leisure time for loading offers."

[1] Report of General Coffee, Nov. 4, 1813 ; Niles, v. 218.

Meanwhile Jackson fortified a point on the Coosa, about thirty-five miles from his base on the Tennessee, and named it Fort Strother. There he expected to be joined by a division of east Tennessee militia under General Cocke, approaching from Chattanooga, as he hoped, with supplies; but while waiting, he received, November 7, a message from Talladega, a Creek village thirty miles to the southward, reporting that the town, which had refused to join the war-party, was besieged and in danger of capture by a large body of hostile warriors. Jackson instantly started to save Talladega, and marched twenty-four miles November 8, surrounding and attacking the besieging Creeks the next morning.

" The victory was very decisive," reported Jackson to Governor Blount,[1] November 11; " two hundred and ninety of the enemy were left dead, and there can be no doubt but many more were killed who were not found. . . . In the engagement we lost fifteen killed, and eighty-five wounded."

Coffee estimated the number of Indians, on their own report,[2] at about one thousand. Jackson mentioned no wounded Indians, nor the number of hostile Creeks engaged. Male Indians. except infants, were invariably killed, and probably not more than five or six hundred were in the battle, for Coffee thought very few escaped unhurt.

At Talladega Jackson was sixty miles from the

[1] Jackson to Blount, Nov. 11, 1813; Niles, v. 267.
[2] Parton's Jackson, i. 445.

Hickory Ground, and still nearer to several large Indian towns, but he had already passed the limit of his powers. News arrived that the army of eastern Tennessee had turned eastward toward the Tallapoosa, and that his expected supplies were as remote as ever. Returning to Fort Strother November 10, Jackson waited there in forced inactivity, as Harrison had waited at Fort Meigs, anxious only to avoid the disgrace of retreat. For two weeks the army had lived on the Indians. A month more passed in idle starvation, until after great efforts a supply train was organized, and difficulties on that account ceased; but at the same moment the army claimed discharge.

The claim was reasonable. Enlisted Dec. 10, 1812, for one year, the men were entitled to their discharge Dec. 10, 1813. Had Jackson been provided with fresh levies he would doubtless have dismissed the old; but in his actual situation their departure would have left him at Fort Strother to pass the winter alone. To prevent this, he insisted that the men had no right to count as service, within the twelve months for which they had enlisted, the months between May and October when they were dismissed to their homes. The men, unanimous in their own view of the contract, started to march home December 10; and Jackson, in a paroxysm of anger, planted two small pieces of artillery in their path and threatened to fire on them. The men, with good-temper, yielded for the moment; and Jackson, quickly recognizing his helplessness, gave way, and allowed them to depart

December 12, with a vehement appeal for volunteers who made no response.

Fort Strother was then held for a short time by east Tennessee militia, about fourteen hundred in number, whose term of service was a few weeks longer than that of the west Tennesseeans. Jackson could do nothing with them, and remained idle. The Governor of Tennessee advised him to withdraw to the State frontier; but Jackson, while admitting that his campaign had failed, declared that he would perish before withdrawing from the ground he considered himself to have gained.[1] Fortunately he stood in no danger. The Creeks did not molest him, and he saw no enemy within fifty miles.

While Jackson was thus brought to a stand-still, Major-General Cocke of east Tennessee, under greater disadvantages, accomplished only results annoying to Jackson. Cocke with twenty-five hundred three-months militia took the field at Knoxville October 12, and moving by way of Chattanooga reached the Coosa sixty or seventy miles above Camp Strother. The nearest Creek Indians were the Hillabees, on a branch of the Tallapoosa about sixty miles from Cocke's position, and the same distance from Jackson. The Hillabees, a group of four small villages, numbered in 1800 one hundred and seventy warriors.[2] Unaware that the Hillabees were making

[1] Blount to Jackson, Dec. 22, 1813; Parton's Jackson, i. 479, 480–484.

[2] Hawkins's Sketch, pp. 43, 44.

their submission to Jackson, and were to receive his promise of protection, Cocke sent a large detachment, which started November 12 into the Indian country, and surprised one of the Hillabee villages November 18, massacring sixty-one warriors, and capturing the other inmates, two hundred and fifty in number, without losing a drop of blood or meeting any resistance.[1]

Jackson was already displeased with General Cocke's conduct, and the Hillabee massacre increased his anger. Cocke had intentionally kept himself and his army at a distance in order to maintain an independent command.[2] Not until Jackson's troops disbanded and marched home, December 12, did Cocke come to Fort Strother. There his troops remained a month, guarding Jackson's camp, until January 12, 1814, when their three months' term expired.

While five thousand men under Jackson and Cocke wandered about northern Alabama, able to reach only small and remote villages, none of which were actively concerned in the outbreak, the Georgians organized a force to enter the heart of the Creek country. Brigadier-General John Floyd commanded the Georgia army, and neither Major-General Pinckney nor any United States troops belonged to it. Jackson's battle of Talladega was fought November 9; Cocke's expedition against the Hillabees started

[1] Cocke to the Secretary of War, Nov. 28, 1813 ; Niles, v. 282, 283.

[2] Cocke to White ; Parton's Jackson, i. 451.

November 12, and surprised the Hillabee village November 18. Floyd entered the hostile country November 24. The Georgians though nearest were last to move, and moved with the weakest force. Floyd had but nine hundred and forty militia, and three or four hundred friendly warriors of the Lower Creek villages.

Floyd had heard that large numbers of hostile Indians were assembled at Autossee, — a town on the Tallapoosa River near Tuckaubatchee, in the centre of the Upper Creek country. He crossed the Chattahoochee November 24 with five days rations, and marched directly against Autossee, arriving within nine or ten miles without meeting resistance. At half-past six on the morning of November 29 he formed his troops for action in front of the town.[1]

The difference between the Northwestern Indians and the Creeks was shown in the battle of Autossee compared with Tippecanoe. Floyd was weaker than Harrison, having only militia and Indians, while Harrison had a regular regiment composing one third of his rank-and-file. The Creeks were probably more numerous than the Tippecanoe Indians, although in both cases the numbers were quite unknown. Probably the Creeks were less well armed, but they occupied a strong position and stood on the defensive. Floyd reported that by nine o'clock he drove the Indians from their towns and burned their houses, —

[1] Floyd to Pinckney, Dec. 4, 1813; Niles, v. 283.

supposed to be four hundred in number. He estimated their loss at two hundred killed. His own loss was eleven killed and fifty-four wounded. That of Harrison at Tippecanoe was sixty-one killed or mortally wounded, and one hundred and twenty-seven not fatally injured. The Creeks hardly inflicted one fourth the loss caused by the followers of the Shawnee Prophet.

General Floyd, — himself among the severely wounded, — immediately after the battle ordered the troops to begin their return march to the Chattahoochee. The Georgia raid into the Indian country was bolder, less costly, and more effective than the Tennessee campaign; but at best it was only a raid, like the Indian assault on Fort Mims, and offered no immediate prospect of regular military occupation. Another attempt, from a third quarter, had the same unsatisfactory result.

The successor of General Wilkinson at New Orleans and Mobile, and in Military District No. 7, was Brigadier-General Thomas Flournoy. Under his direction an expedition was organized from Fort Stoddert, commanded by Brigadier-General Claiborne of the Mississippi volunteers. Claiborne was given the Third United States Infantry, with a number of militia, volunteers, and Choctaw Indians, — in all about a thousand men. He first marched to a point on the Alabama River, about eighty-five miles above Fort Stoddert, where he constructed a military post, called Fort Claiborne. Having established his base there, he marched, December 13, up the river till he reached, December 23, the Holy Ground, where the half-breed Weatherford lived.   There Claiborne approached within about fifty miles of the point which Floyd reached a month before, but for want of co-operation he could not maintain his advantage.   He attacked and captured Weatherford's town, killing thirty Indians, with a loss of one man ; but after destroying the place he retreated, arriving unharmed at Fort Claiborne, on the last day of the year.

Thus the year 1813 ended without closing the Creek war.   More than seven thousand men had entered the Indian country from four directions ; and with a loss of thirty or forty lives had killed, according to their reports, about eight hundred Indians, or one fifth of the hostile Creek warriors ; but this carnage had fallen chiefly on towns and villages not responsible for the revolt.   The true fanatics were little harmed, and could offer nearly as much resistance as ever.   The failure and excessive expense of the campaign were the more annoying, because they seemed beyond proportion to the military strength of the fanatics.   Major-General Pinckney wrote to the War Department at the close of the year : [1] —

" The force of the hostile Creeks was estimated by the best judges to have consisted of three thousand five hundred warriors ; of these it is apprehended that about one thousand have been put *hors de combat.*"

[1] Pinckney to Armstrong, Dec. 28, 1813; MSS. War Department Archives.

To Andrew Jackson, Pinckney wrote, Jan. 19, 1814,[1]

" Your letter, dated December 26, did not reach me until the last evening. Your preceding dispatches of December 14 had led me to conclude what would probably soon be the diminished state of your force. I therefore immediately ordered to your support Colonel Williams's regiment of twelve-months men, and wrote to the Governor of Tennessee urging him to complete the requisition of fifteen hundred for the time authorized by law. I learn from the person who brought your letter that Colonel Williams's regiment is marching to join you ; if the fifteen hundred of the quota should also be furnished by Governor Blount, you will in my opinion have force sufficient for the object to be attained. The largest computation that I have heard of the hostile Creek warriors, made by any competent judge, is four thousand. At least one thousand of them have been killed or disabled ; they are badly armed and supplied with ammunition ; little doubt can exist that two thousand of our men would be infinitely superior to any number they can collect."

Jackson at Fort Strother on the departure of the east Tennesseeans, January 14, received a reinforcement of sixty-day militia, barely nine hundred in number.[2] Determined to use them to the utmost, Jackson started three days afterward to co-operate with General Floyd in an attack on the Tallapoosa villages, aiming at a town called Emuckfaw, some forty miles north of Tuckaubatchee. The move-

[1] Pinckney to Jackson, Jan. 19, 1814 ; MSS. War Department Archives.

[2] Parton, i. 864.

ment was much more dangerous than any he had
yet attempted. His own force was fresh, motley,
and weak, numbering only nine hundred and thirty
militia, including "a company of volunteer officers
headed by General Coffee, who had been abandoned
by his men," and assisted by two or three hundred
friendly Creeks and Cherokees. The sixty-day militia were insubordinate and unsteady, the march was
long, and the Creek towns at which he aimed were
relatively large. Emuckfaw was one of seven villages
belonging to Ocfuskee, the largest town in the Creek
nation, — in 1800 supposed to contain four hundred
and fifty warriors.[1]

As far as Enotachopco Creek, twelve miles from
Emuckfaw, Jackson had no great danger to fear;
but beyond that point he marched with caution. At
daylight, January 22, the Indians, who were strongly
encamped at about three miles distance, made an
attack on Jackson's camp, which was repulsed after
half an hour's fighting. Jackson then sent Coffee
with four hundred men to burn the Indian camp, but
Coffee returned without attempting it. "On view-
ing the encampment and its strength the General
thought it most prudent to return to my encampment," reported Jackson.[2] Immediately after Coffee's
return the Indians again attacked, and Coffee sallied
out to turn their flank, followed by not more than
fifty-four men. The Indians were again repulsed with

[1] Hawkins's Sketch, p. 45.

[2] Jackson to Pinckney, Jan. 29, 1814; Niles, v. 427.

a loss of forty-five killed, but Coffee was severely wounded, and Jackson " determined to commence a return march to Fort Strother the following day."

At that moment Jackson's situation was not unlike that of Harrison after the battle of Tippecanoe, and he escaped less happily. Fortifying his camp, he remained during the night of January 22 undisturbed. At half-past ten, January 23, he began his return march, " and was fortunate enough to reach Enotachopco before night, having passed without interruption a dangerous defile occasioned by a hurricane." [1] Enotachopco Creek was twelve or fifteen miles from Emuckfaw Creek, and the Hillabee towns were about the same distance beyond.

At Enotachopco Jackson again fortified his camp. His position was such as required the utmost caution in remaining or moving. So hazardous was the passage of the deep creek and the defile beyond, through which the army had marched in its advance, that Jackson did not venture to return by the same path, but on the morning of January 24 began cautiously crossing the creek at a safer point: —

" The front guard had crossed with part of the flank columns, the wounded were over, and the artillery in the act of entering the creek, when an alarm-gun was heard in the woods. . . . To my astonishment and mortification, when the word was given by Colonel Carrol to halt and form, and a few guns had been fired, I beheld the right and left columns of the rear guard precipitately

[1] Jackson to Pinckney, Jan. 29, 1814; Niles, v. 427.

give way. This shameful retreat was disastrous in the extreme; it drew along with it the greater part of the centre column, leaving not more than twenty-five men, who being formed by Colonel Carrol maintained their ground as long as it was possible to maintain it, and it brought consternation and confusion into the centre of the army, — a consternation which was not easily removed, and a confusion which could not soon be restored to order." [1]

The Indians were either weak or ignorant of warfare, for they failed to take advantage of the panic, and allowed themselves to be driven away by a handful of men. Jackson's troops escaped unharmed, or but little injured, their loss in the engagements of January 22 and 24 being twenty-four men killed and seventy-one wounded. Probably the Creek force consisted of the Ocfuskee warriors, and numbered about half that of Jackson.[2] Coffee supposed them to be eight hundred or a thousand in number, but the exaggeration in estimating Indian forces was always greater than in estimating white enemies in battle. An allowance of one third was commonly needed for exaggeration in reported numbers of European combatants; an allowance of one half was not unreasonable in estimates of Indian forces.

In letting Jackson escape from Emuckfaw the Creeks lost their single opportunity. Jackson never repeated the experiment. He arrived at Fort Strother

---

[1] Jackson to Pinckney, Jan. 29, 1814; Niles, v. 427.

[2] Pickett's Alabama, ii. 336.

in safety January 29, and did not again leave his intrenchment until the middle of March, under much better conditions.

General Floyd was no more successful. Jackson started from Fort Strother for Emuckfaw January 17 ; Floyd left Fort Mitchell, on the Chattahoochee, January 18, for Tuckaubatchee, only forty miles south of Emuckfaw.[1] Floyd's army, like Jackson's, was partly composed of militia and partly of Lower Creek warriors, in all about seventeen hundred men, including four hundred friendly Creeks. From the best information to be obtained at the time, the effective strength of the hostile Indians did not then exceed two thousand warriors,[2] scattered along the Coosa and Tallapoosa rivers ; while experience proved the difficulty of concentrating large bodies of Indians, even when supplies were furnished them. The British commissariat in Canada constantly issued from five to ten thousand rations for Indians and their families, but Proctor never brought more than fifteen hundred warriors into battle. The Creeks, as far as was known, never numbered a thousand warriors in any battle during the war. Floyd, with seventeen hundred men well armed, was able to face the whole Creek nation, and meant to move forward, fortifying military posts at each day's march, until he should establish himself on the Tallapoosa in the centre

[1] Jackson to Pinckney, Jan. 29, 1814; Niles v. 427.

[2] Letter from Milledgeville, March 16, 1814 ; "The War," April 5, 1814.

of the Creek towns, and wait for a junction with Jackson.

When Jackson was repulsed at Emuckfaw January 22, Floyd was about forty miles to the southward, expecting to draw the chief attack of the Indians. Having advanced forty-eight miles from the Chattahoochee he arrived at a point about seven or eight miles south of Tuckaubatchee, where he fortified, on Calibee Creek, a camp called Defiance. There, before daybreak on the morning of January 27, he was sharply attacked, as Harrison was attacked at Tippecanoe, and with the same result. The attack was repulsed, but Floyd lost twenty-two killed and one hundred and forty-seven wounded, — the largest number of casualties that had yet occurred in the Indian war. The Indians "left thirty-seven dead on the field ; from the effusion of blood and the number of head-dresses and war-clubs found in various directions, their loss must have been considerable independent of their wounded." [1]

The battle of Calibee Creek, January 27, was in substance a defeat to Floyd. So decided were his militia in their determination to go home, that he abandoned all his fortified posts and fell back to the Chattahoochee, where he arrived February 1, four days after the battle.[2]

[1] Floyd to Pinckney, Jan. 27, 1814; Niles, v. 411.
[2] Floyd to Pinckney, Feb. 2, 1814 ; Military and Naval Letters, p. 306. Hawkins to Armstrong, June 7, 1814 ; State Papers, Indian Affairs, i. 858.

Six months had then elapsed since the outbreak of hostilities at Burnt Corn; a year since the Little Warrior murders on the Ohio River, yet not a post had been permanently occupied within eighty miles of the fanatical centre at the fork of the Coosa and Tallapoosa.

Pinckney was obliged to apply to the governors of North and South Carolina to furnish him with men and equipments. The Governor of Georgia also exerted himself to supply the deficiencies of the national magazines.[1] By their aid Pinckney was able to collect an army with which to make another and a decisive movement into the Creek country: but before he could act, Jackson succeeded in striking a final blow.

Jackson's success in overcoming the obstacles in his path was due to his obstinacy in insisting on maintaining himself at Fort Strother, which obliged Governor Blount to order out four thousand more militia in January for six months. Perhaps this force alone would have been no more effectual in 1814 than in 1813, but another reinforcement was decisive. The Thirty-ninth regiment of the regular army, authorized by the Act of January 29, 1813, had been officered and recruited in Tennessee, and was still in the State. Major-General Pinckney sent orders, Dec. 23, 1813, to its colonel, John Williams, to join Jackson.[2] The arrival of the Thirty-ninth regi-

[1] Pinckney to the Governor of Georgia, Feb. 20, 1814; Niles, vi. 132.

[2] Pinckney to Colonel Williams, Dec. 23, 1813; MSS. War Department Archives.

ment February 6, 1814, gave Jackson the means of coping with his militia. February 21 he wrote to his quartermaster, Major Lewis, that he meant to use his regulars first to discipline his own army.[1] "I am truly happy in having the Colonel [Williams] with me. His regiment will give strength to my arm, and quell mutiny." His patience with militiamen had been long exhausted, and he meant to make a warning of the next mutineer.

The first victim was no less a person than Major-General Cocke of the east Tennessee militia. Cocke's division of two thousand men, mustered for six months, began January 17 its march from Knoxville to Fort Strother.[2] Learning on the march that the west Tennessee division, mustered at the same time for the same service, had been accepted to serve only three months, Cocke's men mutinied, and Cocke tried to pacify them by a friendly speech. Jackson, learning what had passed, despatched a sharp order to one of Cocke's brigadiers to arrest and send under guard to Fort Strother every officer of whatever rank who should be found exciting the men to mutiny. Cocke was put under arrest when almost in sight of the enemy's country; his sword was taken from him, and he was sent to Nashville for trial.[3] His division came to Fort Strother, and said no more about its term of service.

[1] Parton's Jackson, i. 503.

[2] Parton's Jackson, i. 454.

[3] Cocke's Defence; "National Intelligencer," October, 1852. Parton's Jackson, i. 455. Eaton's Jackson, p. 155.

Having dealt thus with the officers, Jackson selected at leisure a test of strength with the men. The conduct of the Fayetteville company of the Twenty-eighth regiment of west Tennessee light infantry gave him ground for displeasure. Not only had they refused to obey the call for six months' service and insisted on serving for three months or not at all, but they had halted on their march, and had sent their commanding officer to bargain with Jackson for his express adhesion to their terms. Learning that Jackson made difficulties, they marched home without waiting for an official reply. Jackson ordered the whole body to be arrested as deserters, accompanying his order by an offer of pardon to such as returned to duty on their own understanding of the term of service. The company was again mustered, and arrived at Fort Strother not long after the arrival of the Thirty-ninth United States Infantry.

A few weeks later an unfortunate private of the same company, named Woods, refused to obey the officer of the day, and threatened to shoot any man who arrested him. Jackson instantly called a court-martial, tried and sentenced Woods, and March 14 caused him to be shot. The execution was a harsh measure; but Jackson gave to it a peculiar character by issuing a general order in which he misstated facts that made Wood's case exceptional,[1] in order to let the company understand that their comrade was suffering the penalty which they all deserved.

[1] Parton's Jackson, i. 511.

Without giving his army time to brood over this
severity, Jackson ordered a general movement, and
within forty-eight hours after Woods's execution, all
were well on their way toward the enemy.   Jackson
had with him about five thousand men, four fifths of
whom expected their discharge in a month.   He left
them not a day's repose.

Two lines of advance were open to him in approaching the fork of the Coosa and Tallapoosa,
which was always the objective point.   He might
descend the Coosa, or cross to the Tallapoosa by the
way he had taken in January.   He descended the
Coosa thirty miles, and then struck a sudden blow at
the Tallapoosa towns.

The Ocfuskee Indians, elated by their success in
January, collected their whole force, with that of
some neighboring towns, in a bend of the Tallapoosa,
where they built a sort of fortress by constructing
across the neck of the Horse-shoe a breastwork composed of five large logs, one above the other, with
two ranges of port-holes.[1]   The interior was covered
with trees and fallen timber along the river side,
and caves were dug in the bank.   Seven or eight
hundred Indian warriors together with many women
and children were within the enclosure of eighty or a
hundred acres.

Jackson, after leaving a garrison at a new fort
which he constructed on the Coosa, about half way

[1] Col. Gideon Morgan to Governor Blount, April 1, 1814 ;
Niles. vi. 148.

to the Horse-shoe, had somewhat less than three thousand effectives.[1] With these he camped, on the evening of March 28, about six miles northwest of the bend, and the next morning advanced to attack it. "Determined to exterminate them," he reported,[2] he detached Coffee with the mounted force of seven hundred men and six hundred friendly Indians[3] to surround the bend, along the river bank, while Jackson himself with all his infantry took position before the breastwork. At half-past ten o'clock he planted his cannon about two hundred yards[4] from the centre of the work, and began a rapid fire of artillery and musketry, which continued for two hours without producing apparent effect. Meanwhile the Cherokee allies swam the river in the rear of the Creek warriors, who were all at the breastwork, and seizing canoes, brought some two hundred Indians and whites into the Horse-shoe, where they climbed the high ground in the rear of the breastwork and fired on the Creeks, who were occupied in defending their front.

Jackson then ordered an assault on the breastwork, which was carried, with considerable loss, by the Thirty-ninth regiment, in the centre. The Creeks sought shelter in the thickets and under

[1] Eaton's Jackson. p. 156.

[2] Jackson to Pinckney, March 28, 1814; Military and Naval Letters, p. 319.

[3] Coffee to Jackson, April 1, 1814 ; Niles, vi. 148.

[4] Colonel Morgan to Governor Blount, April 1, 1814 ; Niles, vi. 148.

the bluffs, where they were hunted or burned out, and killed. " The slaughter was greater than all we had done before," wrote Coffee ; it was continued all day and the next morning. When the Horse-shoe had been thoroughly cleared, five hundred and fifty-seven dead bodies were counted within the bend ; many were killed in the river, and about twenty were supposed to have escaped. According to Coffee, " we killed not less than eight hundred and fifty or nine hundred of them, and took about five hundred squaws and children prisoners." The proportion of squaws and children to the whole number of Indians showed the probable proportion of warriors among the dead. " I lament that two or three women and children were killed by accident," reported Jackson.[1]

Jackson's loss was chiefly confined to the Thirty-ninth regiment and the friendly Indians, who were most actively engaged in the storm. The Thirty-ninth lost twenty killed and fifty-two wounded. Among the severely wounded was Ensign Samuel Houston, struck by an arrow in the thigh. The major and two lieutenants were killed. The Cherokees lost eighteen killed and thirty-five wounded. The friendly Creeks lost five killed and eleven wounded. The Tennessee militia, comprising two thirds of the army, lost only eight killed and fifty-two wounded. The total loss was fifty-one killed and one hundred and forty-eight wounded.

[1] Jackson to Governor Blount, March 31, 1814; Niles, vi. 147.

Jackson's policy of extermination shocked many humane Americans, and would perhaps have seemed less repulsive had the Creeks shown more capacity for resistance. The proportion between two hundred casualties on one side and seven or eight hundred killed on the other would have been striking in any case, but was especially so where the advantages of position were on the side of the defence. A more serious criticism was that the towns thus exterminated were not the towns chiefly responsible for the outbreak. The Alabamas and the main body of fanatical Creeks escaped.

Jackson was obliged to return to his new fort on the Coosa, a march of five days; and was delayed five days more by preparations to descend the river. When at length he moved southward, scouring the country as he went, he could find no more enemies. He effected his junction with the Georgia troops April 15, and the united armies reached the fork of the Coosa and Tallapoosa April 18, where Major-General Pinckney joined them, April 20, and took command;[1] but the Red Sticks had then fled southward. A few of the hostile leaders, including Weatherford, made submission, but McQueen and the chief prophets escaped to continue the war from Florida. The friendly Creeks did not consider the war to be finished; they reported to Hawkins[2] —

[1] Jackson to Governor Blount, April 18, 1814; Niles, vi. 212. April 25, 1814; Niles, vi. 219.

[2] Hawkins to Pinckney, April 25, 1814; State Papers, Indian Affairs, i. 858.

" They did not believe the hostile Indians were ready for peace, although a part of them had suffered so severely in battle against our armies. They were proud, haughty, brave, and mad by fanaticism. Those of the towns of Tallapoosa below Tuckaubatchee and Alabama had suffered the least, although they were the most culpable ; and it was probable they would mistake our object in offering terms of peace to them."

The number of refugees was never precisely known, but Hawkins reported that eight of the Tallapoosa towns had migrated in a body to Spanish territory,[1] and probably a larger proportion of the Coosa and Alabama towns accompanied them. The Indians themselves gave out that a few more than a thousand Red Stick warriors survived, who meant to die fighting. In May the British admiral Cochrane sent Captain Pigot of the " Orpheus " to the Appalachicola to communicate with the refugee Creek Indians and supply them with arms. Pigot received ten of the principal chiefs on board his vessel May 20, and reported [2] on their authority that " the number of the warriors of the Creek Nation friendly to the English and ready to take up arms was about twenty-eight hundred, exclusive of one thousand unarmed warriors who had been driven by the Americans from their towns into the marshes near Pensacola, and who were expected to rejoin the main body." The Creek

[1] Hawkins to Armstrong, July 19, 1814; State Papers, Indian Affairs, i. 860.

[2] Abstract of Correspondence, Expedition to New Orleans, 1814–1815; MSS. British Archives.

warriors friendly to the Americans were estimated at about twelve hundred, and the fugitive Red Sticks at one thousand. Whatever their number, they included the most fanatical followers of Tecumthe, and their obstinate outlawry caused long and costly difficulties to the United States government.

Meanwhile the whites were conquerors and could take as much of the Creek lands as suited them; but an irregularity of form could not be avoided. Secretary Armstrong first authorized General Pinckney to conclude a treaty of peace with the hostile Creeks, containing a cession of land and other provisions.[1] A few days later Armstrong saw reason to prefer that the proposed treaty with the Creeks should take a form altogether military, and be in the nature of a capitulation.[2] His idea required a treaty with the hostile Creek chiefs;[3] but the hostile Creeks were not a separate organization capable of making a treaty or granting lands of the Creek nation; and besides that difficulty the hostile chiefs had fled, and refused either to submit or negotiate. No chiefs remained except among the friendly Creeks, who could not capitulate because they had never been at war. They had fought in the United States service and

[1] Armstrong to Pinckney, March 17, 1814; State Papers, Indian Affairs, i. 836.

[2] Armstrong to Pinckney, March 20, 1814; State Papers, Indian Affairs, i. 837.

[3] Madison to Armstrong, May 20, 1814; Madison's Works, iii. 399. Madison's Works, iii. 400, 401.

were entitled to reward as allies, not to punishment as enemies.

The solution of this legal problem was entrusted to Andrew Jackson, whose services in the war earned for him the appointment of major-general in the regular army, and the command of Military District No. 7, with headquarters at Mobile. Jackson met the Creek chiefs in July. The Indians, parties to the negotiation, were friendly chiefs, deputies, and warriors, representing perhaps one third of the entire Creek nation. To these allies and friends Jackson presented a paper, originally intended for the hostile Indians, entitled " Articles of Agreement and Capitulation," requiring as indemnity for war expenses a surrender of two thirds of their territory. They were required to withdraw from the southern and western half of Alabama, within the Chattahoochee on the east and the Coosa on the west. The military object of this policy was to isolate them from the Seminoles and Spaniards on one side, and from the Choctaws and Chickasaws on the other. The political object was to surround them with a white population.

Unanimously the Creeks refused to accept the sacrifice. Jackson told them in reply that their refusal would show them to be enemies of the United States; that they might retain their own part of the country, but that the part which belonged to the hostile Indians would be taken by the government; and that the chiefs who would not consent to sign the paper might join the Red Sticks at Pensacola, — although, added Jackson, he should probably overtake and destroy them before they could get there. Such arguments could not be answered. A number of the Creeks at last, after long resistance, signed the capitulation or agreement, although they continued to protest against it, and refused their aid to carry it out.

Jackson's capitulation of Aug. 9, 1814,[1] which, without closing the Creek war, appropriated to the government the larger part of the Creek lands, was nearly simultaneous with a treaty[2] signed July 22 by William Henry Harrison and Lewis Cass, at Greenville in Ohio, with chiefs of the Wyandots, Delawares, Shawanese, Senecas, and Miamis. This treaty contained no land-cession, but established peace between the parties, and obliged the Indian signers to declare war on the British. Neither Harrison's nor Jackson's treaty embraced the chief body of hostile Indians; but Harrison's treaty served another purpose of no small value in appearing to remove an obstacle to negotiation with England.

[1] State Papers, Indian Affairs, i. 826.
[2] State Papers, Indian Affairs, i. 826.

CHAPTER XI.

BADLY as the United States fared in the campaign of 1813, their situation would have been easy had they not suffered under the annoyances of a blockade continually becoming more stringent. The doctrine that coasts could be blockaded was enforced against America with an energy that fell little short of demonstration. The summer was well advanced before the whole naval force to be used for the purpose could be posted at the proper stations. Not until May 26 did Admiral Warren issue at Bermuda his proclamation of "a strict and rigorous blockade of the ports and harbors of New York, Charleston, Port Royal, Savannah, and of the river Mississippi," which completed the blockade of the coast, leaving only the ports of New England open to neutrals. From that time nothing entered or left the blockaded coast except swift privateers, or occasional fast-sailing vessels which risked capture in the attempt. Toward the close of the year Admiral Warren extended his blockade eastward. Notice of the extension was given at Halifax November 16, and by the blockading squadron off New London December 2, thus closing Long Island Sound to all vessels of every description.[1]

The pressure of the blockade was immediately felt. In August[2] superfine flour sold at Boston for $11.87 a barrel, at Baltimore for $6.00, and at Richmond for $4.50. Upland cotton sold at Boston for twenty cents a pound; at Charleston for nine cents. Rice sold at Philadelphia for $12.00 a hundred weight; in Charleston and Savannah for $3.00. Sugar sold in Boston for $18.75 a hundred weight; in Baltimore for $26.50. Already the American staples were unsalable at the places of their production. No rate of profit could cause cotton, rice, or wheat to be brought by sea from Charleston or Norfolk to Boston. Soon speculation began. The price of imported articles rose to extravagant points. At the end of the year coffee sold for thirty-eight cents a pound, after selling for twenty-one cents in August. Tea which could be bought for $1.70 per pound in August, sold for three and four dollars in December. Sugar which was quoted at nine dollars a hundred weight in New Orleans, and in August sold for twenty-one or twenty-two dollars in New York and Philadelphia, stood at forty dollars in December.

More sweeping in its effects on exports than on imports, the blockade rapidly reduced the means of the people. After the summer of 1813, Georgia alone, owing to its contiguity with Florida, succeeded

---

[1] Proclamation and Notice ; Niles, v. 264.

[2] Prices Current; Niles, v. 41.

in continuing to send out cotton. The exports of
New York, which exceeded $12,250,000 in 1811, fell
to $209,000 for the year ending in 1814. The do-
mestic exports of Virginia diminished in four years
from $4,800,000 to $3,000,000 for 1812, $1,819,000
for 1813, and $17,581 for the year ending Sept. 30,
1814. At the close of 1813 exports, except from
Georgia and New England, ceased.[1]

On the revenue the blockade acted with equal
effect.   Owing to the increase of duties and to
open ports, the New England States rather increased
than diminished their customs receipts. Until the
summer of 1813, when the blockade began in earnest, New York showed the same result; but after
that time the receipts fell, until they averaged less
than $50,000 a month instead of $500,000, which
would have been a normal average if peace had been
preserved. Philadelphia suffered sooner.   In 1810
the State of Pennsylvania contributed more than
$200,000 a month to the Treasury; in 1813 it con-
tributed about $25,000 a month.   Maryland, where
was collected in 1812 no less than $1,780,000 of net
revenue, paid only $182,000 in 1813, and showed an
actual excess of expenditures in 1814.   After the
summer, the total net revenue collected in every
port of the United States outside of New England
did not exceed $150,000 a month, or at the rate of
$1,800,000 a year.[2]

[1] Table No. II.; Pitkin, p. 56.
[2] Table No. I.; Pitkin, p. 415.

No ordinary operations of war could affect the United States so severely as this inexorable blockade. Every citizen felt it in every action of his life. The farmer grew crops which he could not sell, while he paid tenfold prices for every necessity. While the country was bursting with wealth, it was ruined. The blockade was but a part of the evil. The whole coast was systematically swept of the means of industry. Especially the Virginians and Marylanders felt the heavy hand of England as it was felt nowhere else except on the Niagara River. A large British squadron occupied Chesapeake Bay, and converted it into a British naval station. After the month of February, 1813, the coasts of Virginia and Maryland enjoyed not a moment's repose. Considering the immense naval power wielded by England, the Americans were fortunate that their chief losses were confined to the farm-yards and poultry of a few islands in Chesapeake Bay, but the constant annoyance and terror were not the less painful to the people who apprehended attack.

Fortunately the British naval officers showed little disposition to distinguish themselves, and their huge line-of-battle ships were not adapted to river service. The squadron under the general command of Admiral Sir John Borlase Warren seemed contented for the most part to close the bay to commerce. The only officer in the fleet who proved the energy and capacity to use a part of the great force lying idle at Lynnhaven Bay was Rear-Admiral Sir George

Cockburn, whose efficiency was attested by the execration in which his name was held for fifty years in the United States. His duties were not of a nature to make him popular, and he was an admiral of the old school, whose boisterous energy seemed to take needless pleasure in the work.

Early in April, 1813, Admiral Warren sent Cockburn with a light flotilla to the head of Chesapeake Bay to destroy everything that could serve a warlike purpose, and to interrupt, as far as possible, communication along the shore.[1] The squadron consisted of only one light frigate, the "Maidstone," thirty-six guns; two brigs, the "Fantome" and "Mohawk;" and three or four prize schooners, with four or five hundred seamen, marines, and soldiers. With this petty force Cockburn stationed himself at the mouth of the Susquehanna River, and soon threw Maryland into paroxysms of alarm and anger. Taking possession of the islands in his neighborhood, he obtained supplies of fresh food for the whole British force in Chesapeake Bay. He then scoured every creek and inlet above his anchorage. He first moved into the Elk River, and sent his boats, April 28, with one hundred and fifty marines, to Frenchtown, — a village of a dozen buildings, which had acquired a certain importance for the traffic between Baltimore and Philadelphia since the stoppage of transit by sea. Without losing a man, the expedition drove

[1] Admiral Warren to J. W. Croker, May 28, 1813; London "Gazette," July 6, 1813.

away the few Americans who made a show of resistance, and burned whatever property was found,
" consisting of much flour, a large quantity of army
clothing, of saddles, bridles, and other equipments
for cavalry, etc., together with various articles of mer-
chandise," besides five vessels lying near the place.[1]

Cockburn next sent the same force to destroy a
battery lately erected at Havre de Grace. The attack was made on the morning of May 3, and like
the attack on Frenchtown, met with only resistance
enough to offer an excuse for pillage. The militia
took refuge in the woods; Cockburn's troops destroyed or carried away the arms and cannon, and
set fire to the town of some sixty houses, " to cause
the proprietors (who had deserted them and formed
part of the militia who had fled to the woods) to
understand and feel what they were liable to bring
upon themselves by building batteries and acting
toward us with so much useless rancor." [2]   While
engaged in this work Cockburn was told that an
extensive cannon-foundry existed about four miles
up the Susquehanna River; and he immediately
started for it in his boats.   He met no resistance,
and destroyed the foundry with several small vessels.   His handful of men passed the day undisturbed on the banks of the Susquehanna, capturing
fifty-one cannon, mostly heavy pieces, with one hun-

[1] Warren's Report of May 28, 1813; London "Gazette."
[2] Cockburn to Warren, May 3, 1813; London "Gazette," July
6, 1813.

dred and thirty stand of small arms. The party then returned to their ships, " where we arrived at ten o'clock, after being twenty-two hours in constant exertion, without nourishment of any kind ; and I have much pleasure in being able to add that, excepting Lieutenant Westphall's wound, we have not suffered any casualty whatever."

These expeditions cleared every inlet in the Upper Chesapeake except the Sassafras River on the eastern shore. During the night of May 5 Cockburn sent his boats into the Sassafras. Militia in considerable numbers assembled on both banks and opened a fire which Cockburn described as " most heavy," aided by one long gun. Cockburn landed, dispersed the militia, and destroyed Fredericktown and Georgetown, with the vessels and stores he found there. This expedition cost him five men wounded, one severely. The next day, May 6, he reported to Admiral Warren, —

" I had a deputation from Charleston in the Northeast River to assure me that that place is considered by them at your mercy, and that neither guns nor militia-men shall be suffered there ; and as I am assured that all the places in the upper part of Chesapeake Bay have adopted similar resolutions, and as there is now neither public property, vessels, nor warlike stores remaining in this neighborhood, I propose returning to you with the light squadron to-morrow morning."

Thus in the course of a week, and without loss of life on either side, Cockburn with a few boats and

one hundred and fifty men terrorized the shores of
the Upper Chesapeake, and by his loud talk and ran-
dom threats threw even Baltimore into a panic, causing every one to suspend other pursuits in order to
garrison the city against an imaginary attack. The
people, harassed by this warfare, remembered with
extreme bitterness the marauding of Cockburn and
his sailors; but where he met no resistance he paid
in part for what private property he took, and as
far as was recorded, his predatory excursions cost the
Marylanders not a wound.

For six weeks after Cockburn's return to Warren's
station at Lynnhaven Bay, the British fleet remained
inactive. Apparently the British government aimed
at no greater object than that of clearing from
Chesapeake Bay every vessel not engaged in British
interests under British protection. The small craft
and privateers were quickly taken or destroyed; but
the three chief depots of commerce and armaments
— Norfolk, Baltimore, and Washington — required a
greater effort. Of these three places Norfolk seemed
most open to approach, and Admiral Warren determined to attack it.

The British navy wished nothing more ardently
than to capture or destroy the American frigates.
One of these, the "Constellation," lay at Norfolk,
where it remained blockaded throughout the war.
Admiral Warren could earn no distinction so great
as the credit of capturing this frigate, which not only
threatened to annoy British commerce should she

escape to sea, but even when blockaded in port required a considerable squadron to watch her, and neutralized several times her force.

Another annoyance drew Warren's attention to Norfolk. June 20, fifteen gunboats issued from the harbor before daylight, and under cover of darkness approached within easy range of a becalmed British frigate, the " Junon" of forty-six guns. For half an hour, from four o'clock till half-past four, the gunboats maintained, according to the official report of Commodore Cassin who commanded them, " a heavy, galling fire at about three quarters of a mile distance." [1] Their armament was not mentioned, but probably they, like the gunboats on the Lakes, carried in part long thirty-two and twenty-four-pound guns. The attack was intended to test the offensive value of gunboats, and the result was not satisfactory. The fire of fifteen heavy guns for half an hour on a defenceless frigate within easy range should have caused great injury, but did not. When a breeze rose and enabled the " Junon " and a neighboring frigate, the " Barrosa," to get under weigh, the gunboats were obliged to retire with the loss of one man killed and two wounded. The " Junon " also had one man killed, but received only one or two shots in her hull.[2]

The "Constellation" lay, under the guns of two forts and with every possible precaution, five miles up the

[1] Cassin to Secretary Jones, June 21, 1813; Niles, iv. 291.

[2] James, ii. 55.

Elizabeth River, at the Portsmouth navy-yard. The utmost pains had been taken to provide against approach by water. Whatever incompetence or neglect was shown elsewhere, Norfolk was under the command of able officers in both services, who neglected no means of defence. General Wade Hampton had fortified the interior line immediately below the town, where two strong forts were constructed under the direction of Captain Walker Keith Armistead of the Engineers, the first graduate of the West Point Academy in 1803. Five miles below these forts, where the river widened into Hampton Roads, Brigadier-General Robert Taylor of the Virginia militia, and Captain John Cassin commanding at the navy-yard, established a second line of defence, resting on Craney Island on the left, supported by fifteen or twenty gun-boats moored across the channel. A battery of seven guns was established on the island covering the approach to the gunboats, so that the capture of the island was necessary to the approach by water. The force on the island consisted of about seven hundred men, of whom less than a hundred were State troops. The rest were infantry of the line, riflemen, seamen, and marines.[1] The town and forts were strongly garrisoned, and a large body of State militia was constantly on service.

To deal with the defences of Norfolk, Admiral Warren brought from Bermuda, according to newspaper account, a detachment of battalion marines

[1] Report of Robert Taylor, July 4, 1813; Niles, iv. 324.

eighteen hundred strong; three hundred men of the
One Hundred-and-second regiment of the line, commanded by Lieut.-Colonel Charles James Napier,
afterward a very distinguished officer; two hundred
and fifty chasseurs, or French prisoners of war who
had entered the British service; and three hundred
men of the royal marine artillery,[1] — in all, two thousand six hundred and fifty rank-and-file, or about
three thousand men all told, besides the sailors of
the fleet.   At that time no less than thirteen sail
of British ships, including three ships-of-the-line and
five frigates, lay at anchor within thirteen miles of
Craney Island.

The attack was planned for June 22.   The land
forces were commanded by Sir Sydney Beckwith, but
the general movement was directed by Admiral Warren.[2]   The main attack, led by Major-General Beckwith in person, was to land and approach Craney
Island from the rear, or mainland; the second division, under command of Captain Pechell of the flag-
ship "San Domingo," 74, was to approach the island
in boats directly under fire of the American guns on
the island, but not exposed to those in the gunboats.

The plan should have succeeded.   The island was
held by less than seven hundred men in an open
earthwork easily assaulted from the rear.   The water
was so shallow as to offer little protection against
energetic attack.   The British force was more than

[1] James, ii. 54.

[2] Warren's Report of June 24, 1813; James, ii. 414.

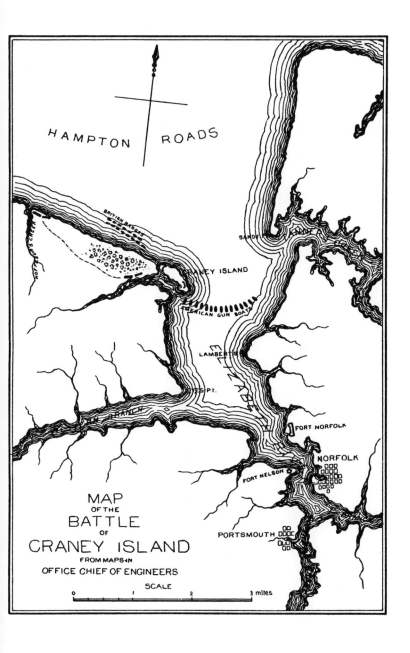

HAMPTON ROADS

BRITISH BARGES

CRANEY ISLAND

AMERICAN GUN BOATS

SANDLIN

LAMBERTS

WESPT.

BRANCH

FORT NORFOLK

NORFOLK

FORT NELSON

PORTSMOUTH

MAP
OF THE
BATTLE
OF
CRANEY ISLAND
FROM MAPS IN
OFFICE CHIEF OF ENGINEERS

SCALE

0   1   2   3 miles

twice the American, and the plan of attack took from the gunboats the chance of assisting the land-battery.

At daylight on the morning of June 22 Beckwith, with about eight hundred men, landed on the main shore outside of Craney Island, and pushed forward to take the island in the rear. Soon afterward Captain Pechell, with about seven hundred men in fifteen boats, approached the island from the north-west along the shore, far out of the reach of the gun-boats. Toward eleven o'clock the British boats came within range of the American battery on the island. Contrary to the opinions of several officers, Captain Pechell insisted on making the attack independently of Beckwith's approach, and pushed on. Two or three hundred yards from land the leading boats grounded in shoal water. Apparently the men might have waded ashore; but " one of the seamen, having plunged his boat-hook over the side, found three or four feet of slimy mud at the bottom;"[1] the leading officer's boat being aground was soon struck by a six-pound shot, the boat sunk, and himself and his crew, with those of two other launches, were left in the water. The other boats took a part of them in, and then quickly retired.

The affair was not improved by the fortunes of Sir Sydney Beckwith, who advanced to the rear of Craney Island, where he was stopped by creeks which he re-ported too deep to ford, and accordingly re-embarked

[1] James, ii. 59.

his troops without further effort; but the true causes
of the failure seemed not to be understood. Napier
thought it due to the division of command between
three heads, Warren, Cockburn, and Beckwith;[1] but
incompetence was as obvious as the division of command. Admiral Warren's official report seemed to
admit that he was also overmatched:[2] —

"Upon approaching the island, from the extreme shoal-
ness of the water on the seaside and the difficulty of
getting across from the land, as well as the island itself
being fortified with a number of guns and men from the
frigate ['Constellation'] and the militia, and flanked
by fifteen gunboats, I considered, in consequence of the
representation of the officer commanding the troops of
the difficulty of their passing over from the land, that
the persevering in the attempt would cost more men
than the number with us would permit, as the other forts
must have been stormed before the frigate and dockyard
could be destroyed. I therefore directed the troops to
be re-embarked."

On neither side were the losses serious. The
American battery inflicted less injury than was to be
expected. Fifteen British boats containing at least
eight hundred men, all told, remained some two hours
under the fire of two twenty-four-pound and four six-
pound guns, at a range differently estimated from
one hundred to three hundred yards, but certainly
beyond musketry fire, for the American troops had

[1] Napier's Life, i. 221.

[2] Warren's Report of June 24, 1813; London "Gazette," Aug.
10, 1813.

to wade out before firing. Three boats were sunk; three men were killed, and sixteen were wounded.[1] Sixty-two men were reported missing, twenty-two of whom came ashore from the boats, while forty deserted from Beckwith's land force.[2] The Americans suffered no loss.

To compensate his men for their check at Craney Island, Admiral Warren immediately afterward devised another movement, which proved, what the Craney Island affair suggested, that the large British force in the Chesapeake was either ill constructed or ill led. Opposite Craney Island, ten miles away on the north shore of James River, stood the village of Hampton, a place of no importance either military or commercial. Four or five hundred Virginia militia were camped there, covering a heavy battery on the water's edge. The battery and its defenders invited attack, but Admiral Warren could have no military object to gain by attacking them. His official report[3] said "that the enemy having a post at Hampton defended by a considerable corps commanding the communication between the upper part of the country and Norfolk, I considered it advisable, and with a view to cut off their resources, to direct it to be attacked." Hampton could not fairly be said to "command" communication with Norfolk, a place which lay beyond ten miles of water wholly commanded by

[1] Return, etc.; James, ii. 414, 415.
[2] Colonel Beatty's Report of June 25, 1813 ; Niles, iv. 324.
[3] Warren's Report of June 27, 1813; James, ii. 414.

the British fleet; but Warren was not obliged to
excuse himself for attacking wherever he pleased,
and Hampton served his object best.

At dawn of June 25, Beckwith's troops were set
ashore about two miles above the village, and moved
forward to the road, taking Hampton in the rear,
while Cockburn's launches made a feint from the
front.   The militia, after resistance costing Beckwith
a total loss of nearly fifty men, escaped, and the
British troops entered the town, where they were allowed to do what they pleased with property and
persons.   Lieutenant-Colonel Napier of the One Hundred-and-second regiment, who commanded Beckwith's advance, wrote in his diary that Sir Sydney
Beckwith " ought to have hanged several villains at
Little Hampton; had he so done, the Americans
would not have complained; but every horror was
perpetrated with impunity, — rape, murder, pillage, —
and not a man was punished."   The British officers
in general shared Napier's disgust, but alleged that
the English troops took no part in the outrages, which
were wholly the work of the French chasseurs.

Warren made no attempt to hold the town; the
troops returned two days afterward to their ships, and
the Virginia militia resumed their station; but when
the details of the Hampton affair became known, the
story roused natural exasperation throughout the
country, and gave in its turn incitement to more violence in Canada.   Admiral Warren and Sir Sydney
Beckwith did not deny the wrong; they dismissed

their Frenchmen from the service, and the United States had no further reason to complain of that corps; but the double mortification seemed to lower the British officers even in their own eyes to the level of marauders.

After the failure to destroy the " Constellation," Admiral Warren could still indulge a hope of destroying the twenty-eight-gun frigate " Adams," and the navy-yard at Washington; for the defence of the Potomac had been totally neglected, and only one indifferent fort, about twelve miles below the Federal city, needed to be captured. July 1 the British squadron entered the Potomac; but beyond rousing a panic at Washington it accomplished nothing, except to gain some knowledge of the shoals and windings that impeded the ascent of the river. Leaving the Potomac, Warren turned up Chesapeake Bay toward Annapolis and Baltimore, but made no attempt on either place. During the rest of the year he cruised about the bay, meeting little resistance, and keeping the States of Virginia and Maryland in constant alarm.

Cockburn was more active. In the month of July he was detached with a squadron carrying Napier's One Hundred-and-second regiment, and arrived, July 12, off Ocracoke Inlet, where he captured two fine privateers, — the " Atlas " and " Anaconda." Thence he sailed southward, and established himself for the winter on Cumberland Island, near the Florida boundary, where he vexed the Georgians. Besides the

property consumed or wasted, he gave refuge to many
fugitive slaves, whom he assisted to the West Indies
or Florida. " Strong is my dislike," wrote Napier,
" to what is perhaps a necessary part of our job :
namely, plundering and ruining the peasantry. We
drive all their cattle, and of course ruin them. *My*
hands are clean ; but it is hateful to see the poor
Yankees robbed, and to be the robber."

Compared with the widespread destruction which
war brought on these regions half a century afterward, the injury inflicted by the British navy in
1813 was trifling, but it served to annoy the Southern
people, who could offer no resistance, and were harassed by incessant militia-calls. To some extent the
same system of vexation was pursued on the Northern
coast. The Delaware River was blockaded and its
shores much annoyed. New York was also blockaded, and Nantucket with the adjacent Sounds became
a British naval station. There Sir Thomas Hardy,
Nelson's favorite officer, commanded, in his flag-ship
the " Ramillies." Hardy did not encourage marauding such as Cockburn practised, but his blockade
was still stringent, and its efficiency was proved by
the failure of Decatur's efforts to evade it.

Decatur commanded a squadron composed of the
" United States," its prize frigate the " Macedonian,"
and the sloop-of-war " Hornet," which lay in the harbor of New York, waiting for a chance to slip out.
Impatient at the steady watch kept by the British
fleet off Sandy Hook, Decatur brought his three ships

through the East River into Long Island Sound. He reached Montauk Point, May 29, only to find Hardy's squadron waiting for him. June 1 he made an attempt to run out, but was chased back, and took refuge in the harbor of New London. A large British squadron immediately closed upon the harbor, and Decatur not only lost hope of getting to sea but became anxious for the safety of his ships. He withdrew them as far as he could into the river, five miles above the town, and took every precaution to repel attack. The British officers were said to have declared that they would get the "Macedonian" back "even if they followed her into a cornfield." They did not make the attempt, but their vigilance never relaxed, and Decatur was obliged to remain all summer idle in port. He clung to the hope that when winter approached he might still escape; but in the month of December the country was scandalized by the publication of an official letter from Decatur to the Secretary of the Navy, charging the people of New London with the responsibility for his failure.

"Some few nights since," he wrote,[1] Dec. 20, 1813, "the weather promised an opportunity for this squadron to get to sea, and it was said on shore that we intended to make the attempt. In the course of the evening two blue lights were burned on both the points at the harbor's mouth as signals to the enemy; and there is not a doubt but that they have, by signals and otherwise, instantaneous information of our movements. Great but unsuc-

[1] Niles, v. 302.

cessful exertions have been made to detect those who
communicated with the enemy by signal. . . . Notwithstanding these signals have been repeated, and have
been seen by twenty persons at least in this squadron,
there are men in New London who have the hardihood
to affect to disbelieve it, and the effrontery to avow
their disbelief."

Decatur's charge roused much ill feeling, and remained a subject of extreme delicacy with the people
of New London. Perhaps Decatur would have done
better not to make such an assertion until he could
prove its truth. That blue lights, as well as other
lights, were often seen, no one denied; but whether
they came from British or from American hands, or
were burned on sea or on shore, were points much
disputed. The town of New London was three miles
from the river's mouth, and Decatur's squadron then
lay at the town. At that distance the precise position
of a light in line with the British fleet might be mis-
taken. Decatur's report, if it proved anything, proved
that the signals were concerted, and were burnt from
" both the points at the river's mouth." If the British admiral wanted information, he could have found
little difficulty in obtaining it; but he would hardly
have arranged a system of signals as visible to Decatur as to himself. Even had he done so, he might
have employed men in his own service as well as
Americans for the purpose. Decatur's letter admitted that he had made great exertions to detect the
culprits, but without success.

The rigor of the British blockade extended no farther north than the Vineyard and Nantucket. Captain Broke in the "Shannon," with a companion frigate, cruised off Boston harbor rather to watch for ships-of-war than to interfere with neutral commerce. Along the coast of Maine an illicit trade with the British provinces was so actively pursued that one of the few American sloops-of-war, the "Enterprise," cruised there, holding smugglers, privateers, and petty marauders in check. On no other portion of the coast would an armed national vessel have been allowed to show itself, but the "Enterprise," protected by the bays and inlets of Maine, and favored by the absence of a blockade, performed a useful service as a revenue cutter. She was not a first-rate vessel. Originally a schooner, carrying twelve guns and sixty men, she had taken part in the war with Tripoli. She was afterward altered into a brig, and crowded with sixteen guns and a hundred men. In 1813 she was commanded by Lieutenant William Burrows, a Pennsylvanian, who entered the navy in 1799, and, like all the naval heroes, was young, — not yet twenty-eight years old.

On the morning of September 5, as the "Enterprise" was cruising eastward, Burrows discovered in a bay near Portland a strange brig, and gave chase. The stranger hoisted three English ensigns, fired several guns, and stood for the "Enterprise." Perhaps escape would have been impossible; but the British captain might, without disgrace, have declined to

fight, for he was no match for the American. The
" Enterprise " measured about ninety-seven feet in
length ; the " Boxer," as the British brig was named,
measured about eighty-four. The " Enterprise "
was nearly twenty-four feet in extreme width ; the
" Boxer " slightly exceeded twenty-two feet. The
" Enterprise " carried fourteen eighteen-pound carronades and two long-nines ; the " Boxer " carried twelve
eighteen-pound carronades and two long-sixes. The
" Enterprise " had a crew of one hundred and two
men ; the " Boxer " had only sixty-six men on board.
With such odds against him, the British captain
might have entertained some desperate hope of success, but could not have expected it.

The behavior of Captain Blyth of the " Boxer "
showed consciousness of his position, for he nailed
his colors to the mast, and told his men that they
were not to be struck while he lived. The day was
calm, and the two brigs manœuvred for a time before
coming together; but at quarter-past three in the afternoon they exchanged their first broadside within
a stone's throw of one another. The effect on both
vessels was destructive. Captain Blyth fell dead,
struck full in the body by an eighteen-pound shot.
Lieutenant Burrows fell, mortally wounded, struck by
a canister shot. After another broadside, at half-past
three the " Enterprise " ranged ahead, crossed the
" Boxer's " bow, and fired one or two more broadsides, until the " Boxer " hailed and surrendered, her
colors still nailed to the mast.

Considering the disparity of force, the two brigs suffered nearly in equal proportion. The " Boxer " lost seven men killed or mortally wounded ; the " Enterprise " lost four. The " Boxer " had thirteen wounded, not fatally ; the " Enterprise " had eight. The " Boxer's " injuries were not so severe as to prevent her captors from bringing her as a prize to Portland ; and no incident in this quasi-civil war touched the sensibilities of the people more deeply than the common funeral of the two commanders, — both well known and favorites in the service, buried, with the same honors and mourners, in the graveyard at Portland overlooking the scene of their battle.

Neither the battle between the " Enterprise " and " Boxer," nor any measures that could be taken by sea or land, prevented a constant traffic between Halifax and the New-England ports not blockaded. The United States government seemed afraid to interfere with it. The newspapers asserted that hundreds of Americans were actually in Halifax carrying on a direct trade, and that thousands of barrels of flour were constantly arriving there from the United States in vessels carrying the Swedish or other neutral flag. In truth the government could do little to enforce its non-intercourse, and even that little might prove mischievous. Nothing could be worse than the spirit of the people on the frontier. Engaged in a profitable illicit commerce, they could only be controlled by force, and any force not overwhelming merely provoked violence or treason. The Navy

Department had no vessels to send there, and could not have prevented their capture if vessels in any number had been sent. The Secretary of War had abandoned to the State governments the defence of the coast. When Armstrong allotted garrisons to the various military districts, he stationed one regiment, numbering three hundred and fifty-two effectives, besides two hundred and sixty-three artillerists, in Military District No. 1, which included the whole coast north of Cape Cod, with the towns of Boston, Marblehead, Salem, Gloucester, Portsmouth, Portland, and Eastport.   Such a provision was hardly sufficient for garrisoning the fort at Boston.   The government doubtless could spare no more of its small army, but for any military or revenue purpose might almost as well have maintained in New England no force whatever.

CHAPTER XII.

DURING the month of April, 1813, four American frigates lay in Boston Harbor fitting for sea. The "President" and "Congress" returned to that port Dec. 31, 1812. The "Constitution," after her battle with the "Java," arrived at Boston February 27, 1813. The "Chesapeake" entered in safety April 9, after an unprofitable cruise of four months. The presence of these four frigates at Boston offered a chance for great distinction to the British officer stationed off the port, and one of the best captains in the service was there to seize it. In order to tempt the American frigates to come out boldly, only two British frigates, the "Shannon" and "Tenedos," remained off the harbor. They were commanded by Captain P. B. V. Broke of the "Shannon." Broke expected Rodgers with his ships, the "President" and "Congress," to seize the opportunity for a battle with two ships of no greater force than the "Shannon" and "Tenedos;" but either Rodgers did not understand the challenge or did not trust it, or took a different view of his duties, for he went to sea on the night of April 30, leaving Broke greatly chagrined and inclined to be somewhat indignant with him for escaping.[1]

After May 1, Broke on the watch outside, as he ran in toward Nahant, could see the masts of only the "Constitution" and "Chesapeake" at the Charlestown navy-yard, and his anxiety became the greater as he noticed that the "Chesapeake" was apparently ready for sea.[2]   May 25 Broke sent away his consort, the "Tenedos," to cruise from Cape Sable southward, ostensibly because the two frigates cruising separately would have a better chance of intercepting the "Chesapeake" than if they kept together.[3]   His stronger reason was to leave a fair field for the "Chesapeake" and "Shannon," as he had before kept all force at a distance except the "Shannon" and "Tenedos" in order to tempt Rodgers to fight.[4]   That there might be no second misunderstanding, he sent several messages to Captain Lawrence commanding the "Chesapeake," inviting a combat.

Nothing showed so clearly that at least one object of the war had been gained by the Americans as the habit adopted by both navies in 1813 of challenging ship-duels.   War took an unusual character when officers like Hardy and Broke countenanced such a practice, discussing and arranging duels between matched ships, on terms which implied that England

[1] Broke to Lawrence, June 1, 1813; Broke's Life, 159.   Niles, v. 29.

[2] Broke's Life, pp. 150, 151.   [3] Broke's Life, p. 156.

[4] Broke's Life, pp. 160, 383.

admitted half-a-dozen American frigates to be equal
in value to the whole British navy. The loss of a
British frigate mattered little to a government which
had more than a hundred such frigates actually at
sea, not to speak of heavier ships ; but the loss
of the " Chesapeake " was equivalent to destroying
nearly one fourth of the disposable American navy.
Already the " Constellation " was imprisoned at Norfolk ; the " United States " and " Macedonian " were
blockaded for the war ; the " Congress " though at
sea was unseaworthy and never cruised again ; the
" Adams " was shut in the Potomac ; the " Essex "
was in the Pacific. The United States Navy consisted, for active service on the Atlantic, of only
the " President," 44, at sea ; the " Constitution," 44,
replacing her masts at the Charlestown navy-yard ;
the " Chesapeake," 38, ready for sea ; and a few
sloops-of-war. Under such circumstances, British
officers who like Broke considered every American
frigate bound to offer them equal terms in a duel,
seemed to admit that the American service had
acquired the credit it claimed.

The first duty of a British officer was to take risks ;
the first duty of an American officer was to avoid
them, and to fight only at his own time, on his own
terms. Rodgers properly declined to seek a battle
with Broke's ships. Captain James Lawrence of the
" Chesapeake" was less cautious, for his experience in
the war led him to think worse of the British navy than
it deserved. Lawrence commanded the " Hornet " in

Bainbridge's squadron at the time of the "Java's" capture. Bainbridge and Lawrence blockaded the "Bonne Citoyenne," a twenty-gun sloop-of-war at San Salvador in Brazil. Lawrence sent a message to the captain of the "Bonne Citoyenne" inviting him to come out and meet the "Hornet." The British captain declined, doubtless for proper reasons; but the reason he gave seemed to Lawrence insufficient, for it was merely that Commodore Bainbridge, in spite of his pledged word, might interfere.[1] Bainbridge sailed about Christmas, and was absent till January 3, capturing the "Java" in the interval. January 6 he sailed for Boston, leaving Lawrence in the "Hornet" still blockading the "Bonne Citoyenne," which showed no more disposition to fight the "Hornet" in Bainbridge's absence than before, although the British captain's letter had said that "nothing could give me greater satisfaction than complying with the wishes of Captain Lawrence" if the single alleged objection were removed.

The conduct of the "Bonne Citoyenne" — a vessel at least the equal of the "Hornet"[2] — gave Lawrence a low opinion of the British service, and his respect was not increased by his next experience. A British seventy-four arrived at San Salvador, January 24, and obliged the "Hornet" to abandon the "Bonne Citoyenne." During the next month the little vessel cruised northward along the Brazil coast, making a

---

[1] Letter of Captain Greene; James, Appendix, no. 35.
[2] James, p. 209.

few prizes, until February 24 off the mouth of De-
merara River, at half-past three o'clock in the afternoon, Captain Lawrence discovered a sail approaching him. Within the bar at the mouth of the river,
seven or eight miles distant, he saw another vessel
at anchor. Both were British sloops-of-war. The
one at anchor was the " Espiègle," carrying eighteen thirty-two-pound carronades. The other, approaching on the " Hornet's " weather-quarter, was
the " Peacock," carrying eighteen twenty-four-pound
carronades, two long-sixes, and one or two lighter
pieces.

The " Peacock," according to British report,[1] had
long been " the admiration of her numerous visitors,"
and was remarkable for the elegance of her fittings;
but in size she was inferior to the " Hornet." Lawrence reported his ship to be four feet the longer,
but the British believed the " Hornet " to measure
one hundred and twelve feet in length, while the
" Peacock " measured one hundred.[2] Their breadth
was the same. The " Hornet " carried eighteen thirty-
two-pounders, while the British captain, thinking his
sloop too light for thirty-twos, had exchanged them
for twenty-fours, and carried only sixteen. The
American crew numbered one hundred and thirty-
five men fit for duty ; the British numbered one
hundred and twenty-two men and boys.

At ten minutes past five, Lawrence tacked and

[1] James, p. 202.

[2] James, p. 206; Roosevelt's Naval War of 1812, p. 48.

stood for the brig. Fifteen minutes afterward the two vessels, sailing in opposite directions, passed each other and exchanged broadsides within a stone's-throw. The British fire, even at point-blank range of forty or fifty feet, did no harm, while the "Hornet's" broadside must have decided the battle; for although both vessels instantly wore, and Lawrence at thirty-five minutes past five ran his enemy close aboard, the "Peacock" almost immediately struck at thirty-nine minutes past five in a sinking condition, and actually went down immediately afterward, carrying with her nine of the "Peacock's" wounded and three of the "Hornet's" crew.

The ease of this victory was beyond proportion to the odds. The British captain and four men were killed outright, thirty-three officers and men were wounded, and the brig was sunk in an action of less than fifteen minutes; while the "Hornet" lost one man killed and two wounded, all aloft, and not a shot penetrated her hull. If the facility of this triumph satisfied Lawrence of his easy superiority in battle, the conduct of the "Espiègle" convinced him that the British service was worse than incompetent. Lawrence, expecting every moment to see the "Espiègle" get under weigh, made great exertions to put his ship in readiness for a new battle, but to his astonishment the British brig took no notice of the action.[1] Subsequent investigation showed that the "Espiègle" knew nothing of the battle until the next day; but

[1] Lawrence's Report of March 19, 1813; Niles, iv. 84.

Lawrence, assuming that the British captain must have seen or heard, or at least ought to have suspected what was happening, conceived that cowardice was a trait of the British navy.

When Lawrence reached New York he became famous for his victory, and received at once promotion. The "Hornet," given to Captain Biddle, was attached to Decatur's squadron and blockaded at New London, while Lawrence received command of the "Chesapeake." Lawrence was then thirty-two years old; he was born in New Jersey in 1781, entered the navy in 1798, and served in the war with Tripoli. He was first lieutenant on the "Constitution," and passed to the grade of commander in 1810, commanding successively the "Vixen," the "Wasp," the "Argus," and the "Hornet." His appointment to the "Chesapeake" was an accident, owing to the ill health of Captain Evans, who commanded her on her recent cruise. The "Chesapeake's" reputation for ill luck clung to her so persistently that neither officers nor men cared greatly to sail in her, and Lawrence would have preferred to remain in the "Hornet;"[1] but his instructions were positive, and he took command of the "Chesapeake" about the middle of May. Most of the officers and crew were new. The old crew on reaching port, April 9, had been discharged, and left the ship, dissatisfied with their share of prize-money, and preferring to try the

[1] Biography; from "The Portfolio." Niles, Supplement to vol. v. p. 29. Cooper's Naval History, ii. 247.

privateer service. The new crew was unequal in
quality and required training ; they neither knew
their officers nor each other.

Lawrence's opponent, Captain Broke of the " Shannon," was an officer whose courage could as little
be questioned as his energy or skill. Among all
the commanders in the British service Broke had
profited most by the lessons of the war. More
than seven years' experience of his ship and crew
gave him every advantage of discipline and system.
Nearly every day the officers at the Charlestown
navy-yard could see the " Shannon " outside, prac-
tising her guns at floating targets as she sailed
about the bay. Broke's most anxious wish was to
fight the " Chesapeake," which he considered to be
of the same size with the " Shannon." [1] The two frigates were the same length within a few inches, —
between one hundred and fifty, and one hundred and
fifty-one feet. Their breadth was forty feet within
a few inches. The " Chesapeake " carried eighteen
thirty-two-pound carronades on the spar-deck ; the
" Shannon " carried sixteen. Each carried twenty-
eight long eighteen-pounders on the gun-deck. The
"Chesapeake" carried also two long twelve-pounders
and a long eighteen-pounder, besides a twelve-pound
carronade. The " Shannon " carried four long nine-
pounders, a long six-pounder, and three twelve-pound
carronades. The " Chesapeake's " only decided advantage was in the number of her crew, which con-

[1] Broke's Life, p. 333.

sisted of three hundred and seventy-nine men, while the "Shannon" carried three hundred and thirty all told.

Broke sent the "Tenedos" away May 25, but Lawrence was not aware of it, and wrote, May 27, to Captain Biddle of the "Hornet" a letter, showing that till the last moment he hoped not to sail in the "Chesapeake:" [1] —

"In hopes of being relieved by Captain Stewart, I neglected writing to you according to promise; but as I have given over all hopes of seeing him, and the 'Chesapeake' is almost ready, I shall sail on Sunday, provided I have a chance of getting out clear of the 'Shannon' and 'Tenedos,' who are on the look-out."

Sunday, May 30, the ship was ready, though the crew was not as good or as well disciplined as it should have been, and showed some discontent owing to difficulties about prize-money. On the morning of June 1 the frigate was lying in President's Roads, when between eight and nine o'clock the second lieutenant, George Budd, reported a sail in sight. Captain Lawrence went up the main rigging, and having made out the sail to be a large frigate, ordered the crew to be mustered, and told them he meant to fight. At midday he stood down the harbor and out to sea. The "Shannon," outside, stood off under easy sail, and led the way until five o'clock, when she luffed and waited till the "Chesapeake" came up. As the wind was westerly, Lawrence had the

[1] Cooper's Naval History, ii. 247.

choice of position, but he made no attempt to profit by his advantage, although it might have been decisive. Bringing the " Chesapeake " with a fresh breeze directly down on the " Shannon's " quarter, at half-past five he luffed, at about fifty yards distance, and ranged up abeam on the " Shannon's " starboard side.

The " Shannon " opened fire as her guns began to bear, but discharged only her two sternmost guns when the " Chesapeake " replied. The two ships ran on about seven minutes, or about the length of time necessary for two discharges of the first guns fired, when, some of the " Shannon's " shot having cut away the "Chesapeake's " foretopsail tie and jib-sheet, the ship came up into the wind and was taken aback. Lying with her larboard quarter toward the " Shannon's " side, at some forty or fifty yards distance, she began to drift toward her enemy. None of the " Chesapeake's " guns then bore on the " Shannon," and the American frigate wholly ceased firing.

From the moment the " Chesapeake " was taken aback she was a beaten ship, and the crew felt it. She could be saved only by giving her headway, or by boarding the " Shannon ; " but neither expedient was possible. The effort to make sail forward was tried, and proved futile. The idea of boarding was also in Lawrence's mind, but the situation made it impracticable. As the " Chesapeake " drifted stern-foremost toward the " Shannon," every gun in the British broadside swept the American deck diago-

nally from stern to stem, clearing the quarter-deck
and beating in the stern-ports, while the musketry
from the " Shannon's " tops killed the men at the
" Chesapeake's " wheel, and picked off every officer,
sailor, or marine in the after-part of the ship. Boarders could not be rallied under a fire which obliged
them to seek cover. The men on the spar-deck left
their stations, crowding forward or going below.

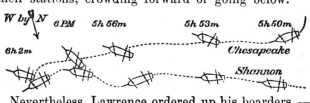

Nevertheless, Lawrence ordered up his boarders, —
he could do nothing else; but the affair hurried
with such rapidity to its close that almost at the
same instant the " Chesapeake's " quarter touched
the " Shannon " amidships. From the moment when
the " Chesapeake " was taken aback until the moment
when she fell foul, only four minutes were given for
Lawrence to act. Before these four minutes were
at an end, he was struck and mortally wounded by
a musket-ball from the " Shannon." His first lieutenant, Ludlow, had already been carried below,
wounded. His second lieutenant, Budd, was stationed below. His third lieutenant, Cox, improperly
assisted Lawrence to reach the gun-deck. Not an
officer remained on the spar-deck, and neither an
officer nor a living man was on the quarter-deck
when the " Chesapeake's " quarter came against the

"Shannon's" gangway, as though inviting the British captain to take possession.

As the ships fouled, Broke ran forward and called for boarders. With about twenty men he stepped on the "Chesapeake's" quarter-deck, and was followed by thirty more before the ships parted. The error should have cost him his life and the lives of all who were with him, for the Americans might easily have killed every man of the boarding-party in spite of the fire from the "Shannon." For several moments Broke was in the utmost peril, not only from the American crew but from his own. His first lieutenant, Watt, hastening to haul down the American ensign, was killed by the discharge of a cannon from the "Shannon;" and when Broke, leaving the "Chesapeake's" quarter-deck, went forward to clear the forecastle, enough of the American crew were there to make a sharp resistance. Broke himself was obliged to take part in the scuffle. According to his report, he "received a severe sabre-wound at the first onset, whilst charging a part of the enemy who had rallied on their forecastle." According to another British account he was first knocked down with the butt-end of a musket, and then was cut by a broadsword. Of his fifty boarders, not less than thirty-seven were killed or wounded.[1]

Had the American crew been in a proper state of discipline, the struggle would have taken an extraordinary character, and the two ships might have re-

[1] Life of Broke, p. 203.

newed the combat, without officers, and in a more
or less unmanageable condition.   Fortunately for
Broke, his fifty men outnumbered the Americans on
the spar-deck, while the men below, for the most
part, would not come up.   About a score of sailors
and marines were on the forecastle, and about a
dozen more rushed up from below, led by the second lieutenant, George Budd, as soon as he, at his
station on the main-deck, learned what was happening above; but so rapidly did the whole affair pass,
that in two minutes the scuffle was over, the Americans were killed or thrown down the hatchway, and
the ship was helpless, with its spar-deck in the hands
of Broke's boarders.   The guns ceased firing, and the
crew below surrendered after some musket-shots up
and down the hatchways.

The disgrace to the Americans did not consist so
much in the loss of a ship to one of equal force, as in
the shame of suffering capture by a boarding-party
of fifty men.   As Lawrence lay wounded in the cockpit, he saw the rush of his men from the spar-deck
down the after-ladders, and cried out repeatedly and
loudly, "Don't give up the ship! blow her up!"
He was said to have added afterward: "I could have
stood the wreck if it had not been for the boarding."

Doubtless the "Shannon" was the better ship, and
deserved to win.   Her crew could under no circumstances have behaved like the crew of the "Chesapeake."   In discipline she was admittedly superior;
but the question of superiority in other respects was

not decided. The accident that cut the "Chesapeake's" jib-sheet and brought her into the wind was
the only decisive part of the battle, and was mere
ill luck, such as pursued the "Chesapeake" from the
beginning. As far as could be seen, in the favorite
American work of gunnery the "Shannon" showed
no superiority.

On that point the reports agreed. The action began at half-past five o'clock in the afternoon at close
range. In seven minutes the "Chesapeake" forged
ahead, came into the wind and ceased firing, as none
of her guns could be made to bear. Seven minutes
allowed time at the utmost for two discharges of
some of her guns. No more guns were fired from the
"Chesapeake" till she drifted close to the "Shannon." Then her two sternmost guns, the thirteenth
and fourteenth on the main deck, again bore on the
enemy, and were depressed and fired by Lieutenant
Cox while the boarders were fighting on the spar-
deck.[1] Thus the number of discharges from the
"Chesapeake's" guns could be known within reasonable certainty. She carried in her broadside nine
thirty-two-pounders and fourteen or fifteen eighteen-
pounders, besides one twelve-pounder, — twenty-five
guns. Assuming them to have been all discharged
twice, although the forward guns could scarcely have
been discharged more than once, the "Chesapeake"
could have fired only fifty-two shot, including the

[1] Evidence of Midshipman Edmund Russell; Court-Martial
of Lieutenant Cox. MSS. Navy Department Archives.

two eighteen-pounders fired by Lieutenant Cox at the close.

According to the official report nearly every shot must have taken effect. The " Shannon" was struck by thirteen thirty-two-pound shot; the " Chesapeake" fired only eighteen, if she discharged every gun twice. The " Shannon " was struck by twelve eighteen-pound shot, fourteen bar-shot, and one hundred and nineteen grape-shot; the " Chesapeake's " fifteen eighteen-pounders could hardly have done more in the space of seven minutes. In truth, every shot that was fired probably took effect.

The casualties showed equal efficiency of fire, and when compared with other battles were severe. When the " Guerriere " struck to the " Constitution " in the previous year, she had lost in half an hour of close action twenty-three killed or mortally wounded and fifty-six more or less injured. The " Shannon" seems to have lost in eleven minutes, before boarding, twenty-seven men killed or mortally wounded and nineteen more or less injured.[1]

The relative efficiency of the " Shannon's " gunnery was not so clear, because the " Shannon's " battery continued to fire after the " Chesapeake" ceased. As the " Chesapeake " drifted down on the " Shannon " she was exposed to the broadside of the British frigate, while herself unable to fire a gun.

" The shot from the ' Shannon's ' aftermost guns now had a fair range along the ' Chesapeake's ' decks," said

[1] List of killed and wounded ; Life of Broke, p. 203.

the British account,[1] " beating in the stern-ports and
sweeping the men from their quarters. The shots from
the foremost guns at the same time entering the ports
from the mainmast aft did considerable execution."

Broke's biographer[2] said that the "Chesapeake"
fired but one broadside, and then coming into the
wind drifted down, "exposed while making this crippled and helpless movement to the 'Shannon's' second and most deliberate broadside." The "Chesapeake" was very near, almost touching the British
frigate during the four or five minutes of this fire,
and every shot must have taken effect. Broke ordered the firing to cease when he boarded, but one
gun was afterward discharged, and killed the British
first lieutenant as he was lowering the American flag
on the "Chesapeake's" quarter-deck.

The "Shannon's" fire lasted eleven or twelve minutes. She carried twenty-five guns in broadside.[3]
Eight of these were thirty-two-pound carronades,
and the official report showed that the "Chesapeake" was struck by twenty-five thirty-two-pound
shot, showing that three full broadsides were fired
from the "Shannon," and at least one gun was
discharged four times. The "Shannon's" broadside also carried fourteen eighteen-pounders, which
threw twenty-nine shot into the "Chesapeake," besides much canister and grape. Considering that
at least half the "Shannon's" shot were fired at so

[1] James, p. 216.   [2] Life of Broke, p. 170.
[3] Broke's letter of challenge ; James, Appendix, p. 36.

close a range that they could not fail to take effect, nothing proved that her guns were better served than those of the " Chesapeake." The " Shannon," according to the British account, fired twice as many shot under twice as favorable conditions, but the injury she inflicted was not twice the injury inflicted in return. Setting aside the grape-shot, the " Chesapeake" struck the " Shannon" thirty-nine times; the " Shannon" struck the " Chesapeake" fifty-seven times. Including the grape-shot, which Broke used freely, the " Shannon" probably did better, but even with a liberal allowance for grape and canister, nothing proved her superiority at the guns.

The loss in men corresponded with the injury to the ships. The " Shannon" lost eighty-three killed and wounded; the " Chesapeake" lost one hundred and forty-six. Thirty-three of the " Shannon's" men were killed or died of their wounds; sixty-one of the " Chesapeake's" number were killed or mortally wounded.

The injuries suffered by the " Chesapeake" told the same story, for they were chiefly in the stern, and were inflicted by the " Shannon's" second and third broadsides, after the " Chesapeake" ceased firing. The " Chesapeake's" bowsprit received no injury, and not a spar of any kind was shot away. The " Shannon" carried her prize into Halifax with all its masts standing, and without anxiety for its safety.

The news of Broke's victory was received in England and by the British navy with an outburst of pleasure that proved the smart of the wound inflicted by Hull, Decatur, and Bainbridge.   The two official expressions of Broke's naval and civil superiors probably reflected the unexaggerated emotion of the service.

"At this critical moment," wrote Admiral Warren[1] by a curious coincidence the day before his own somewhat less creditable defeat at Craney Island, "you could not have restored to the British naval service the preeminence it has always preserved, or contradicted in a more forcible manner the foul aspersions and calumnies of a conceited, boasting enemy, than by the brilliant act you have performed."

A few days later he wrote again:[2] —

"The relation of such an event restores the history of ancient times, and will do more good to the service than it is possible to conceive."

In Parliament, July 8, John Wilson Croker said:[3]

"The action which he [Broke] fought with the 'Chesapeake' was in every respect unexampled.   It was not — and he knew it was a bold assertion which he made — to be surpassed by any engagement which graced the naval annals of Great Britain."

The Government made Broke a baronet, but gave him few other rewards, and his wound was too serious to permit future hard service.   Lawrence died June 5, before the ships reached Halifax.   His first lieutenant, Ludlow, also died.   Their bodies were

[1] Broke's Life, p. 298.   [2] Broke's Life, p. 300.
[3] Cobbett's Debates, xxvi. 1160.

brought to New York and buried September 16, with formal services at Trinity Church.

By the Americans the defeat was received at first with incredulity and boundless anxiety, followed by extreme discouragement. The news came at a dark moment, when every hope had been disappointed and the outlook was gloomy beyond all that had been thought possible.

"I remember," wrote Richard Rush in later life, — "what American does not! — the first rumor of it. I remember the startling sensation. I remember at first the universal incredulity. I remember how the post-offices were thronged for successive days by anxious thousands; how collections of citizens rode out for miles on the highway, accosting the mail to catch something by anticipation. At last, when the certainty was known, I remember the public gloom; funeral orations and badges of mourning bespoke it. 'Don't give up the ship!' — the dying words of Lawrence — were on every tongue."

Six weeks afterward another American naval captain lost another American vessel-of-war by reason of the same over-confidence which caused Lawrence's mistakes, and in a manner equally discreditable to the crew. The "Argus" was a small brig, built in 1803, rating sixteen guns. In the summer of 1813 she was commanded by Captain W. H. Allen, of Rhode Island, who had been third officer to Barron when he was attacked in the "Chesapeake" by the "Leopard." Allen was the officer who snatched a coal from the galley and discharged the only gun that was fired that day. On leaving the "Chesapeake,"

Allen was promoted to be first officer in the "United
States." To his exertions in training the men to
the guns, Decatur attributed his superiority in gunnery over the "Macedonian." To him fell one of
the most distinguished honors that ever came to the
share of an American naval officer, — that of successfully bringing the "Macedonian" to port. Promoted
to the rank of captain, he was put in command of
the "Argus," and ordered to take William Henry
Crawford to his post as Minister to France.

On that errand the "Argus" sailed, June 18, and
after safely landing Crawford, July 11, at Lorient
in Brittany, Captain Allen put to sea again, three
days afterward, and in pursuance of his instructions
cruised off the mouth of the British Channel. During
an entire month he remained between the coast of
Brittany and the coast of Ireland, destroying a score
of vessels and creating a panic among the ship-owners
and underwriters of London. Allen performed his
task with as much forbearance as the duty permitted,
making no attempt to save his prizes for the sake
of prize-money, and permitting all passengers to take
what they claimed as their own without inspection or
restraint. The English whose property he destroyed
spoke of him without personal ill-feeling.

The anxiety and labor of such a service falling on
a brig of three hundred tons and a crew of a hundred men, and the impunity with which he defied
danger, seemed to make Allen reckless. On the
night of August 13 he captured a brig laden with

wine from Oporto. Within sight of the Welsh coast
and within easy reach of Milford Haven, he burned his
prize, not before part of his crew got drunk on the
wine. The British brig "Pelican," then cruising in
search of the "Argus," guided by the light of the
burning prize, at five o'clock on the morning of August 14 came down on the American brig; and Captain Allen, who had often declared that he would run
from no two-masted vessel, waited for his enemy.

According to British measurements, the "Argus"
was ninety-five and one-half feet long; the "Pelican,"
one hundred. The "Argus" was twenty-seven feet,
seven and five-eighths inches in extreme breadth ; the
"Pelican" was thirty feet, nine inches. The "Argus"
carried eighteen twenty-four-pound carronades, and
two long twelve-pounders ; the "Pelican" carried
sixteen thirty-two-pound carronades, four long six-
pounders, and a twelve-pound carronade. The number of the "Argus's" crew was disputed. According
to British authority, it was one hundred and twenty-
seven,[1] while the "Pelican" carried one hundred and
sixteen men and boys.[2]

At six o'clock in the morning, according to American reckoning,[3] — at half-past five according to the
British report, — the "Argus" wore, and fired a
broadside within grape-distance, which was returned

[1] Report of Captain Maples, Aug. 14, 1813; James, Appendix no. 42, p. lxv.

[2] James, pp. 275-282.

[3] Report of Lieutenant Watson, March 2, 1815; Niles, viii. 43.

with cannon and musketry. Within five minutes
Captain Allen was struck by a shot which carried
away his left leg, mortally wounding him; and five
minutes afterward the first lieutenant was wounded
on the head by a grape-shot. Although the second
lieutenant fought the brig well, the guns were sur-
prisingly inefficient. During the first fifteen minutes
the "Argus" had the advantage of position, and at
eighteen minutes after six raked the "Pelican" at
close range, but inflicted no great injury on the enemy's hull or rigging, and killed at the utmost but
one man, wounding only five. According to an English account,[1] "the 'Argus' fought well while the can-
nonading continued, but her guns were not levelled
with precision, and many shots passed through the
'Pelican's' royals." The "Pelican," at the end of
twenty-five minutes, succeeded in cutting up her opponent's rigging so that the "Argus" lay helpless
under her guns. The "Pelican" then took a position on her enemy's starboard quarter, and raked
her with eight thirty-two-pound carronades for nearly
twenty minutes at close range, without receiving a
shot in return except from musketry. According to
the report of the British captain, the action "was
kept up with great spirit on both sides forty-three
minutes, when we lay her alongside, and were in the
act of boarding when she struck her colors." [2]

[1] Niles, v. 118.
[2] Report of Captain Maples, Aug. 14, 1813; Niles, v. 118.
James, Appendix no. 42.

The "Argus" repeated the story of the "Chesa-peake," except that the action lasted three quarters of an hour instead of fifteen minutes. During that time, the "Pelican" should have fired all her broad-side eight or ten times into the "Argus" at a range so close that no shot should have missed. Sixty thirty-two-pound shot fired into a small brig less than one hundred feet long should have shivered it to atoms. Nine thirty-two-pound shot from the "Hor-net" seemed to reduce the "Peacock" to a sinking condition in fifteen minutes; yet the "Argus" was neither sunk nor dismasted. The British account of her condition after the battle showed no more injury than was suffered by the "Peacock," even in killed and wounded, by one or at the utmost two broadsides of the "Hornet."

"The 'Argus' was tolerably cut up in her hull. Both her lower masts were wounded, although not badly, and her fore-shrouds on one side nearly all destroyed; but like the 'Chesapeake,' the 'Argus' had no spar shot away. Of her carronades several were disabled. She lost in the action six seamen killed; her commander, two midshipmen, the carpenter, and three seamen mortally, her first lieutenant and five seamen severely, and eight others slightly wounded, — total twenty-four; chiefly, if not wholly by the cannon-shot of the 'Pelican.'"[1]

The "Pelican" lost seven men killed or wounded, chiefly by musketry. On both sides the battle showed little skill with the guns; but perhaps the

[1] James, p. 273.

"Pelican," considering her undisputed superiority during half the combat, showed even less than the "Argus." As in the "Chesapeake's" battle, the discredit of the defeated ship lay in surrender to boarders.

Two such defeats were calculated to shake confidence in the American navy. That Allen should have been beaten in gunnery was the more strange, because his training with the guns gave him his chief credit with Decatur. Watson, the second lieutenant of the "Argus," attributed the defeat to the fatigue of his crew. Whatever was the immediate cause, no one could doubt that both the "Chesapeake" and "Argus" were sacrificed to the over-confidence of their commanders.

CHAPTER XIII.

THE people of the Atlantic coast felt the loss of the "Chesapeake" none too keenly. Other nations had a history to support them in moments of mortification, or had learned by centuries of experience to accept turns of fortune as the fate of war. The American of the sea-coast was not only sensitive and anxious, but he also saw with singular clearness the bearing of every disaster, and did not see with equal distinctness the general drift of success. The loss of the "Chesapeake" was a terrible disaster, not merely because it announced the quick recovery of England's pride and power from a momentary shock, but also because it threatened to take away the single object of American enthusiasm which redeemed shortcomings elsewhere. After the loss of the "Chesapeake," no American frigate was allowed the opportunity to fight with an equal enemy. The British frigates, ordered to cruise in company, gave the Americans no chance to renew their triumphs of 1812.

Indeed, the experience of 1813 tended to show that the frigate was no longer the class of vessel best suited to American wants. Excessively expensive compared with their efficiency, the "Constitution,"

" President," and " United States " could only with difficulty obtain crews ; and when after much delay they were ready for sea, they could not easily evade a blockading squadron. The original cost of a frigate varied from two hundred thousand dollars to three hundred thousand ; that of a sloop-of-war, like the " Hornet," " Wasp," or " Argus," varied between forty and fifty thousand dollars. The frigate required a crew of about four hundred men ; the sloop carried about one hundred and fifty. The annual expense of a frigate in active service was about one hundred and thirty-four thousand dollars ; that of the brig was sixty thousand. The frigate required much time and heavy timber in her construction ; the sloop could be built quickly and of ordinary material. The loss of a frigate was a severe national disaster ; the loss of a sloop was not a serious event.

For defensive purposes neither the frigate nor the brig counted heavily against a nation which employed ships-of-the-line by dozens ; but even for offensive objects the frigate was hardly so useful as the sloop-of-war. The record of the frigates for 1813 showed no results equivalent to their cost. Their cruises were soon told. The " President," leaving Boston April 30, ran across to the Azores, thence to the North Sea, and during June and July haunted the shores of Norway, Scotland, and Ireland, returning to Newport September 27, having taken thirteen prizes. The " Congress," which left Boston with the " President," cruised nearly eight months in the Atlantic,

and returned to Boston December 14, having captured but four merchantmen. The " Chesapeake,"
which sailed from Boston Dec. 13, 1812, cruised four
months in the track of British commerce, past Ma-
deira and Cape de Verde, across the equator, and
round through the West Indies, returning to Boston
April 9, having taken six prizes; at the beginning
of her next cruise, June 1, the " Chesapeake " was
herself captured. The adventures of the " Essex "
in the Pacific were such as might have been equally
well performed by a sloop-of-war, and belonged rather
to the comparative freedom with which the frigates
moved in 1812 than to the difficult situation that
followed. No other frigates succeeded in getting to
sea till December 4, when the " President " sailed
again. The injury inflicted by the frigates on the
Atlantic was therefore the capture of twenty-three
merchantmen in a year. At the close of 1813, the
" President " and the " Essex " were the only frigates
at sea; the " Constitution " sailed from Boston only
Jan. 1, 1814; the " United States " and " Macedonian " were blockaded at New London; the " Constellation " was still at Norfolk; the " Adams " was
at Washington, and the " Congress " at Boston.

When this record was compared with that of the
sloops-of-war the frigates were seen to be luxuries.
The sloop-of-war was a single-decked vessel, rigged
sometimes as a ship, sometimes as a brig, but never
as a sloop, measuring about one hundred and ten feet
in length by thirty in breadth, and carrying usually

eighteen thirty-two-pound carronades and two long twelve-pounders. Of this class the American navy possessed in 1812 only four examples, — the " Hornet," the " Wasp," the " Argus," and the " Syren." The " Wasp" was lost Oct. 18, 1812, after capturing the " Frolic." The " Syren " remained at New Orleans during the first year of the war, and then came to Boston, but saw no ocean service of importance during 1813. The " Hornet " made three prizes, including the sloop-of-war " Peacock," and was then blockaded with the " United States " and " Macedonian ; " but the smaller vessel could do what the frigates could not, and in November the " Hornet " slipped out of New London and made her way to New York, where she waited an opportunity to escape to sea. The story will show her success. Finally, the " Argus " cruised for a month in the British Channel, and made twenty-one prizes before she was captured by the " Pelican."

The three frigates, " President," " Congress," and " Chesapeake," captured twenty-three prizes in the course of the year, and lost the " Chesapeake." The two sloops, the " Hornet " and " Argus," captured twenty-four prizes, including the sloop-of-war " Peacock," and lost the " Argus."

The government at the beginning of the war owned four smaller vessels, — the " Nautilus " and " Vixen " of fourteen guns, and the " Enterprise " and " Viper " of twelve. Another brig, the " Rattlesnake," sixteen, was bought. Experience seemed to prove that these

were of little use. The "Nautilus" fell into the
hands of Broke's squadron July 16, 1812, within a
month after the declaration of war. The "Vixen"
was captured Nov. 22, 1812, by Sir James Yeo. The
"Viper," Jan. 17, 1813, became prize to Captain
Lumley in the British frigate "Narcissus." The
"Enterprise" distinguished itself by capturing the
"Boxer," and was regarded as a lucky vessel, but
was never a good or fast one.[1] The "Rattlesnake,"
though fast, was at last caught on a lee shore by the
frigate "Leander," July 11, 1814, and carried into
Halifax.[2]

In the enthusiasm over the frigates in 1812, Congress voted that six forty-fours should be built, besides four ships-of-the-line. The Act was approved
Jan. 2, 1813. Not until March 3 did Congress pass
an Act for building six new sloops-of-war. The loss
of two months was not the only misfortune in this
legislation. Had the sloops been begun in January,
they might have gone to sea by the close of the year.
The six sloops were all launched within eleven months
from the passage of the bill, and the first of them, the
"Frolic," got to sea within that time, while none of
the frigates or line-of-battle ships could get to sea
within two years of the passage of the law. A more
remarkable oversight was the building of only six
sloops, when an equal number of forty-fours and four

[1] Lieutenant Creighton to Secretary Jones, March 9, 1814;
Niles, vi. 69.

[2] Niles, vi. 391.

seventy-fours were ordered. Had Congress voted twenty-four sloops, the proportion would not have been improper; but perhaps the best policy would have been to build fifty such sloops, and to prohibit privateering. The reasons for such a course were best seen in the experiences of the privateers.

The history of the privateers was never satisfactorily written. Neither their number, their measurements, their force, their captures, nor their losses were accurately known. Little ground could be given for an opinion in regard to their economy. Only with grave doubt could any judgment be reached even in regard to their relative efficiency compared with government vessels of the same class. Yet their experience was valuable, and their services were very great.

In the summer of 1812 any craft that could keep the sea in fine weather set out as a privateer to intercept vessels approaching the coast. The typical privateer of the first few months was the pilot-boat, armed with one or two long-nine or twelve-pound guns. Of twenty-six privateers sent from New York in the first four months of war, fifteen carried crews of eighty men or less. These small vessels especially infested the West Indies, where fine weather and light breezes suited their qualities. After the seas had been cleared of such prey as these petty marauders could manage, they were found to be unprofitable, — too small to fight and too light to escape. The typical privateer of 1813 was a larger vessel, — a

brig or schooner of two or three hundred tons, armed
with one long pivot-gun, and six or eight lighter
guns in broadside ; carrying crews which varied in
number from one hundred and twenty to one hundred
and sixty men ; swift enough to escape under most
circumstances even a frigate, and strong enough to
capture any armed merchantman.

After the war was fairly begun, the British mercantile shipping always sailed either under convoy
or as armed " running ships " that did not wait for
the slow and comparatively rare opportunities of
convoy, but trusted to their guns for defence. The
new American privateer was adapted to meet both
chances. Two or three such craft hanging about a
convoy could commonly cut off some merchantman,
no matter how careful the convoying man-of-war
might be. By night they could run directly into the
fleet and cut out vessels without even giving an
alarm, and by day they could pick up any craft that
lagged behind or happened to stray too far away.
Yet the " running ships " were the chief objects of
their search, for these were the richest prizes ; and
the capture of a single such vessel, if it reached
an American port in safety, insured success to the
cruise. The loss of these vessels caused peculiar
annoyance to the British, for they sometimes carried
considerable amounts of specie, and usually were
charged with a mail which was always sunk and lost
in case of capture.

As the war continued, experience taught the own-

ers of privateers the same lesson that was taught to
the government. The most efficient vessel of war
corresponded in size with the "Hornet" or the new
sloops-of-war building in 1813. Tonnage was so arbitrary a mode of measurement that little could be
learned from the dimensions of five hundred tons
commonly given for these vessels; but in a general
way they might be regarded as about one hundred
and fifteen or one hundred and twenty feet long on
the spar-deck and thirty-one feet in extreme breadth.
Unless such vessels were swift sailers, particularly
handy in working to windward, they were worse than
useless; and for that reason the utmost effort was
made both by the public and private constructors to
obtain speed. At the close of the war the most
efficient vessel afloat was probably the American
sloop-of-war, or privateer, of four or five hundred
tons, rigged as a ship or brig, and carrying one
hundred and fifty or sixty men, with a battery va-
rying according to the ideas of the captain and owners, but in the case of privateers almost invariably
including one "long Tom," or pivot-gun.

Yet for privateering purposes the smaller craft
competed closely with the larger. For ordinary service no vessel could do more effective work in a more
economical way than was done by Joshua Barney's
"Rossie" of Baltimore, or Boyle's "Comet" of the
same port, or Champlin's "General Armstrong" of
New York, — schooners or brigs of two or three hundred tons, uncomfortable to their officers and crews,

but most dangerous enemies to merchantmen. Vessels of this class came into favor long before the war, because of their speed, quickness in handling, and economy during the experience of twenty years in blockade-running and evasion of cruisers. Such schooners could be built in any Northern sea-port in six weeks or two months at half the cost of a government cruiser.

The government sloop-of-war was not built for privateering purposes. Every government vessel was intended chiefly to fight, and required strength in every part and solidity throughout. The frame needed to be heavy to support the heavier structure; the quarters needed to be thick to protect the men at the guns from grape and musketry; the armament was as weighty as the frame would bear. So strong were the sides of American frigates that even thirty-two-pound shot fired at forty or fifty feet distance sometimes failed to penetrate, and the British complained as a grievance that the sides of an American forty-four were thicker than those of a British seventy-four.[1] The American ship-builders spared no pains to make all their vessels in every respect — in size, strength, and speed — superior to the vessels with which they were to compete; but the government ship-carpenter had a harder task than the private ship-builder, for he was obliged to obtain greater speed at the same time that he used heavier material than the British constructors. As far as the navy

[1] James, p. 18.

carpenters succeeded in their double object, they did so by improving the model and increasing the proportions of the spars.

The privateer was built for no such object. The last purpose of a privateer was to fight at close range, and owners much preferred that their vessels, being built to make money, should not fight at all unless much money could be made. The private armed vessel was built rather to fly than to fight, and its value depended far more on its ability to escape than on its capacity to attack. If the privateer could sail close to the wind, and wear or tack in the twinkling of an eye; if she could spread an immense amount of canvas and run off as fast as a frigate before the wind; if she had sweeps to use in a calm, and one long-range gun pivoted amidships, with plenty of men in case boarding became necessary, — she was perfect. To obtain these results the builders and sailors ran excessive risks. Too lightly built and too heavily sparred, the privateer was never a comfortable or a safe vessel. Beautiful beyond anything then known in naval construction, such vessels roused boundless admiration, but defied imitators. British constructors could not build them, even when they had the models; British captains could not sail them; and when British admirals, fascinated by their beauty and tempted by the marvellous qualities of their model, ordered such a prize to be taken into the service, the first act of the carpenters in the British navy-yards was to reduce to their own standard the long masts, and to strengthen the hull and sides till the vessel should be safe in a battle or a gale. Perhaps an American navy-carpenter must have done the same; but though not a line in the model might be altered, she never sailed again as she sailed before. She could not bear conventional restraints.

Americans were proud of their privateers, as they well might be; for this was the first time when in competition with the world, on an element open to all, they proved their capacity to excel, and produced a creation as beautiful as it was practical. The British navy took a new tone in regard to these vessels. Deeply as the American frigates and sloops-of-war had wounded the pride of the British navy, they never had reduced that fine service to admitted inferiority. Under one pretext or another, every defeat was excused. Even the superiority of American gunnery was met by the proud explanation that the British navy, since Trafalgar, had enjoyed no opportunity to use their guns. Nothing could convince a British admiral that Americans were better fighters than Englishmen; but when he looked at the American schooner he frankly said that England could show no such models, and could not sail them if she had them. In truth, the schooner was a wonderful invention. Not her battles, but her escapes won for her the open-mouthed admiration of the British captains, who saw their prize double like a hare and slip through their fingers at the moment when capture was sure. Under any ordinary condition of wind and weather, with an open sea, the schooner, if only she could get to windward, laughed at a frigate.

As the sailing rather than the fighting qualities of the privateer were the chief object of her construction, those were the points best worth recording; but the newspapers of the time were so much absorbed in proving that Americans could fight, as to cause almost total neglect of the more important question whether Americans could sail better than their rivals. All great nations had fought, and at one time or another every great nation in Europe had been victorious over every other; but no people, in the course of a thousand years of rivalry on the ocean, had invented or had known how to sail a Yankee schooner. Whether ship, brig, schooner, or sloop, the American vessel was believed to outsail any other craft on the ocean, and the proof of this superiority was incumbent on the Americans to furnish. They neglected to do so. No clear evidence was ever recorded of the precise capacities of their favorite vessels. Neither the lines of the hull, the dimensions of the spars, the rates of sailing by the log in different weather, the points of sailing, — nothing precise was ever set down.

Of the superiority no doubts could be entertained. The best proof of the American claim was the British admission. Hardly an English writer on marine affairs — whether in newspapers, histories, or novels — failed to make some allusion to the beauty and speed of American vessels. The naval literature of Great

Britain from 1812 to 1860 was full of such material.
The praise of the invention was still commonly accompanied by some expression of dislike for the in-
ventor, but even in that respect a marked change
followed the experiences of 1812–1814. Among the
Englishmen living on the island of Jamaica, and
familiar with the course of events in the West Indies
from 1806 to 1817, was one Michael Scott, born in
Glasgow in 1789, and in the prime of his youth at
the time of the American war. In the year 1829,
at the age of forty, he began the publication in
" Blackwood's Magazine " of a series of sketches
which rapidly became popular as " Tom Cringle's
Log." Scott was the best narrator and probably the
best informed man who wrote on the West Indies at
that period ; and his frequent allusions to the United
States and the war threw more light on the social
side of history than could be obtained from all official
sources ever printed.

" I don't like Americans," Scott said ; " I never did
and never shall like them. I have seldom met an American gentleman in the large and complete sense of the
term. I have no wish to eat with them, drink with them,
deal with or consort with them in any way ; but let me
tell the whole truth, — *nor fight* with them, were it not
for the laurels to be acquired by overcoming an enemy
so brave, determined, and alert, and every way so worthy
of one's steel as they have always proved."

The Americans did not fight the War of 1812 in
order to make themselves loved. According to Scott's

testimony they gained the object for which they did fight. " In gunnery and small-arm practice we were as thoroughly weathered on by the Americans during the war as we overtopped them in the bull-dog courage with which our boarders handled those genuine English weapons, — the cutlass and the pike." Superiority in the intellectual branches of warfare was conceded to the Americans ; but even in regard to physical qualities, the British were not inclined to boast.

" In the field," said Scott, " or grappling in mortal combat on the blood-slippery quarter-deck of an enemy's vessel, a British soldier or sailor is the bravest of the brave.   No soldier or sailor of any other country, saving and excepting those damned Yankees, can stand against them."

Had English society known so much of Americans in 1807, war would have been unnecessary.

Yet neither equality in physical courage nor superiority in the higher branches of gunnery and small-arms was the chief success of Americans in the war. Beyond question the schooner was the most conclusive triumph.   Readers of Michael Scott could not forget the best of his sketches, — the escape of the little American schooner " Wave " from two British cruisers, by running to windward under the broadside of a man-of-war.   With keen appreciation Scott detailed every motion of the vessels, and dwelt with peculiar emphasis on the apparent desperation of the attempt.   Again and again the thirty-two-pound shot,

as he described the scene, tore through the slight
vessel as the two crafts raced through the heavy seas
within musket-shot of one another, until at last the
firing from the corvette ceased. " The breeze had
taken off, and the ' Wave,' resuming her superiority
in light winds, had escaped." Yet this was not the
most significant part of " Tom Cringle's " experience.
The " Wave," being afterward captured at anchor,
was taken into the royal service and fitted as a ship-
of-war. Cringle was ordered by the vice-admiral to
command her, and as she came to report he took a
look at her : —

" When I had last seen her she was a most beautiful
little craft, both in hull and rigging, as ever delighted
the eye of a sailor ; but the dock-yard riggers and carpenters had fairly bedevilled her, at least so far as ap-
pearances went. First they had replaced the light rail
on her gunwale by heavy solid bulwarks four feet high,
surmounted by hammock nettings at least another foot ;
so that the symmetrical little vessel that formerly floated
on the foam light as a sea-gull now looked like a clumsy,
dish-shaped Dutch dogger. Her long, slender wands of
masts which used to swing about as if there were neither
shrouds nor stays to support them were now as taut and
stiff as church-steeples, with four heavy shrouds of a
side, and stays and back-stays, and the Devil knows
what all."

" If them heave-'emtaughts at the yard have not
taken the speed out of the little beauty I am a
Dutchman " was the natural comment, — as obvious
as it was sound.

The reports of privateer captains to their owners were rarely published, and the logs were never printed or deposited in any public office. Occasionally, in the case of a battle or the loss of guns or spars or cargo in a close pursuit, the privateer captain described the causes of his loss in a letter which found its way into print; and from such letters some idea could be drawn of the qualities held in highest regard, both in their vessels and in themselves. The first and commonest remark was that privateers of any merit never seemed to feel anxious for their own safety so long as they could get to windward a couple of gunshots from their enemy. They would risk a broadside in the process without very great anxiety. They chiefly feared lest they might be obliged to run before the wind in heavy weather. The little craft which could turn on itself like a flash and dart away under a frigate's guns into the wind's eye long before the heavy ship could come about, had little to fear on that point of sailing; but when she was obliged to run to leeward, the chances were more nearly equal. Sometimes, especially in light breezes or in a stronger wind, by throwing guns and weighty articles overboard privateers could escape; but in heavy weather the ship-of-war could commonly outcarry them, and more often could drive them on a coast or into the clutches of some other man-of-war.

Of being forced to fly to leeward almost every privateer could tell interesting stories. A fair example of

such tales was an adventure of Captain George Coggeshall, who afterward compiled, chiefly from newspapers, an account of the privateers, among which he
preserved a few stories that would otherwise have
been lost.[1] Coggeshall commanded a two-hundred-
ton schooner, the "David Porter," in which he made
the run to France with a cargo and a letter-of-marque.
The schooner was at Bordeaux in March, 1814, when
Wellington's army approached.   Afraid of seizure by
the British if he remained at Bordeaux, Coggeshall
sailed from Bordeaux for La Rochelle with a light
wind from the eastward, when at daylight March 15,
1814, he found a large ship about two miles to windward.   Coggeshall tried to draw his enemy down to
leeward, but only lost ground until the ship was not
more than two gunshots away.   The schooner could
then not run to windward without taking the enemy's
fire within pistol-shot, and dared not return to Bordeaux.   Nothing remained but to run before the wind.
Coggeshall got out his square-sail and studding-sails
ready to set, and when everything was prepared he
changed his course and bore off suddenly, gaining a
mile in the six or eight minutes lost by the ship in
spreading her studding-sails.   He then started his
water-casks, threw out ballast, and drew away from
his pursuer, till in a few hours the ship became a
speck on the horizon.

   Apparently a similar but narrower escape was made
by Captain Champlin of the " Warrior," a famous

   [1] Coggeshall's History of American Privateers, p. 188.

privateer-brig of four hundred and thirty tons, mounting twenty-one guns and carrying one hundred and fifty men.[1] Standing for the harbor of Fayal, Dec. 15, 1814, he was seen by a British man-of-war lying there at anchor. The enemy slipped her cables and made sail in chase. The weather was very fresh and squally, and at eight o'clock in the evening the ship was only three miles distant. After a run of about sixty miles, the man-of-war came within grape-shot distance and opened fire from her two bow-guns. Champlin luffed a little, got his long pivot-gun to bear, and ran out his starboard guns as though to fight, which caused the ship to shorten sail for battle. Then Champlin at two o'clock in the morning threw overboard eleven guns, and escaped. The British ship was in sight the next morning, but did not pursue farther.

Often the privateers were obliged to throw everything overboard at the risk of capsizing, or escaped capture only by means of their sweeps. In 1813 Champlin commanded the " General Armstrong," a brig of two hundred and forty-six tons and one hundred and forty men. Off Surinam, March 11, 1813, he fell in with the British sloop-of-war " Coquette," which he mistook for a letter-of-marque, and approached with the intention of boarding. Having come within pistol-shot and fired his broadsides, he discovered his error. The wind was light, the two vessels had no headway, and for three quarters of an

[1] Extract of letter from Captain Champlin ; Niles, viii. 110.

hour, if Champlin's account could be believed, he lay within pistol-shot of the man-of-war. He was struck by a musket-ball in the left shoulder; six of his crew were killed and fourteen wounded; his rigging was cut to pieces; his foremast and bowsprit injured, and several shots entered the brig between wind and water, causing her to leak; but at last he succeeded in making sail forward, and with the aid of his sweeps crept out of range. The sloop-of-war was unable to cripple or follow him.[1]

Sometimes the very perfection of the privateer led to dangers as great as though perfection were a fault. Captain Shaler of the "Governor Tompkins," a schooner, companion to the "General Armstrong," chased three sail Dec. 25, 1812, and on near approach found them to be two ships and a brig. The larger ship had the appearance of a government transport; she had boarding-nettings almost up to her tops, but her ports appeared to be painted, and she seemed prepared for running away as she fought. Shaler drew nearer, and came to the conclusion that the ship was too heavy for him; but while his first officer went forward with the glass to take another look, a sudden squall struck the schooner without reaching the ship, and in a moment, before the light sails could be taken in, "and almost before I could turn round, I was under the guns, not of a transport, but of a large frigate, and not more than a quarter of a mile from her." With impudence that warranted punishment,

[1] Extract from log, March 11, 1813; Niles, iv. 133.

Shaler fired his little broadside of nine or twelve pounders into the enemy, who replied with a broad-side of twenty-four-pounders, killing three men, wound-ing five, and causing an explosion on deck that threw confusion into the crew ; but the broadside did no serious injury to the rigging. The schooner was then just abaft the ship's beam, a quarter of a mile away, holding the same course and to windward. She could not tack without exposing her stern to a raking fire, and any failure to come about would have been cer-tain destruction. Shaler stood on, taking the ship's fire, on the chance of outsailing his enemy before a shot could disable the schooner. Side by side the two vessels raced for half an hour, while twenty-four-pound shot fell in foam about the schooner, but never struck her, and at last she drew ahead beyond range. Even then her dangers were not at an end. A calm followed ; the ship put out boats ; and only by throw-ing deck-lumber and shot overboard, and putting all hands at the sweeps, did Shaler " get clear of one of the most quarrelsome companions that I ever met with." [1]

The capacities of the American privateer could to some extent be inferred from its mishaps. Notwith-standing speed, skill, and caution, the privateer was frequently and perhaps usually captured in the end. The modes of capture were numerous. April 3, 1813, Admiral Warren's squadron in the Chesapeake cap-tured by boats, after a sharp action, the privateer

[1] Shaler's Report of Jan. 1, 1813 ; Niles, v. 429.

"Dolphin" of Baltimore, which had taken refuge in the Rappahannock River. April 27 the "Tom" of Baltimore, a schooner of nearly three hundred tons, carrying fourteen guns, was captured by his Majesty's ships "Surveillante" and "Lyra" after a smart chase. Captain Collier of the "Surveillante" reported: "She is a remarkably fine vessel of her class, and from her superior sailing has already escaped from eighteen of his Majesty's cruisers." May 11, the "Holkar" of New York was driven ashore off Rhode Island and destroyed by the "Orpheus" frigate. May 19, Captain Gordon of the British man-of-war "Ratler," in company with the schooner "Bream," drove ashore and captured the "Alexander" of Salem, off Kennebunk, "considered the fastest sailing privateer out of the United States," according to Captain Gordon's report.[1] May 21, Captain Hyde Parker of the frigate "Tenedos," in company with the brig "Curlew," captured the "Enterprise" of Salem, pierced for eighteen guns. May 23, the "Paul Jones," of sixteen guns and one hundred and twenty men, fell in with a frigate in a thick fog off the coast of Ireland, and being crippled by her fire surrendered. July 13, Admiral Cockburn captured by boats at Ocracoke Inlet the fine privateer-brig "Anaconda" of New York, with a smaller letter-of-marque. July 17, at sea, three British men-of-war, after a chase of four hours, captured the "Yorktown" of twenty guns and one hundred and forty men. The schooner

[1] London Gazette for 1813, p. 1574.

" Orders in Council " of New York, carrying sixteen guns and one hundred and twenty men, was captured during the summer, after a long chase of five days, by three British cutters that drove her under the guns of a frigate. The " Matilda," privateer of eleven guns and one hundred and four men, was captured off San Salvador by attempting to board the British letter-of-marque " Lyon " under the impression that she was the weaker ship.

In these ten instances of large privateers captured or destroyed in 1813, the mode of capture happened to be recorded ; and in none of them was the privateer declared to have been outsailed and caught by any single British vessel on the open seas. Modes of disaster were many, and doubtless among the rest a privateer might occasionally be fairly beaten in speed, but few such cases were recorded, although British naval officers were quick to mention these unusual victories. Unless the weather gave to the heavier British vessel-of-war the advantage of carrying more sail in a rough sea, the privateer was rarely outsailed.

The number of privateers at sea in 1813 was not recorded. The list of all private armed vessels during the entire war included somewhat more than five hundred names.[1] Most of these were small craft, withdrawn after a single cruise. Not two hundred were so large as to carry crews of fifty men. Nearly two hundred and fifty, or nearly half the whole number of privateers, fell into British hands. Prob-

[1] Emmons's Navy of the United States, pp. 170–197.

ably at no single moment were more than fifty sea-going vessels on the ocean as privateers, and the number was usually very much less; while the large privateer-brigs or ships that rivalled sloops-of-war in size were hardly more numerous than the sloops themselves.

The total number of prizes captured from the British in 1813 exceeded four hundred, four fifths of which were probably captured by privateers, national cruisers taking only seventy-nine. If the privateers succeeded in taking three hundred and fifty prizes, the whole number of privateers could scarcely have exceeded one hundred. The government cruisers " President," " Congress," " Chesapeake," " Hornet," and "Argus" averaged nearly ten prizes apiece. Privateers averaged much less; but they were ten times as numerous as the government cruisers, and inflicted four times as much injury.

Such an addition to the naval force of the United States was very important. Doubtless the privateers contributed more than the regular navy to bring about a disposition for peace in the British classes most responsible for the war. The colonial and shipping interests, whose influence produced the Orders in Council, suffered the chief penalty. The West India colonies were kept in constant discomfort and starvation by swarms of semi-piratical craft darting in and out of every channel among their islands; but the people of England could have borne with patience the punishment of the West Indies had not the American cruisers inflicted equally severe retribution nearer home.

Great Britain was blockaded. No one could deny that manifest danger existed to any merchant-vessel that entered or left British waters. During the summer the blockade was continuous. Toward the close of 1812 an American named Preble, living in Paris, bought a small vessel, said to have belonged in turn to the British and French navy, which he fitted as a privateer-brig, carrying sixteen guns and one hundred and sixty men. The " True-Blooded Yankee," commanded by Captain Hailey, sailed from Brest March 1, 1813, and cruised thirty-seven days on the coasts of Ireland and Scotland, capturing twenty-seven valuable vessels ; sinking coasters in the very bay of Dublin ; landing and taking possession of an island off the coast of Ireland, and of a town in Scotland, where she burned seven vessels in the harbor. She returned safely to Brest, and soon made another cruise. At the same time the schooner " Fox " of Portsmouth burned or sunk vessel after vessel in the Irish Sea, as they plied between Liverpool and Cork. In May, the schooner " Paul Jones " of New York, carrying sixteen guns and one hundred and twenty men, took or destroyed a dozen vessels off the Irish coast, until she was herself caught in a fog by the frigate " Leonidas," and captured May 23 after a chase in which five of her crew were wounded.

While these vessels were thus engaged, the brig

" Rattlesnake " of Philadelphia, carrying sixteen guns and one hundred and twenty men, and the brig " Scourge " of New York, carrying nine guns and one hundred and ten men, crossed the ocean and cruised all the year in the northern seas off the coasts of Scotland and Norway, capturing some forty British vessels, and costing the British merchants and ship-owners losses to the amount of at least two million dollars. In July the " Scourge " fell in with Commodore Rodgers in the " President," and the two vessels remained several days in company off the North Cape, while the British admiralty sent three or four squadrons in search of them without success. July 19, after Rodgers had been nearly a month in British waters, one of these squadrons drove him away, and he then made a circuit round Ireland before he turned homeward. At the same time, from July 14 to August 14, the " Argus " was destroying vessels in the British Channel at the rate of nearly one a day. After the capture of the " Argus," August 14, the " Grand Turk " of Salem, a brig carrying sixteen guns and one hundred and five men, cruised for twenty days in the mouth of the British Channel without being disturbed. Besides these vessels, others dashed into British waters from time to time as they sailed forward and back across the ocean in the track of British commerce.

No one disputed that the privateers were a very important branch of the American navy; but they suffered under serious drawbacks, which left doubtful the balance of merits and defects. Perhaps their chief advantage compared with government vessels was their lightness, — a quality which no government would have carried to the same extent. The long-range pivot-gun was another invention of the privateer, peculiarly successful and easily adapted for government vessels. In other respects, the same number or even half the number of sloops-of-war would have probably inflicted greater injury at less cost. The "Argus" showed how this result could have been attained. The privateer's first object was to save prizes; and in the effort to send captured vessels into port the privateer lost a large proportion by recapture. Down to the moment when Admiral Warren established his blockade of the American coast from New York southward, most of the prizes got to port. After that time the New England ports alone offered reasonable chance of safety, and privateering received a check.[1] During the war about twenty-five hundred vessels all told were captured from the British. Many were destroyed; many released as cartels; and of the remainder not less than seven hundred and fifty, probably one half the number sent to port, were recaptured by the British navy. Most of these were the prizes of privateers, and would have been destroyed had they been taken by government vessels. They were usually the most valuable prizes, so that the injury that might have

[1] Memorial of Baltimore merchants, Feb. 19, 1814; State Papers, Naval Affairs, p. 300.

been inflicted on British commerce was diminished
nearly one half by the system which encouraged
private war as a money-making speculation.

Another objection was equally serious. Like all
gambling ventures, privateering was not profitable.
In the list of five hundred privateers furnished by the
Navy Department,[1] three hundred were recorded as
having never made a prize. Of the remainder, few
made their expenses. One of the most successful
cruises of the war was that of Joshua Barney on the
Baltimore schooner " Rossie " at the outbreak of hostilities, when every prize reached port. Barney sent
in prizes supposed to be worth fifteen hundred thousand dollars ; but after paying charges and duties
and selling the goods, he found that the profits were
not sufficient to counterbalance the discomforts, and
he refused to repeat the experiment. His experience
was common. As early as November, 1812, the owners of twenty-four New York privateers sent to Congress a memorial declaring that the profits of private
naval war were by no means equal to the hazards,
and that the spirit of privateering stood in danger
of extinction unless the government would consent
in some manner to grant a bounty for the capture
or destruction of the enemy's property.

If private enterprise was to fail at the critical
moment, and if the government must supply the deficiency, the government would have done better to
undertake the whole task. In effect, the government

[1] Emmons's Navy of the United States.

in the end did so. The merchants asked chiefly for a
reduction of duties on prize-goods. Gallatin pointed
out the serious objections to such legislation, and the
little probability that the measure would increase the
profits of privateering or the number of privateers.
The actual privateers, he said, were more than enough
for the food offered by the enemy's trade, and privateering, like every other form of gambling, would
always continue to attract more adventurers than it
could support.[1]

Congress for the time followed Gallatin's advice,
and did nothing ; but in the summer session of 1813,
after Gallatin's departure for Europe, the privateer
owners renewed their appeal, and the acting Secretary
of the Treasury, Jones, wrote to the chairman of the
Naval Committee July 21, 1813,[2] —

" The fact is that . . . privateering is nearly at an
end ; and from the best observation I have been enabled
to make, it is more from the deficiency of remuneration
in the net proceeds of their prizes than from the vigilance
and success of the enemy in recapturing."

In deference to Jones's opinion, Congress passed an
Act, approved Aug. 2, 1813, reducing one third the
duties on prize-goods. Another Act, approved August 3, granted a bounty of twenty-five dollars for
every prisoner captured and delivered to a United
States agent by a private armed vessel. A third Act,

[1] Gallatin to Langdon Cheves, Dec. 8, 1812; Annals, 1812–
1813, p. 434.

[2] Annals, 1813–1814, i. 473.

approved August 2, authorized the Secretary of the
Navy to place on the pension list any privateersman
who should be wounded or disabled in the line of
his duty.

These complaints and palliations tended to show
that the privateer cost the public more than the equivalent government vessel would have cost. If instead
of five hundred privateers of all sizes and efficiency,
the government had kept twenty sloops-of-war constantly at sea destroying the enemy's commerce, the
result would have been about the same as far as concerned injury to the enemy, while in another respect
the government would have escaped one of its chief
difficulties.   Nothing injured the navy so much as
privateering. Seamen commonly preferred the harder
but more profitable and shorter cruise in a privateer,
where fighting was not expected or wished, to the
strict discipline and murderous battles of government
ships, where wages were low and prize-money scarce.
Of all towns in the United States, Marblehead was
probably the most devoted to the sea; but of nine
hundred men from Marblehead who took part in the
war, fifty-seven served as soldiers, one hundred and
twenty entered the navy, while seven hundred and
twenty-six went as privateersmen.[1]   Only after much
delay and difficulty could the frigates obtain crews.
The "Constitution" was nearly lost by this cause at
the beginning of the war; and the loss of the "Chesapeake" was supposed to be chiefly due to the deter-

[1] Roads's Marblehead, p. 255.

mination of the old crew to quit the government
service for that of the privateers.

Such drawbacks raised reasonable doubts as to the
balance of advantages and disadvantages offered by
the privateer system. Perhaps more careful inquiry
might show that, valuable as the privateers were, the
government would have done better to retain all military and naval functions in its own hands, and to
cover the seas with small cruisers capable of pursuing
a system of thorough destruction against the shipping
and colonial interests of England.

CHAPTER XIV.

GALLATIN and Bayard, having sailed from the Delaware May 9, arrived at St. Petersburg July 21, only to find that during the six months since the Czar offered to mediate, Russia had advanced rapidly in every direction except that of the proposed mediation. Napoleon after being driven from Russia in December, 1812, passed the winter in Paris organizing a new army of three hundred thousand men on the Elbe, between Dresden and Magdeburg, while a second army of more than one hundred thousand was to hold Hamburg and Bremen. Russia could not prevent Napoleon from reconstructing a force almost as powerful as that with which he had marched to Moscow, for the Russian army had suffered very severely and was unfit for active service; but the Czar succeeded in revolutionizing Prussia, and in forcing the French to retire from the Vistula to the Elbe, while he gained a reinforcement of more than one hundred thousand men from the fresh and vigorous Prussian army. Even with that assistance the Czar could not cope with Napoleon, who, leaving Paris April 17, during the month of May fought furious battles at Lützen and Bautzen, which forced the allied Russian and Prussian armies back from the Elbe to the Oder.

At that point Austria interfered so energetically as to oblige Napoleon to accept an armistice for the purpose of collecting new forces. During the armistice the Czar stationed himself at Gitschin in Bohemia, nine hundred miles from St. Petersburg, and about the same distance from London by the path that couriers were obliged to take. When Gallatin and Bayard reached St. Petersburg, July 21, the armistice, which had been prolonged until August 10, was about to expire, and the Czar could not be anxious to decide subordinate questions until the issue of the coming campaign should be known.

Meanwhile the government of England had in May, with many friendly expressions, declined the Russian mediation.[1] Castlereagh probably hoped that this quiet notification to Lieven, the Russian envoy in London, would end the matter; but toward the month of July news reached London that the American commissioners, Gallatin and Bayard, had arrived at Gothenburg on their way to Russia, and Castlereagh then saw that he must be more explicit in his refusal. Accordingly he took measures for making the matter clear not only to the Russian government but also to the American commissioners.

With the Russian government he was obliged by the nature of their common relations to communi-

[1] Diary of J. Q. Adams, June 22, 1813, ii. 479.

cate officially, and he wrote instructions to Lord Cathcart, dated July 5, directing communication to be made.

"I am afraid," said Castlereagh's letter,[1] "this tender of mediation which on a question of maritime right cannot be listened to by Great Britain, however kindly and liberally intended, will have had the unfortunate effect of protracting the war with the United States. It is to be lamented that the formal offer was made to America before the disposition of the British government was previously sounded as to its acceptance of a mediation. It has enabled the President to hold out to the people of America a vague expectation of peace, under which he may reconcile them with less repugnance to submit to the measures of the Government. This evil, however, cannot now be avoided, and it only remains to prevent this question from producing any embarrassment between Great Britain and Russia."

Embarrassment between Great Britain and Russia was no new thing in European politics, and commonly involved maritime objects for which the United States were then fighting. Castlereagh had much reason for wishing to avoid the danger. The most fortunate result he could reasonably expect from the coming campaign was a defeat of Bonaparte that should drive him back to the Rhine. Then Russia and Austria would probably offer terms to Napoleon; England would be obliged to join in a European Congress; Napoleon would raise the question of mari-

[1] Castlereagh to Cathcart, July 5, 1813; MSS. British Archives.

time rights, and on that point he would be supported by Russian sympathies. Napoleon and Russia might insist that the United States should take part in the Congress, and in that case England might be obliged to retire from it. Castlereagh felt uneasy at the prospect, and ordered Cathcart to " press the Emperor of Russia in the strongest manner not to push his personal interference on this point further." Cathcart was to use his utmost endeavors to persuade the Czar " pointedly to discountenance a design so mischievously calculated to promote the views of France."

Another week of reflection only increased Castlereagh's anxieties, and caused the British government to take a step intended to leave the Czar no opening for interference. July 13 Castlereagh wrote Cathcart new instructions,[1] directing him to present a formal note acquainting the Czar that the Prince Regent was " ready immediately to name plenipotentiaries to meet and treat with the American plenipotentiaries in the earnest desire " of peace, either in London or at Gothenburg ; although he could " not consent that these discussions should be carried on in any place which might be supposed to imply that they were in any way connected with any other negotiations." He wrote privately to Cathcart that the mere knowledge of the intervention of a third power in any arrangement with the

[1] Castlereagh to Cathcart, July 13, 1813 ; MSS. British Archives.

United States would probably decide the British people against it.[1]

Thus in July, 1813, when the war was barely a year old, Castlereagh reached the point of offering to negotiate directly with the United States. This advantage was gained by the Russian offer of mediation, and was intended not to pacify America but to silence Alexander and Roumanzoff. Castlereagh was frank and prompt in his declarations. His offer of direct negotiation was dated July 13, at a time when Alexander Baring received a letter from Gallatin announcing his arrival at Gothenburg and inviting assistance for the proposed mediation. Baring consulted Castlereagh, and wrote, July 22, a long letter to Gallatin, to inform the American commissioners what the British government had done and was willing to do. " Before this reaches you," said Baring,[2] " you will have been informed that this mediation has been refused, with expressions of our desire to treat separately and directly here; or, if more agreeable to you, at Gothenburg." To leave no room for misunderstanding, Baring added that if the American commissioners were obliged by their instructions to adhere pertinaciously to the American demands in respect to impressments, he should think negotiation useless.

[1] Castlereagh to Cathcart, July 14, 1813; Castlereagh Papers, Third Series, i. 35.

[2] Baring to Gallatin, July 22, 1813; Gallatin's Writings, i. 546.

In regular succession all these expressions of British policy were received at St. Petersburg in the Czar's absence, and in the doubtful state of mind which followed the battles of Lützen and Bautzen. Alexander had left Count Roumanzoff at St. Petersburg, continuing to act as Chancellor of the Empire and Foreign Secretary; but in truth the Minister of Foreign Affairs, as far as the Czar then required such an officer, was Count Nesselrode, who attended Alexander in person and received his orders orally. Nesselrode at that time was rather an agent than an adviser; but in general he represented the English alliance and hostility to Napoleon, while Roumanzoff represented the French alliance and hostility to England.

Of English diplomacy Americans knew something, and could by similarity of mind divine what was not avowed. Of French diplomacy they had long experience, and their study was rendered from time to time more easy by Napoleon's abrupt methods. Of Russian diplomacy they knew little or nothing. Thus far Minister Adams had been given his own way. He had been allowed to seem to kindle the greatest war of modern times, and had been invited to make use of Russia against England; but the Czar's reasons for granting such favor were mysterious even to Adams, for while Napoleon occasionally avowed motives, Alexander never did. Russian diplomacy moved wholly in the dark.

Only one point was certain. For reasons of his own, the Czar chose to leave Roumanzoff nominally

in office until the result of the war should be decided,
although Roumanzoff was opposed to the Czar's policy. The chancellor did not stand alone in his hostility to the war; probably a majority of the Russian
people shared the feeling. Even the army and its
old General Koutousoff, though elated with an immense triumph, grumbled at being obliged to fight
the battles of Germany, and would gladly have returned to their own soil. The Czar himself could not
afford to break his last tie with the French interest, but was wise to leave a path open by which he
could still retreat in case his war in Germany failed.
If Napoleon should succeed once more in throwing
the Russian army back upon Russian soil, Alexander
might still be obliged to use Roumanzoff's services
if not to resume his policy. Such a suspicion might
not wholly explain Alexander's course toward Roumanzoff and Koutousoff, but no one could doubt that
it explained the chancellor's course toward the Czar.
Indeed, Roumanzoff made little concealment of his
situation or his hopes. Adams could without much
difficulty divine that the failure of the Czar in Germany would alone save Roumanzoff in St. Petersburg,
and that the restoration of Roumanzoff to power was
necessary to reinvigorate the mediation.

Castlereagh's first positive refusal to accept the
mediation was notified to Count Lieven in May, and
was known to Roumanzoff in St. Petersburg about the
middle of June. Early in July the Czar received it,
and by his order Nesselrode, in a despatch to Lieven

dated July 9, expressed " the perfect satisfaction
which his Imperial Majesty felt in the reasons which
actuated the conduct of this [British] government on
a point of so much delicacy and importance." [1] The
Czar was then in the midst of difficulties. The result
of the war was doubtful, and depended on Austria.

Just as news of the armistice arrived in St. Petersburg, Minister Adams went to Roumanzoff, June
22, to inform him of Gallatin's and Bayard's appointment. Roumanzoff in return gave Adams explicit information of England's refusal to accept the
Czar's offer. Adams immediately recorded it in his
Diary : [2] —

" He [Roumanzoff] said that he was very sorry to say
he had received since he had seen me [June 15] further
despatches from Count Lieven, stating that the British
government, with many very friendly and polite assurances that there was no mediation which they should so
readily and cheerfully accept as that of the Emperor of
Russia, had however stated that their differences with the
United States of America involving certain principles of
the internal government of England were of a nature
which they did not think suitable to be settled by a
mediation."

Adams expected this answer, and at once assumed it to be final; but Roumanzoff checked him.
" It would now be for consideration," he continued,
" whether, after the step thus taken by the American

[1] Castlereagh to Cathcart, Sept. 1, 1813 ; MSS. British
Archives.

[2] Diary of J. Q. Adams, June 22, 1813, ii. 479.

government [in sending commissioners to St. Peters-
burg], it would not be advisable to renew the propo-
sition to Great Britain; upon which he should write
to the Emperor." Not because of any American request, but wholly of his own motion, Roumanzoff proposed to keep the mediation alive. His motives were
for Adams to fathom. The chancellor did not avow
them, but he hinted to Adams that the chances of
war were many. " Perhaps it might be proper not
to be discouraged by the ill success of his first ad-
vances. After considerations might produce more
pacific dispositions in the British government. Unexpected things were happening every day; 'and in
our own affairs,' said the count, ' a very general report prevails that an armistice has taken place.'" A
Congress had been proposed, and the United States
were expressly named among the Powers to be invited
to it.

Adams reported this conversation to his Government in a despatch dated June 26,[1] and waited for his
two new colleagues, who arrived July 21. Personally
the colleagues were agreeable to Adams, and the proposed negotiation was still more so, for the President sent him official notice that in case the negotiations were successful, Adams's services would be
required as minister in London; but with the strongest inducements to press the mediation, Adams could
not but see that he and his colleagues depended on

[1] Adams to Monroe, June 26, 1813; MSS. State Department
Archives.

Roumanzoff, and that Roumanzoff depended not on Alexander, but on Napoleon. Roumanzoff's only chance of aiding them was by clinging to office until the Czar should be weary of war.

Unwilling as Gallatin was to be thus made the sport of imperial policy, he was obliged, like his colleagues, to submit. Two days after their arrival, Roumanzoff told them that he meant, if possible, to begin the whole transaction anew.

"The count said he regretted much that there was such reason to believe the British would decline the mediation; but on transmitting the copy of the credential letter to the Emperor, he would determine whether to renew the proposal, as the opposition in England might make it an embarrassing charge against the Ministry if they should under such circumstances reject it." [1]

Roumanzoff had written soon after June 22 to ask the Czar whether, on the arrival of the American commissioners, the offer of mediation should be renewed. The Czar, overwhelmed with business, wrote back, about July 20, approving Roumanzoff's suggestion, and authorizing him to send a despatch directly to Count Lieven in London renewing the offer. The Czar's letter was communicated to Adams August 10 [2] by Roumanzoff, who was evidently much pleased and perhaps somewhat excited by it.

Such a letter warranted some excitement, for Roumanzoff could regard it only as a sign of hesitation

[1] Diary of J. Q. Adams, July 23, 1813, ii. 489.
[2] Diary of J. Q. Adams, July 23, 1813, ii. 501.

and anxiety.   Alexander was in a degree pledged to
England to press the mediation no further.   While
he assured England through Nesselrode, July 9, that
he was perfectly satisfied with the British reasons
for refusing his offer of mediation " on a point of so
much delicacy and importance," he authorized Roumanzoff only ten days afterward to annoy England a
second time with an offer which he had every reason
to know must be rejected ; and he did this without
informing Nesselrode.

Gallatin and Bayard found themselves, August 10,
condemned to wait two or three months for the British answer, which they knew must be unfavorable,
because Gallatin received August 17 Baring's letter
announcing the determination of Castlereagh to negotiate separately.   Roumanzoff's conduct became
more and more mysterious to the commissioners.
He did not notify them of Castlereagh's official offer
to negotiate directly.   He confounded Adams, August
19, by flatly denying his own information, given two
months before, that England rejected mediation in
principle because it involved doctrines of her internal government.   Roumanzoff insisted that England
had never refused to accept the mediation, although
he held in his hands at least two despatches from
Lieven, written as late as July 13, officially communicating England's determination to negotiate directly
or not at all.   Castlereagh, foreseeing the possibility
of misunderstanding, had read to Lieven the instructions of July 13 for communication to Roumanzoff,

besides authorizing Cathcart to show them *in extenso* to the Czar.[1] In denying that such instructions had been given, Roumanzoff could not have expected the American commissioners to believe him.

The motive of Roumanzoff's persistence might be open to the simple explanation that the chancellor hoped to recover power, and within a few months to re-establish his policy of ˙antagonism to England. Alexander's conduct could be explained by no such obvious interest. When Castlereagh's letters of July 13 and 14 reached Cathcart at the Czar's headquarters in Bohemia about August 10, they arrived at the most critical moment of the war. On that day the armistice expired. The next day Austria declared war on Napoleon. The combined armies of Russia, Prussia, and Austria concentrated behind the mountains, and then marched into Saxony. While starting on that campaign, August 20, the Czar was told by Lord Cathcart the reasons why his offer of mediation was rejected, and answered at once that in this case he could do nothing more.[2] Cathcart wrote to Nesselrode a formal note on the subject August 23 or 24, but did not at once communicate it,[3] because the campaign had then begun ; the great battle of Dresden was fought August 26 and 27, and the allies, again beaten, retired into Bohemia August 28. The

[1] Castlereagh to Cathcart, July 14, 1813 ; Castlereagh's Papers, Third Series, i. 35.

[2] Diary of J. Q. Adams, Nov. 23, 1813, ii. 539, 542.

[3] Diary of J. Q. Adams, April 2, 1814, ii. 593.

Czar saw his best military adviser Moreau killed by his side at Dresden, and he returned to Töplitz in no happy frame of mind.

At Töplitz, September 1, Cathcart delivered to Nesselrode his formal note,[1] refusing Russian mediation and communicating the offer of England to negotiate directly. In an ordinary condition of government Nesselrode should have taken care that the British note should be made known without delay to the American commissioners at St. Petersburg, but the Czar kept in his own hands the correspondence with Roumanzoff and the Americans, and neither he nor Nesselrode communicated Cathcart's act to Roumanzoff.[2] Possibly their silence was due to the new military movements. August 29 the French marshal Vandamme with forty thousand men, pursuing the allies into Bohemia, was caught between the Prussians and Austrians August 30 and crushed. During the month of September severe fighting, favorable to the allies, occurred, but no general advance was made by the allied sovereigns.

Alexander next received at Töplitz toward September 20 a letter from Roumanzoff enclosing a renewal of the offer of mediation, to be proposed in a despatch to Lieven, read by Roumanzoff to the American commissioners August 24, and sent to London August 28. The Czar must have known the futility of this new step, as well as the mistake into which Roumanzoff

[1] Cathcart to Nesselrode, Sept. 1, 1813 ; State Papers, iii. 622.
[2] Diary of J. Q. Adams, April 23, 1814, ii. 599.

had been led, and the awkward attitude of the American commissioners. Only a fortnight before, he had received Cathcart's official note, and a few days earlier he had assured Cathcart that he should do no more in the matter. Yet, September 20, Alexander wrote with his own hand a note of four lines to Roumanzoff, approving his despatch to Lieven, and begging him to follow up the affair as he had begun it.[1]

The Czar's letter of September 20 completed the embroglio, which remained unintelligible to every one except himself. Cathcart was the most mystified of all the victims to the Czar's double attitude. At the time when Alexander thus for the second time authorized Roumanzoff to disregard the express entreaties of the British government, Cathcart was making an effort to explain to Castlereagh the Czar's first interference. If Castlereagh understood his minister's ideas, he was gifted with more than common penetration.

" I believe the not communicating the rescript of the Emperor concerning the American plenipotentiaries to have been the effect of accident," wrote Cathcart[2] from Töplitz September 25; " but what is singular is that notwithstanding his [Nesselrode's] letter of the ninth [July], by the Emperor's command, to Count Lieven, this communication from and instruction to Roumanzoff was not known to Count Nesselrode till this day, when I mentioned it to him, having received no caution to do

[1] Diary of J. Q. Adams, Sept. 10, 1813, ii. 531.

[2] Cathcart to Castlereagh, Sept. 25, 1813 ; MSS. British Archives.

otherwise, and he was not at all pleased with it. It was during the advance to Dresden. But I cannot help thinking that there must have been some policy of Roumanzoff's stated in regard to keeping hold of the mediation, which, whether it was detailed or not, would not escape the Emperor's penetration, and upon which he may have been induced to act as far as sanctioning the proposal of treating at *London* under Russia's mediation, which the Prince Regent's government might accept or reject as they pleased; and that not wishing to go at that time into a discussion of maritime rights with either Nesselrode or me, he afterward forgot it."

Cathcart's style was involved, but his perplexity was evident. His remarks related only to the Czar's first letter to Roumanzoff, written about July 20, not " during the advance to Dresden." He knew nothing of the Czar's second letter to Roumanzoff, dated September 20, renewing the same authority, only five days before Cathcart's labored attempt to explain the first. Of the second letter, as of the first, neither Nesselrode nor Cathcart was informed.

The Czar's motive in thus ordering each of his two ministers to act in ignorance and contradiction of the other's instructions perplexed Roumanzoff as it did Cathcart. Lieven first revealed to Roumanzoff the strange misunderstanding by positively refusing to present to Castlereagh the chancellor's note of August 28 renewing the offer of mediation. Roumanzoff was greatly mortified. He told Gallatin that the mediation had been originally the Czar's own idea; that it had been the subject of repeated dis-

cussions at his own motion, and had been adopted
notwithstanding Roumanzoff's hints at the possibility
of English reluctance.[1]   The chancellor sent Lieven's
despatch immediately to the Czar without comment,
requesting the Czar to read it and give his orders.
The British officials, unwilling to blame Alexander,
attacked Roumanzoff.   Lord Walpole, who came directly from Bohemia to St. Petersburg to act as
British ambassador, said " he was as sure as he
was of his own existence, and he believed he could
prove it, that Roumanzoff had been cheating us all."[2]
Cathcart wrote, December 12, to Castlereagh, —

" I think Nesselrode knows nothing of the delay of
communicating with the American mission ; that it was
an intrigue of the chancellor's, if it is one ; and that
during the operations of war the Emperor lost the clew
to it, so that something has been unanswered."[3]

Perhaps the Czar's conduct admitted of several
interpretations.   He might wish to keep the mediation alive in order to occupy Roumanzoff until the
campaign should be decided ; or he might in his good
nature prefer to gratify his old favorite by allowing
him to do what he wished ; or he took this method
of signifying to Roumanzoff his disgrace and the
propriety of immediate retirement.   Apparently Roumanzoff took the last view, for he sent his resignation
to the Czar, and at the close of the year quitted his

[1] Diary of J. Q. Adams, Nov. 3, 1813, ii. 541.
[2] Diary of J. Q. Adams, April 2, 1814, ii. 591.
[3] Cathcart to Castlereagh, Dec. 12, 1813 ; Castlereagh Papers.

official residence at the Department of Foreign Affairs, telling Gallatin that he remained in office only till he should receive authority to close the American mission.

The American commissioners in private resented Alexander's treatment, but were unable to leave Russia without authority. Gallatin learned, October 19, that the Senate had refused to confirm his appointment, but he remained at St. Petersburg, chiefly in deference to Roumanzoff's opinion, and probably with ideas of assisting the direct negotiation at London or elsewhere. Meanwhile the campaign was decided, October 18, by Napoleon's decisive overthrow at Leipzig, which forced him to retreat behind the Rhine. Still the Czar wrote nothing to Roumanzoff, and the American commissioners remained month after month at St. Petersburg. Not until Jan. 25, 1814, did Gallatin and Bayard begin their winter journey to Amsterdam, where they arrived March 4 and remained a month. Then Gallatin received, through Baring, permission to enter England, and crossed the Channel to hasten if he could the direct negotiation which Castlereagh had offered and Madison accepted.

The diplomatic outlook had changed since March, 1813, when the President accepted the offer of Russian mediation ; but the change was wholly for the worse. England's triumphs girdled the world, and found no check except where Perry's squadron blocked the way to Detroit. The allied armies crossed the Rhine in December and entered France on the east. At the same time Wellington after a long campaign drove Joseph from Spain, and entering France from the south pressed against Bordeaux. The government and people of England, in their excitement and exultation at daily conquests, thought as little as they could of the American war. Society rarely mentioned it. Newspapers alone preserved a record of British feelings toward the United States during the year 1813. The expressions of newspapers, like those of orators, could not be accepted without allowance, for they aimed at producing some desired effect, and said either more or less than the truth ; as a rule, they represented the cool opinion neither of the person who uttered nor of the audience who heard them ; but in the absence of other records, public opinion was given only in the press, and the London newspapers alone furnished evidence of its character.

The " Morning Chronicle " — the only friend of the United States in the daily press of England — showed its friendship by silence. Whatever the liberal opposition thought in private, no one but Cobbett ventured in public to oppose the war. Cobbett having become a radical at the time of life when most men become conservative, published in his " Weekly Register " many columns of vigorous criticism on the American war without apparent effect, although in truth he expressed opinions commonly held by intelligent people. Even Lord Castlereagh, Cobbett's antipathy, shared some of Cobbett's least popular opinions in the matter of the American war.

English society, whatever shades of diversity might exist, was frank and free in expressing indifference or contempt. Of the newspapers which made a duty of reflecting what was believed to be the prevailing public opinion, the "Times," supposed to favor the interests of Wellesley and Canning, was probably the ablest. During the early part of the war, the "Times" showed a disposition to criticise the Ministry rather than the Americans. From the "Times" came most of the bitter complaints, widely copied by the American press, of the naval defeats suffered by the "Guerriere," the "Java," and the "Macedonian." British successes were belittled, and abuse of Americans was exaggerated, in order to deprive ministers of credit. "The world has seen President Madison plunge into a war from the basest motives, and conduct it with the most entire want of ability," said the "Times" of February 9, 1813. "The American government has sounded the lowest depth of military disgrace, insomuch that the official records of the campaign take from us all possibility of exulting in our victories over such an enemy." The "Times" found in such reflections a reason for not exulting in ministerial victories, but it bewailed defeats the more loudly, and annoyed the Ministry by the violence of its attacks on naval administration.

As the year passed, and England's triumph in

Europe seemed to overshadow the world, the "Times," probably recognizing the uselessness of attacking the Ministry, showed worse temper toward the United States. The Americans were rarely mentioned, and always with language of increasing ill humor. " Despicable in the cabinet, ridiculous in the field," [1] the Americans disappeared from sight in the splendor of victory at Vittoria and Leipzig. No wish for peace was suggested, and if the " Times " expressed the true feelings of the respectable middle class, as it was supposed to aim at doing, no wish for peace could be supposed to exist.

Of the ministerial papers the " Courier" was the best, and of course was emphatic in support of the American war. The Ministry were known to be lukewarm about the United States, and for that reason they thought themselves obliged to talk in public as strongly as the strongest against a peace. When the Russian mediation called for notice, May 13, the " Courier " at once declared against it : —

" Before the war commenced, concession might have been proper; we always thought it unwise. But the hour of concession and compromise is passed. America has rushed unnecessarily and unnaturally into war, and she must be made to feel the effects of her folly and injustice ; peace must be the consequence of punishment, and retraction of her insolent demands must precede negotiation. The thunders of our cannon must first strike terror into the American shores."

[1] The Times, Oct. 17, 1813.

The " Courier " felt that Americans were not Englishmen, and could not forgive it, but was unable to admit that they might still exercise a considerable influence on human affairs: —

" They have added nothing to literature, nothing to any of the sciences; they have not produced one good poet, not one celebrated historian! Their statesmen are of a mixed breed, — half metaphysicians, half politicians; all the coldness of the one with all the cunning of the other. Hence we never see anything enlarged in their conceptions or grand in their measures." [1]

These reasons were hardly sufficient to prove the right of impressing American seamen. The literary, metaphysical, or social qualities of Americans, their " enlarged conceptions," and the grandeur or littleness of their measures, had by common consent ceased to enter into discussion, pending a settlement of the simpler issue, whether Americans could fight. For a long time the English press encouraged the belief that Americans were as incapable of fighting as of producing poets and historians. Their naval victories were attributed to British seamen. Perhaps the first turn of the tide was in November, 1813, when news of Perry's victory on Lake Erie crossed in London the news of Napoleon's defeat at Leipzig. Perry's victory, like those of Hull, Decatur, and Bainbridge, was too complete for dispute: " It may, however, serve to diminish our vexation at this occurrence to learn that the flotilla in question was not

[1] The Courier, July 27, 1813.

any branch of the British navy, . . . but a local force, a kind of mercantile military." [1]

By a curious coincidence, Castlereagh's official letter to Monroe, offering direct negotiation, was dated the same day, November 4, when news of the victory at Leipzig met in London news of the defeat on Lake Erie, and Castlereagh probably meant to allow no newspaper prejudices to obstruct a peace; but public opinion was slow to recover its balance. When news arrived that the Americans had captured Malden, recovered Detroit, and destroyed Proctor's army on the Thames, the "Courier" showed the first symptom of change in opinion by expressing a somewhat simple-minded wish to hear no more about the Americans : —

"The intelligence is unpleasant, but we confess that we do not view, and have never from the beginning of the war viewed, the events in America with any very powerful interest. The occurrences in Europe will no doubt produce a very decisive effect upon the American government; and unless it is more obstinate and stupid in its hostility than even *we* think it, it will do as the other allies of Bonaparte have done, — abandon him."

If the national extravagance could be expected to show its full force in one direction rather than in another, naturalized Americans taken in arms were certain to produce it. The issue was regularly raised after Van Rensselaer's defeat at Queenston in 1812. When the American prisoners arrived at Quebec,

[1] The Courier, Nov. 4, 1813.

they were mustered, and twenty-three native-born subjects of Great Britain, belonging to the First, Sixth, and Thirteenth U. S. Infantry, were taken from the ranks and shipped to England to be put on trial as British subjects for bearing arms against their king. The American agent in London reported to the President that the men had arrived there for the reason given. Secretary Armstrong, May 15, 1813, then ordered twenty-three British soldiers into close confinement as hostages. The British government directed Sir George Prevost to put double the number of Americans in close confinement, and Sir George, in giving notice of this measure to General Wilkinson, October 17, 1813,[1] added : —

"I have been further instructed by his Majesty's government to notify to you for the information of the government of the United States that the commanders of his Majesty's armies and fleets on the coasts of America have received instructions to prosecute the war with unmitigated severity against all cities, towns, and villages belonging to the United States, and against the inhabitants thereof, if, after this communication shall have been made to you, and a reasonable time given for its being transmitted to the American government, that government shall unhappily not be deterred from putting to death any of the soldiers who now are or who may hereafter be kept as hostages for the purposes stated in the letter from Major-General Dearborn."

[1] Prevost to Wilkinson, Oct. 17, 1813 ; State Papers, Foreign Relations, iii. 635. Bathurst to Prevost, Aug. 12, 1813; State Papers, Foreign Relations, iii. 641.

The limit of retaliation was soon reached, for the number of prisoners was small on both sides. The British government somewhat carefully refrained from committing itself too far; but the press treated the matter as though it were vital.

"If Mr. Madison," said the "Courier" of July 24, "dare to retaliate by taking away the life of one English prisoner in revenge for a British subject fully proved to be such being taken in the act of voluntarily bearing arms against his country, America puts herself out of the protection of the law of nations, and must be treated as an outlaw. An army and navy acting against her will then be absolved from all obligation to respect the usages and laws of war. Hostilities may be carried on against her in any mode until she is brought to a proper sense of her conduct."

The "Morning Post" of December 28 called for the execution of British subjects taken in arms, and for retaliation on retaliation in defiance of "the brutal wretches who, after betraying, are still suffered to govern America." The "Times" of May 24 spoke with hardly less vehemence. Probably such talk was not shared by the government, for the government never tested its sincerity by bringing the men to trial; but at the close of 1813 public opinion in England was supposed to be tending toward extreme measures against the United States. The approaching fall of Napoleon threatened to throw America outside the pale of civilization. Englishmen seemed ready to accept the idea that Madison and Napoleon should be coupled together, and that no peace should be made which did not include the removal of both from office and power.   Of all periods in American history this was probably the least adapted to negotiation, but while England was at the moment of her most extravagant sense of power, President Madison received and accepted Castlereagh's offer to negotiate, and Gallatin went with Bayard to London to hasten the approach of peace.

CHAPTER XV.

CONGRESS assembled Dec. 6, 1813, at a time of general perplexity. The victories of Perry and Harrison, September 10 and October 5, had recovered Detroit and even conquered a part of West Canada, but their successes were already dimmed by the failures of Wilkinson and Hampton before Montreal, and the retreat of both generals November 13 within United States territory. In the Creek country the Georgians had failed to advance from the east, and Jackson was stopped at Fort Strother by want of supplies and men. At sea the navy was doing little, while the British blockade from New London southward was becoming more and more ruinous to the Southern and Middle States, and through them to the government. Abroad the situation was not yet desperate. The latest news from Europe left Napoleon at Dresden, victorious for the moment, before the great battles of October. From the American commissioners at St. Petersburg no news had arrived, but England's refusal to accept mediation was unofficially known. With this material the President was obliged to content himself in framing his Annual Message.

The Message sent to Congress December 7 began by expressing regret that the British government had disappointed the reasonable anticipation of discussing and, if possible, adjusting the rights and pretensions in dispute. From France nothing had been received on the subjects of negotiation. Madison congratulated Congress on the success of the navy upon the ocean and the Lakes, and the victory won by Harrison and R. M. Johnson in Canada. He mentioned briefly the failure of the armies on the St. Lawrence, and at greater length the success of Jackson on the Coosa; and he entered in detail into the retaliatory measures taken on either side in regard to naturalized soldiers. The finances were treated with more show of confidence than was warranted by the prospects of the Treasury; and the Message closed by a succession of paragraphs which seemed written in a spirit of panegyric upon war : —

" The war has proved moreover that our free government like other free governments, though slow in its early movements, acquires in its progress a force proportioned to its freedom; and that the Union of these States, the guardian of the freedom and safety of all and of each, is strengthened by every occasion that puts it to the test. In fine, the war with its vicissitudes is illustrating the capacity and the destiny of the United States to be a great, a flourishing, and a powerful nation."

The rule that feeble and incompetent governments acquire strength by exercise, and especially in war, had been as well understood in 1798 as it was in

1813, and had been the chief cause of Republican antipathy to war ; but had Madison publicly expressed the same sentiment in 1798 as in 1813, he would have found himself in a better position to enforce the rights for which he was struggling when the extreme discontent of nearly one third of the States contradicted his congratulations on " the daily testimony of increasing harmony throughout the Union." Whatever the ultimate result of the war might be, it had certainly not thus far strengthened the Union. On the contrary, public opinion seemed to be rapidly taking the shape that usually preceded a rupture of friendly relations between political societies. Elections in the Middle States showed that the war, if not actually popular, had obliged the people there to support the government for fear of worse evils. New Jersey by a small majority returned to its allegiance, and the city of New York elected a Republican to represent it in Congress; but the steady drift of opinion in the Middle States toward the war was simultaneous with an equally steady drift in the Eastern States against it.

The evidences of chronic discontent in the Eastern States were notorious. Less than a month before Madison wrote his Annual Message, Governor Chittenden of Vermont, by proclamation November 10, recalled the State militia from national service : [1]

" He cannot conscientiously discharge the trust reposed in him by the voice of his fellow-citizens, and by the

[1] Proclamation of Nov. 10, 1813; Niles, v. 212.

Constitution of this and the United States, without an unequivocal declaration that in his opinion the military strength and resources of this State must be reserved for its own defence and protection exclusively, excepting in cases provided for by the Constitution of the United States, and then under orders derived only from the commander-in-chief."

The intercourse between the Eastern States and the enemy was notorious. The Federalist press of Massachusetts, encouraged by Russian and English success in Europe, discussed the idea of withdrawing the State from all share in the war, and making a separate arrangement with England. The President's first act, after sending to Congress his Annual Message, was to send a special Message incidentally calling attention to the want of harmony that paralyzed the energy of the government.

The special and secret Message of December 9 asked Congress once more to impose an embargo. Considering the notorious antipathy of the Eastern States to the system of embargo, the new experiment was so hazardous as to require proof of its necessity. That it was directed against the commerce of the New England States was evident, for the blockade answered the purposes of embargo elsewhere. The Message seemed to propose that all commerce should cease because any commerce must favor the enemy; in effect, it urged that New England should be forbidden to sell or buy so long as the rest of the country was prevented from doing so.

"The tendency of our commercial and navigation laws in their present state to favor the enemy," said Madison,[1] "and thereby prolong the war, is more and more developed by experience. Supplies of the most essential kinds find their way not only to British ports and British armies at a distance, but the armies in our neighborhood with which our own are contending derive from our ports and outlets a subsistence attainable with difficulty if at all from other sources. Even the fleets and troops infesting our coasts and waters are by like supplies accommodated and encouraged in their predatory and incursive warfare. Abuses having a like tendency take place in our import trade. British fabrics and products find their way into our ports under the name and from the ports of other countries, and often in British vessels disguised as neutrals by false colors and papers. . . . To shorten as much as possible the duration of the war, it is indispensable that the enemy should feel all the pressure that can be given to it."

Although Madison pointed to the notorious supply of food for the British forces in Canada as one of the motives for imposing an embargo, no one supposed that motive to be decisive. Other laws already forbade and punished such communication with the enemy; and experience proved that a general embargo would be no more effective than any special prohibition. The idea that England could be distressed by an embargo seemed still less likely to influence Government. Congress knew that Russia, Prussia, Denmark, Sweden and Norway, Spain, and

[1] Message of Dec. 9, 1813; Annals, 1813–1814, p. 2031.

South America were already open to English commerce, and that a few days must decide whether Napoleon could much longer prevent Great Britain from trading with France. The possibility of distressing England by closing Boston and Salem, New Bedford and Newport to neutral ships was not to be seriously treated.

Whatever was the true motive of the President's recommendation, Congress instantly approved it. The next day, December 10, the House went into secret session, and after two days of debate passed an Embargo Act by a vote of eighty-five to fifty-seven, which quickly passed the Senate by a vote of twenty to fourteen, and received the President's approval December 17, being the first legislation adopted at the second session of the Thirteenth Congress.[1] The Act was at once enforced with so much severity that within a month Congress was obliged to consider and quickly adopted another Act[2] relieving from its operation the people of Nantucket, who were in a state of starvation, all communication with the main land having been forbidden by the law ; but nothing proved that the illicit communication with Canada ceased.

This beginning of legislation at a time when the crisis of the war could be plainly seen approaching suggested much besides want of harmony. The em-

[1] Act laying an Embargo, Dec. 17, 1813 ; Annals, 1813–1814, p. 2781.

[2] Act of Jan. 25, 1814; Annals, 1813–1814, p. 2788.

bargo strengthened the antipathy of New England to
the war,—a result sufficiently unfortunate; but it also
led to a number of other consequences that were
doubtless foreseen by the Administration, since they
were prophesied by the Federalists. The Act was
approved December 17. Hardly had it gone into
operation when the British schooner " Bramble " arrived at Annapolis, December 30, bringing a letter
from Castlereagh to Monroe offering to negotiate
directly, though declining mediation. Important as
this news was, it did not compare with that in the
newspapers brought by the " Bramble." These contained official reports from Germany of great battles
fought at Leipzig October 16, 18, and 19, in which the
allies had overwhelmed Napoleon in defeat so disastrous that any hope of his continuing to make head
against them in Germany was at an end. Except
France, the whole continent of Europe already was
open to British commerce, or soon must admit it.
From that moment the New England Federalists no
longer doubted their own power. Their tone rose ;
their opposition to the war became more threatening ;
their schemes ceased to be negative, and began to
include plans for positive interference ; and the embargo added strength to their hatred of Madison and
the Union.

Madison was seldom quick in changing his views,
but the battle of Leipzig was an event so portentous
that optimism could not face it. Other depressing
news poured in. Fort George was evacuated ; Fort

Niagara was disgracefully lost; Lewiston, Black Rock, and Buffalo were burned, and the region about Niagara was laid waste ; blue lights were seen at New London. Every prospect was dark, but the battle of Leipzig was fatal to the last glimmer of hope that England could be brought to reason, or that New England could be kept quiet. A change of policy could not safely be delayed.

Castlereagh's offer was instantly accepted. January 5 Monroe replied, with some complaint at the refusal of mediation, that the President acceded to the offer of negotiating at Gothenburg. The next day Madison sent the correspondence to Congress, with a warning not to relax " vigorous preparations for carrying on the war." A week afterward, January 14, he nominated J. Q. Adams, J. A. Bayard, Henry Clay, and Jonathan Russell as commissioners to negotiate directly with Great Britain, and the Senate confirmed the nominations, January 18, with little opposition except to Jonathan Russell's further nomination as Minister to Sweden, which was confirmed by the narrow vote of sixteen to fourteen. Three weeks later, February 8, Albert Gallatin was added to the commission, George W. Campbell being nominated to the Treasury.

The prompt acceptance of Castlereagh's offer, the addition of Henry Clay to the negotiators, and the removal of Gallatin from the Treasury showed that diplomacy had resumed more than its old importance. The hope of peace might serve to quiet New England for a time, but mere hope with so little to nourish it could not long pacify any one, if the embargo was to remain in force. Several signs indicated there also a change of policy. Besides the embargo, and in support of its restrictions, Madison had recommended the passage of bills prohibiting collusive captures, ransoming vessels captured by the enemy, and interference by the courts, as well as the introduction of British woollens, cottons, and spirits. The bill prohibiting woollens and other articles was reported to the Senate December 30, the day when the " Bramble " reached Annapolis. The Senate waited nearly a month, till January 27, and then passed the bill, January 31, by a vote of sixteen to twelve. The House referred it to the Committee on Foreign Relations February 3, where it remained. On the other hand, the bill prohibiting ransoms was introduced in the House December 30, and passed January 26 by a vote of eighty to fifty-seven. The Senate referred it January 28 to the Committee on Foreign Relations, which never reported it. The fate of these measures foreshadowed the destiny of the embargo.

Yet the President clung to his favorite measure with a degree of obstinacy that resembled desperation. Congress showed by its indifference to the two supplementary bills that it had abandoned the President's system as early as January, but the embargo continued throughout the winter, and the month of March passed without its removal. The news from Europe at the close of that month left no doubt that

Napoleon could offer little effectual resistance even
in France to the allies, whose armies were known to
have crossed the Rhine, while Wellington advanced
on Bordeaux. Holland was restored to her ancient
independence, and Napoleon was understood to have
accepted in principle, for a proposed Congress at
Mannheim, the old boundaries of France as a basis
of negotiation. In theory, the overthrow of Napoleon
should have not essentially affected the embargo or
the Non-importation Acts, which were expected to
press upon England independently of Napoleon's Continental system; but in practice the embargo having
produced no apparent effect on Europe during the
war, could not be expected to produce an effect after
England had succeeded in conquering France, and
had abandoned her blockades as France had abandoned her decrees. For that reason avowedly Madison at last yielded, and sent a Message to Congress
March 31, recommending that the system of commercial restriction should cease : —

" Taking into view the mutual interests which the
United States and the foreign nations in amity with her
have in a liberal commercial intercourse, and the extensive changes favorable thereto which have recently
taken place ; taking into view also the important advantages which may otherwise result from adapting the
state of our commercial laws to the circumstances now
existing," —

Taking into view only these influences, Madison
seemed to ignore the supposed chief motive of the

embargo in stopping supplies for Canada, and to admit that embargo was an adjunct of Napoleon's Continental system; but in truth Madison's motives, both
political and financial, were deeper and more decisive
than any he alleged. His retreat was absolute. He
recommended that Congress should throw open the
ports, and should abandon all restriction on commerce
beyond a guaranty of war duties for two years after
peace as a measure of protection to American manufactures. The failure of the restrictive system was
not disguised.

The House received the Message with a mixed
sense of relief and consternation, and referred it to
Calhoun's committee, which reported April 4 a bill
for repealing the Embargo and Non-importation Acts,
together with the reasons which led the committee to
unite with the Executive in abandoning the restrictive
system.

Calhoun had always opposed the commercial policy
of Jefferson and Madison. For him the sudden Executive change was a conspicuous triumph; but he
showed remarkable caution in dealing with the House.
Instead of attempting to coerce the majority, according to his habit, by the force of abstract principles,
he adopted Madison's reasoning and softened his
own tone, seeming disposed to coax his Southern
and Western friends from making a display of useless
ill-temper. " Men cannot go straight forward," he
said, " but must regard the obstacles which impede
their course. Inconsistency consists in a change of

conduct when there is no change of circumstances which justify it." The changes in the world's circumstances required a return to free trade; but the manufactures would not be left unprotected, — on the contrary, "he hoped at all times and under every policy they would be protected with due care." [1]

As an example of political inconsistency, as Calhoun defined it, his pledge to protect American manufactures deserved to be remembered; but hardly had Calhoun's words died on the echoes of the House when another distinguished statesman offered a prospective example even more striking of what Calhoun excused. Daniel Webster rose, and in the measured and sonorous tones which impressed above all the idea of steadfastness in character, he pronounced a funeral oration over the restrictive system: —

" It was originally offered to the people of this country as a kind of political faith; it was to be believed, not examined; . . . it was to be our political salvation, nobody knew exactly how; and any departure from it would lead to political ruin, nobody could tell exactly why."

Its opponents had uniformly contended that it was auxiliary to Napoleon's Continental system, in co-operation with Napoleon's government; and its abandonment with the fall of Napoleon showed the truth. While thus exulting in the overthrow of the first "American system," Webster qualified his triumph by adding that he was, "generally speaking," not the

[1] Annals, 1813–1814, p. 1965.

enemy of manufactures; he disliked only the rearing
them in hot-beds : —

" I am not in haste to see Sheffields and Birminghams
in America. . . . I am not anxious to accelerate the approach of the period when the great mass of American
labor shall not find its employment in the field; when the
young men of the country shall be obliged to shut their
eyes upon external Nature, — upon the heavens and the
earth, — and immerse themselves in close and unwhole-
some workshops; when they shall be obliged to shut their
ears to the bleatings of their own flocks upon their own
hills, and to the voice of the lark that cheers them at the
plough, that they may open them in dust and smoke and
steam, to the perpetual whirl of spools and spindles and
the grating of rasps and saws."

Potter of Rhode Island, where the new manufactures centred, spoke hotly against the change.   Much
Federalist capital had been drawn into the manufacturing business as well as into speculation in all
articles of necessity which the blockade and the embargo made scarce.   At heart the Federalists were
not unanimous in wishing for a repeal of the restrictive system, and Potter represented a considerable
class whose interests were involved in maintaining
high prices.   He admitted that the average duties
would still give American manufactures an advantage
of thirty-six per cent, without including freight and
marine risks, but he insisted that the bill was intended to encourage importations of British goods
" that we do not want and can do very well without,

in order to raise a revenue from the people in an indirect way."

Probably Potter's explanation of the change in system was correct. The necessities of the Treasury were doubtless a decisive cause of Madison's step; but these necessities were foreseen by the Federalists when Madison recommended the embargo, and the neglect to give them due weight exposed the Administration to grave reproach. " A government which cannot administer the affairs of a nation," said Webster, " without producing so frequent and such violent alterations in the ordinary occupations and pursuits of private life, has in my opinion little claim to the regard of the community."

The Republicans made no attempt to defend themselves from such criticisms. Among the small number who refused to follow Calhoun was Macon, who sat in his seat during the debate writing to his friend Judge Nicholson.

" Those who voted the embargo so very lately," he said,[1] "and those or him who recommended it must, I think, feel a little sore under Webster's rubs. . . . I have not for a long time seen the Feds look in so good humor. They have all a smile on their countenances, and look at each other as if they were the men which had brought this great and good work about. . . . The Republicans have not the most pleasing countenances. Those who support the bill do not look gay or very much delighted with their majority, and those who expect to be in the minority have a melancholy gloom over their faces."

[1] Macon to Nicholson, April 6, 1814; Nicholson MSS.

That the system of commercial restrictions had failed was admitted, but the failure carried no conviction of error to its friends. Physical force had also apparently failed. The Southern Republicans had no choice but to adopt strong measures, giving to the government powers which in their opinion they had no constitutional right to confer; but they remained unshaken in their opinions.

" I confess to you," wrote Macon, " that the parties seem by their acts to be approaching each other, and I fear that tough times is a strong argument with many of us to stretch the Constitution; and the difference between expediency and constitutionality becomes every day less. Notwithstanding this, I do not despair of the republic, because my dependence has always been on the people; and their influence was felt in laying the embargo, and probably that of the Executive in repealing it."

No one understood or represented so well as Macon the instincts and ideas of the Southern people at that time, and he never represented them more truly than in the matter of the embargo. Virginia and the Carolinas were with him at heart. Macon's hopes for the republic depended on his confidence in the people; and that confidence in its turn depended on his belief that the people were still true to a dogma which the Government had abandoned as impracticable. The belief was well founded, as the course of events proved. The House, April 7, by a vote of one hundred and fifteen to thirty-seven, passed the bill repealing the Embargo and Non-importation Acts ; the Senate also passed it, April 12, by a vote of twenty-six to four; the President, April 14, approved it; and from that day the restrictive system, which had been the cardinal point of Jefferson's and Madison's statesmanship, seemed to vanish from the public mind and the party politics of the country. Yet so deeply riveted was the idea of its efficacy among the Southern people, that at the next great crisis of their history they staked their lives and fortunes on the same belief of their necessity to Europe which had led them into the experiment of coercing Napoleon and Canning by commercial deprivations ; and their second experiment had results still more striking than those which attended their first.

The explanation of this curious popular trait certainly lay in the nature of Southern society'; but the experience was common to the whole Union. When the restrictive system was abandoned of necessity in April, 1814, it had brought the country to the verge of dissolution. The Government could neither make war nor peace ; the public seemed indifferent or hostile ; and the same traits which characterized the restrictive system continued to paralyze the efforts of Congress to adopt more energetic methods.

"I will yet hope we may have no more war," wrote Mrs. Madison to Mrs. Gallatin Jan. 7, 1814.[1] "If we do, alas! alas! we are not making ready as we ought

[1] Gallatin MSS.

to do.   Congress trifle away the most precious of their
days, — days that ought to be devoted to the defence
of their divided country."

Mrs. Madison doubtless echoed the language she
heard used at the White House; yet the leaders of
Congress were neither triflers nor idlers, and they
did all that public opinion permitted.   Within a week
after Mrs. Madison's complaint, the military committee of the House reported a bill for encouraging en-
listments.   Viewed as a means of embodying the
whole military strength of the republic to resist
the whole military strength of Great Britain, about
to be released from service in Europe, Troup's
bill [1] was not an efficient measure; but it terrified
Congress.

During the campaign of 1813, as the story has
shown, the Government never succeeded in placing
more than ten or eleven thousand effective rank-and-
file in the field in a single body.   About as many
more were in garrison, and the sick-list was always
large.   Armstrong reported to the Ways and Means
Committee that the aggregate strength of the army
in February, 1813, was 18,945; in June, 27,609; in
December, 34,325; and Jan. 17, 1814, it was 33,822.[2]
Discouraging as this report was, it concealed the
worst part of the situation.   In truth, the abstract
furnished by the adjutant-general's office gave the
number of regular troops in service for January, 1814,

[1] Annals, 1813–1814, p. 928.

[2] Armstrong to Eppes, Feb. 10, 1814; Niles, vi. 94.

not as 33,822, but as 23,614; and to the return a
note was appended, explaining that "although the
numerical force in January, 1814, was 23,614, the actual strength of the army at that time was less than
half that number, arising from the expiration of the
term of service of the troops raised in 1809 and enlisted for five years, and of the twelve and eighteen-
months men enlisted in 1812–1813."[1] The establishment consisted of 58,254 men authorized by law;
but the legal establishment was not half filled. The
European news showed that England would soon be
able to reinforce her army in Canada and take the
offensive. Instead of sixty thousand men, Armstrong
needed twice that number for a moderately safe defence, since every part of the sea-coast stood at the
enemy's mercy, and no adequate defence was possible which did not include an offensive return some-
where on the Canadian frontier. Needing more than
one hundred thousand, — authorized by law to enlist
sixty thousand, — he could depend on less than thirty
thousand men. Yet so far from attempting to increase the establishment, Armstrong hoped only to
fill the ranks.

Troup's bill aimed at that object, purporting to be
"A Bill making further provision for filling of the
ranks of the regular army." No system of draft
was suggested. Troup's committee proposed to treble
the bounty rather than raise the pay, — a system

[1] Note to abstract of regular troops in service, January, 1814;
adjutant-general's office. MSS. War Department Archives.

which might be economical in a long war; but if the war should last only one year, the soldier must gain four fifths of his bounty without return. Troup first' suggested one hundred dollars as bounty, which Congress raised to one hundred and twenty-four dollars, together with three hundred and twenty acres of land as already fixed. The pay of privates remained at ten dollars. Twenty-four dollars of the bounty was to be paid only on the soldier's discharge. Recruiting-agents were to receive eight dollars for each recruit.

Such a provision for filling the ranks could not be called excessive. Even if the whole bounty were added to the pay, and the soldier were to serve but twelve months, he would receive only twenty dollars a month and his land-certificate. If he served his whole term of five years, he received little more than twelve dollars a month. The inducement was not great in such a community as the United States. The chance that such a measure would fill the ranks was small; yet the measure seemed extravagant to a party that had formerly pledged itself against mercenary armies.

If the bill showed the timidity of the Republicans, it called out worse qualities in the Federalists. The speeches of the opposition were for the most part general in their criticisms and denunciations, and deserved little attention; but that of Daniel Webster was doubly interesting, because Webster was not only the ablest but among the most cautious of his party.

His speech [1] suggested much of the famous eloquence
of his later oratory, but dwelt on ideas to which his
later life was opposed, and followed lines of argument
surprising in a statesman of his great intellectual
powers. His chief theme was the duty of government to wage only a defensive war, except on the
ocean. " Give up your futile projects of invasion.
Extinguish the fires that blaze on your inland fron-
tiers." He wished the government to use its forces
only to repel invasion.

" The enemy, as we have seen, can make no permanent
stand in any populous part of the country. Its citizens
will drive back his forces to the line ; but at that line
where defence ceases and invasion begins, they stop.
They do not pass it because they do not choose to pass
it. Offering no serious obstacle to their actual power, it
rises like a Chinese wall against their sentiments and
their feelings."

This advice, which echoed a Federalist idea reasonable or excusable in 1812, was out of place in
January, 1814. The battles of Leipzig and Vittoria
had settled the question of offensive and defensive in
Canada. The offensive had passed into British hands,
and a successful defence was all that the United
States could hope. The interests of New England as
well as of New York and of the whole Union required
that the defensive campaign should, if possible, be
fought on Canadian soil rather than at Plattsburg,
Washington, or New Orleans ; and even the most ex-

---

[1] Annals, 1813–1814, p. 940.

treme Federalist could scarcely be believed blind to
an idea so obvious.

Moderate as the bill was, fifty-eight members voted
against it, while ninety-seven voted in its favor. In
the Senate the bill passed without a division, and received, January 27, the President's approval. Meanwhile the Senate passed bills for converting the
twelve-months regiments into regiments enlisted for
the war, as well as for raising three rifle regiments
for the same term, and any number of volunteers that
in the President's opinion the public service required,
offering to all recruits for these corps the same inducements as to the regular regiments. These bills
produced another and a longer debate, but were
passed without serious opposition. No further addition was made to the regular army, and no other
effort to obtain recruits.

Thus organized, the army consisted of forty-six
regiments of infantry enlisted for five years, — four
rifle regiments; an artillery corps and a regiment of
light artillery; a regiment of dragoons; the engineer
corps, the rangers, and sea-fencibles, — an aggregate
of 62,773 men authorized by law, an increase of only
five thousand men over that of the previous year.

The appropriations for the military establishment
amounted to nearly twenty-five million dollars, the
Federalists alone voting against them. The naval
appropriations amounted to seven millions, and were
voted without opposition. The Secretary of the Navy
discouraged the building of more cruisers, owing to

want of timber and seamen; but Congress showed more than ordinary sagacity by appropriating half a million dollars for the construction of floating batteries with steam-power.

Such provision for the coming campaign offered little evidence of increasing energy to make head against the vastly increased military and naval power of England; but the financial outlook was much worse than the military, and Congress dared not face it. The acting Secretary of the Treasury, William Jones, sent his annual report to the House January 8, and so far as his balance-sheet went, no difficulties were apparent. He had disbursed thirty million dollars during the past fiscal year, and needed nearly forty millions for the current year. These sums were not excessive when compared with the wealth of the country or its exertions at other periods of national danger. Half a century afterward the people of the Southern States, not much more numerous than the people of the Union in 1812, and with a far larger proportion of slaves, supported during four years the burden of an army numbering nearly five hundred thousand men. For the same period the Northern people, not much exceeding twenty millions in number, lent their government more than five hundred million dollars a year. The efforts of 1864, proportioned to the population, were nearly ten times as great as those of 1814, when Secretary Jones looked with well-founded alarm at the prospect of borrowing thirty millions for the year, and of maintaining an army which could scarcely be expected to number forty thousand rank-and-file.

The United States, with a proper currency and untouched resources, should have found no serious difficulty in borrowing thirty or even fifty millions a year in 1814 ; but they were in reality on the verge of bankruptcy, although the national resources were probably ample. The amount of private capital available for loans was uncertain, and the amount of circulating medium was equally doubtful. Timothy Pitkin of Connecticut, perhaps the best authority in Congress, thought that the paid bank capital of the United States did not much exceed sixty millions,[1] and that the notes of these banks in circulation did not reach thirty millions. His estimate of paid bank capital was probably liberal, but his estimate of the circulation was eight or ten millions too small. Had the Treasury been able to count on the use of these resources, they might have answered all necessary purposes ; but between the mistakes of the government and the divisions of the people, the Treasury was left with no sound resources whatever.

The first and fatal blow to the Treasury was the loss of the Bank of the United States, which left the government without financial machinery or a sound bank-note circulation. The next blow, almost equally severe, was the loss of the Massachusetts and Connecticut banks, which were the strongest in the Union.

[1] Speech of Timothy Pitkin, Feb. 10, 1814 ; Annals, 1813–1814, p. 1297.

Whether the responsibility for the loss rested on the Executive, Congress, or the two States might be a subject for dispute ; but whoever was responsible, the effect was ruinous. The New England banks were financial agents of the enemy. The bank capital of Massachusetts including Maine was about twelve and a quarter million dollars ; that of Connecticut exceeded three millions. The whole bank capital of New England reached eighteen millions,[1] or nearly one third of the paid bank capital of the whole country, if Pitkin's estimate was correct. That nearly one third of the national resources should be withdrawn from the aid of government was serious enough ; but in reality the loss was much greater, for New England held a still larger proportion of the specie on which the bank circulation of other States depended.

The system of commercial restrictions was responsible for thus, at the most critical moment of the war, throwing the control of the national finances into the hands of the Boston Federalists. Against the protests of the Federalists, manufactures had been forced upon them by national legislation until New England supplied the Union with articles of necessary use at prices practically fixed by her own manufacturers. From the whole country specie began to flow toward Boston as early as the year 1810, and with astonishing rapidity after the war was declared. The British blockade stimulated the movement, and the embargo

[1] Considerations on Currency, etc. By Albert Gallatin, 1831. Statements II. and III., pp. 101, 103.

of December, 1813, which lasted till April, 1814, cut
off every other resource from the Southern and Western States. Unable longer to send their crops even
to New England for a market, they were obliged to
send specie, and they soon came to the end of their
supply.   The Massachusetts banks, which reported
about $820,000 in specie in 1809, returned more than
$3,680,000 in June, 1812; which rose to $5,780,000
in June, 1813, and reached nearly $7,000,000 in June,
1814. In five years the Massachusetts banks alone
drew more than six million dollars in specie from the
Southern and Middle States,[1] besides what they sent
to Canada in payment for British bills.

No one knew how much specie the country contained.   Gallatin afterward estimated it at seventeen
million dollars,[2] and of that amount the banks of New
England in 1814 probably held nearly ten millions.
The Massachusetts banks, with seven millions in
specie, had a bank-note circulation of less than three
millions.   The Middle, Southern, and Western States
must have had a bank-note circulation approaching
forty millions in paper, with seven or eight millions in
specie to support it,[3] while the paper was constantly
increasing in quantity and the specie constantly diminishing.   Bank paper, as was believed, could not
with safety exceed the proportion of three paper dol-

[1] Schedule, 1803–1837 ; Senate Document No. 38. Massachusetts Legislature, 1838.

[2] Gallatin's Considerations, p. 45.

[3] Gallatin's Considerations, p. 45.   Schedules II. and III.,
pp. 101, 103. Gallatin's Writings, iii. 286, 357, 359.

lars to every specie dollar in the bank vaults; but the banks in 1814 beyond New England were circulating at least four paper dollars to every silver or gold dollar, and in many cases were issuing paper without specie in their possession.

Already the banks of New England were pressing their demands on those of New York, which in their turn called on Philadelphia and Baltimore. The specie drained to New England could find its way back only by means of government loans, which New England refused to make in any large amount. On the other hand, Boston bought freely British Treasury notes at liberal discount, and sent coin to Canada in payment of them.[1] Probably New England lent to the British government during the war more money than she lent to her own. The total amount subscribed in New England to the United States loans was less than three millions.

This situation was well understood by Congress. In the debate of February, 1814, the approaching dangers were repeatedly pointed out. The alarm was then so great that the Committee of Ways and Means reported a bill to incorporate a new national bank with a capital of thirty million dollars, while Macon openly advocated the issue of government paper,[2] declaring that "paper money never was beat." Congress after a diffuse debate passed only a loan bill for twenty-five millions, and an Act for the issue of

[1] Gallatin's Writings, iii. 284.
[2] Annals, 1813–1814, p. 1787.

five million interest-bearing Treasury notes, leaving with the President the option to issue five millions more in case he could not borrow it. The legislation was evidently insufficient, and satisfied no one. " You have authorized a loan for twenty-five millions," said Grundy in the debate of April 2, " and have provided for the expenditure of so much money. Where is the money ? "

Without attempting to answer this question, April 18 Congress adjourned.

CHAPTER XVI.

WHILE Congress was thus employed, much occurred behind the scenes that bore directly on the movements of war. The French minister, Serurier, alone made official reports, and his letters became less interesting as his importance diminished; but occasionally he still threw a ray of light on Madison's troubles. At midsummer in 1813 he was in high spirits.

"Within the past week," Serurier wrote, July 21, 1813,[1] "we have received, one after another, news of the fresh successes at the beginning of the campaign, — the battle of Lützen, the offer of armistice, and the battle of Bautzen. These events, so glorious for France, have been so many thunder-strokes for the enemy in America. Their consternation is equal to their previous confidence, which had no bounds. The Republicans of Congress, on the other hand, have received these news in triumph. All have come to congratulate me, and have told me that they, not less than we, had been victorious at Lützen. The ascendency, henceforward irresistible, which his Majesty is

[1] Serurier to Bassano, July 21, 1813; Archives des Aff. Étr. MSS.

acquiring over his enemies, will, I hope, supply a little tone and vigor to this Government, which had need of them."

When the President returned to Washington, Oct. 25, 1813, Serurier reported with less enthusiasm, but still with confidence, that Madison remained firm:

"He expressed himself in very proper, though very measured, terms on the monstrous coalition that has been renewed against his Majesty. I remarked to him that among our advantages we must doubtless count the fact that the coalition had ten heads, while France had but one. 'And what a powerful head!' replied the President, instantly, with less grace than conviction in his whole countenance."

The vigor of Napoleon postponed for a few months the total downfall of Serurier's influence, but it slowly waned, and he became more and more grateful for consideration shown him. The President's Annual Message, December 7, met his approval. "All agree that nothing more energetic or more warlike has yet come from Mr. Madison's Cabinet." [1] The secret Message of December 9 and the embargo pleased him more.

"Mr. Monroe assured me three days ago," continued Serurier, writing December 10, "that the Government had been informed of supplies to the extent of nearly thirty thousand barrels of flour furnished to Canada from ports of the United States. A rigorous embargo can

[1] Serurier to Bassano, Dec. 10, 1813; Archives des Aff. Etr. MSS.

alone prevent such criminal speculations, and give the war a decisive character which will shorten its duration and assure its success. . . . In this affair is seen a new proof of Mr. Madison's obstinacy (*roideur*) which prevents him from abandoning a measure he has once put forward, and judges to be for the public interest."

The arrival of the "Bramble" with news of the battle of Leipzig, and with Castlereagh's offer to negotiate, left Serurier helpless. "In this state of things," he wrote,[1] January 14, "it would have been difficult for the Executive to refuse to negotiate; and I cannot but think that he accedes to it only with regret and without illusions." In deference to Serurier's opinion, the President appointed Henry Clay as commissioner to treat for peace rather than Crawford, then American envoy to Napoleon; but in the last week of March news arrived from Bordeaux to February 10, announcing that the allies had reached Troyes and were advancing on Paris, while Napoleon had accepted their conditions of negotiation.

"For the moment the public believed everything to be lost," reported Serurier, April 15.[2] "I ought in justice to say that the President and his Cabinet showed more coolness and did not share the universal alarm, and that they continued to show me great confidence in the Emperor's genius. I did not find them excessively disturbed by the march of the allies, or doubtful of our power to

[1] Serurier to Bassano, Jan. 14, 1814; Archives des Aff. Étr. MSS.

[2] Serurier to Bassano, April 15, 1814; Archives des Aff. Étr. MSS.

repulse them; but I know that his Majesty's adhesion
to the preliminary conditions of the allies, and yet more
the Congress of Chatillon, and the irresistible influence
necessarily acquired for the British minister, greatly
(*vivement*) alarmed Mr. Madison. He thought he saw,
in the announcement of our adoption of those conditions,
our renunciation of every kind of power and control
over Spain and Germany, where England was to rule.
He believed that a peace, dictated by Lord Castlereagh,
must already have been signed, and that the United
States were to remain alone on the field of battle. It
was then that Mr. Madison, abruptly and without having in any way prepared the public for it, addressed
to Congress the Message recommending an immediate
repeal of the embargo and a partial repeal of the non-
importation."

While Serurier explained the suddenness of
Madison's action by the need of conciliating the
Continental powers and the manufacturing cities of
England, he added that domestic difficulties had a
large share in the decision. Contraband trade had
become general in the Eastern States. A sort of
civil war, he said, was beginning between the officers of customs and the smugglers; the Government also felt serious anxiety for the success of its
loan, and began to doubt its ability to maintain pay-
ments for the army and navy. Revenue had become
necessary. Such was the terror caused by the French
news that the capitalists who had offered to contract
for the loan began to withdraw their offers and to say
that it was no longer practicable. "Analyze it as

you please," said Serurier, " you will still find that it was the passage of the Rhine and the progress of the allies in France which, in spite of all I could say, decided this retrograde movement of a Government which I have hitherto always found firm, wise, and consequent.   But fear does not reason."

Serurier failed even to obtain permission for French letters-of-marque to be received with their prizes in American ports.   The President recommended it to Congress, but Monroe told Serurier that the committee of Congress had not dared to make a report, being persuaded that it would be rejected.[1]   " Mr. Monroe agreed to all I said ; granted that Congress was in the wrong, and I entirely in the right; but nevertheless Congress has adjourned without considering the question."   Serurier was disposed to advise the withdrawal by France of the liberties granted to American privateers, — a measure which, he might almost have foreseen, was likely in any case soon to be taken.

With the repeal of the embargo ended the early period of United States history, when diplomatists played a part at Washington equal in importance to that of the Legislature or the Executive.   The statecraft of Jefferson and Madison was never renewed. Thenceforward the government ceased to balance between great foreign Powers, and depended on its own resources.   As far as diplomacy had still a part to

[1] Serurier to Bassano, April 25, 1814; Archives des Aff. Étr. MSS.

play in the year 1814, its field of action was in Europe; and there the ablest men in civil life were sent. Gallatin, Bayard, J. Q. Adams, and Crawford were already on the spot; and Henry Clay, after resigning the Speaker's chair, Jan. 19, 1814, sailed for Gothenburg to take part in the negotiation.

President Madison sought in vain for men of equal ability to supply the gaps made by transferring so many of his strongest supporters to Europe. The House of Representatives, January 19, elected Langdon Cheves Speaker; but the choice was a defeat for Madison, whose friends supported Felix Grundy. The Federalists, joining those Republicans who were hostile to commercial restrictions, numbered ninety-four against fifty-nine votes for Grundy, — and the success of Cheves foreshadowed the overthrow of the embargo. In providing for other vacancies the President fared worse. Cheves was a man of ability, and in general policy was a friend of the Administration; but most of the other material upon which the President must depend was greatly inferior to Cheves. The Cabinet needed partial reconstruction, and Madison was at a loss for choice.

The President's favorite candidate for the Treasury, after Gallatin showed his determination to remain abroad, was Alexander James Dallas of Pennsylvania. Dallas was one of Gallatin's strongest personal friends, an old Republican, and a lawyer of undoubted ability. Born in Jamaica in 1759, like Gallatin and Hamilton he had become a citizen of

the United States before the Constitution or the con-
federation was adopted. He had been a leader of
the Republican party in Federalist times, and was
made district-attorney of Pennsylvania by Jefferson ;
but Duane and the "Aurora" destroyed his influence
and left him isolated. In Pennsylvania Dallas commanded no support. Both the senators, Leib and
Lacock, opposed his appointment to the Treasury,
and were able to procure his rejection had Madison
ventured to make it.[1]

Obliged to abandon Dallas, the President offered the
appointment to Richard Rush, the comptroller, who
declined it. At last Madison pitched upon G. W.
Campbell, of Tennessee. Since Crawford's departure
Campbell had represented the Administration in the
Senate, but neither as senator nor as representative
had he won great distinction. Best known for his duel
with Barent Gardenier, his physical courage was more
apparent than his financial fitness. Campbell brought
no strength to the Administration, and rather weakened its character among capitalists ; but Madison
could think of no one better qualified for the place.
The Republicans were at a loss for leaders. " I do
not complain that Campbell is unfit," wrote Macon
to Nicholson ; [2] " indeed, if the choice of secretary
must be made out of Congress, I do not know that
a better could be made." Yet the selection was
unfortunate.

[1] Ingersoll's History, ii. 253.
[2] Macon to Nicholson, Feb. 8, 1814; Nicholson MSS.

Madison was also obliged to select a new attorney-general in place of William Pinkney. Till then the attorney-general had not been regarded as standing on the same footing with other members of the Cabinet. The Secretaries of State and Treasury were paid five thousand dollars a year; those of the War and Navy were paid forty-five hundred; but the attorney-general was paid only three thousand. He had neither office-room nor clerks, and was not required to reside permanently at Washington, but pursued the private business of his profession where he liked, attending to the business of government rather as a counsel under general retainer than as a head of Department. Pinkney lived in Baltimore, and his abilities were so valuable that the President was glad to employ them on any terms, and was not inclined to impose conditions of residence which Pinkney could not accept without a greater sacrifice than he was ready to make.[1] Congress was not so forbearing as the President. John W. Taylor, a member from New York, moved a resolution January 5, directing the Judiciary Committee to inquire into the expediency of requiring the attorney-general to reside in Washington during the session of Congress. The committee reported a bill, January 22, requiring permanent residence from the attorney-general, with an increase of salary. The bill failed to become law, but Pinkney at once resigned.

Madison offered the post to Richard Rush, who

[1] Madison to Pinkney, Jan. 29, 1814; Works, ii. 581.

accepted it. Rush's abilities were more than respectable, and caused regret that he had not accepted the Treasury, for which he was better fitted than Campbell; but these changes did not improve the Cabinet. "His predecessor, Pinkney, I believe considered him the best lawyer in the nation," wrote Macon;[1] "but that Campbell and Rush are equal to Gallatin and Pinkney is not, I imagine, believed by any one who knows them." In the case of Pinkney and Rush, the advantages of permanent residence balanced in part the loss of ability; but no such consideration affected the change of Campbell for Gallatin.

Fortunately Madison lost enemies as well as friends. Time worked steadily in his favor. The old Smith faction, the Clinton party, and the "Aurora" were already broken. Senators who claimed too much independence of action found public opinion setting strongly against them. Samuel Smith and Giles were near the end of their terms, and had no chance of re-election. The legislature of North Carolina, in December, 1813, censured so severely the conduct of Senator Stone that the senator resigned his seat.[2] At the same time, Pennsylvania succeeded in ridding herself of Senator Leib, and Madison was able to punish the postmaster-general, Gideon Granger, whose friendship for Leib made him obnoxious to his party.

[1] Macon to Nicholson, Feb. 17, 1814; Nicholson MSS.
[2] Report and Resolution of Dec. 16, 1814; Niles, v. 356.

Granger was not a member of the Cabinet, but his patronage was the more important because at that time, by some anomaly in the law, it was not subject to approval by the Senate. Early in January one of his best post-offices, that of Philadelphia, became vacant. One senator of the United States had already resigned his seat to become postmaster of New York; and the Pennsylvanians had reason to fear that Leib, whose term was about to expire, would resign to become postmaster of Philadelphia, and that Granger wished to gratify him. Immediately all the Administration Republicans, including members of Congress and of the State legislature, joined in recommending another man, and warned Granger in private that his own removal from office would follow the appointment of Leib.[1] C. J. Ingersoll — a young member from Pennsylvania, among the warmest supporters of Madison and the war — reinforced the threat by moving the House, January 7, for a committee to amend the laws with a view to making postmasters subject to the usual rule of confirmation. The committee was appointed.

Irritated by this treatment, Granger in defiance of President and party appointed Michael Leib to the office, and Leib instantly resigned his seat and hastened to assume the duties of his new post. In this transaction Madison was the chief gainer. Not only did he rid himself of Leib, but he gained a warm

[1] Granger to John Todd, February, 1814; New England "Palladium," March 4, 1814.

ally in the person of Leib's successor; for the Pennsylvania legislature, February 28, transferred Jonathan Roberts from the House to take Leib's place in the Senate. Madison's advantage was not limited by Leib's departure or Roberts's accession. He was able also to punish Granger in a manner at that time almost or quite without parallel. Executive offices ran, as a rule, during good behavior; and although Jefferson made removals of party enemies, neither he nor Madison had ventured to remove party friends, except in cases of misbehavior. Granger's conduct exasperated the Pennsylvanians to a point where no rules were regarded. Eighty-six members of the Pennsylvania legislature joined in addressing a memorial to the President demanding the removal of Granger as the only means of getting rid of Leib, who had not only opposed Madison's election, but who, " when entrusted with one of the highest offices in the gift of the State, . . . acted in direct hostility to her wishes and interests, and aided as far as possible her political enemies." Madison needed little urging. February 25 he nominated to the Senate as postmaster-general the governor of Ohio, Return Jonathan Meigs. After some little delay, the Senate confirmed the appointment, March 17, without a division.

Scarcely was this matter settled, when Congress yielded to Madison's opinion in another instance where for ten years the House had obstinately resisted his wishes. The Yazoo bill became law. For this concession several reasons combined. The Su-

preme Court, through Chief-Justice Marshall, by an
elaborate decision in February, 1810, settled the law
in favor of the claimants. John Randolph's defeat
removed from Congress the chief obstacle to the proposed agreement. The threatening attitude of New
England made every palliative necessary. Under
these inducements, the Senate passed the bill, February 28, by a vote of twenty-four to eight, and the
House passed it, March 26, by a vote of eighty-four to
seventy-six.

Little by little the pressure of necessity compelled
Congress and the country to follow Madison's lead.
Whether for good or for evil, he had his way. His
enemies were overcome and driven from the field;
his friends were rewarded, and his advice followed.
Of revolt within the party he stood no longer in fear.
Already political intrigue and factiousness began to
take a direction which concerned him only so far
as he felt an interest in the choice of his successor.
Three years more would complete Madison's public
career, and in all probability if another President of
the United States were ever elected, he would be one
of Madison's friends; but many persons doubted
whether the country would reach another Presidential election, and the jealousy which actuated New
England against the South was not the only ground
for that opinion. In Madison's immediate circle of
friends, the jealousy between Virginia and New York
threatened to tear the government in pieces. These
States did not, like Massachusetts, threaten to leave

the Union, but their struggles for power promised to bring government to a standstill.

The antipathy of New York for Virginia was not lessened by the success of Virginia in overthrowing Aaron Burr and DeWitt Clinton. The Republican party in New York quickly produced two new aspirants to the Presidency, whose hopes were founded on public weariness of Virginian supremacy. One of the two candidates was Governor Daniel D. Tompkins, whose services as war-governor of New York were great, and were rewarded by great popularity. Governor Tompkins was too remote from the capital to annoy Madison by direct contact with factions or activity in intrigue; but the other rival stood at the centre of Executive patronage. John Armstrong was a man capable of using power for personal objects, and not easily to be prevented from using it as he pleased.

Armstrong was an unusual character. The local influences which shaped Americans were illustrated by the leaders whom New York produced, and by none better than by Armstrong. Virginians could not understand, and could still less trust, such a combination of keenness and will, with absence of conventional morals as the Secretary of War displayed. The Virginians were simple in everything; even their casuistry was old-fashioned. Armstrong's mind belonged to modern New York. The Virginians were a knot of country gentlemen, inspired by faith in rural virtues, and sustained by dislike for the city tendencies of Northern society. Among themselves they were genial, reluctant to offend, and eager to remove causes of offence. The domestic history of the government at Washington repeated the Virginian traits. Jefferson and his friends passed much time in making quarrels, and more in making peace. Unlike Pennsylvania, New York, and New England, Virginia stood stoutly by her own leaders; and however harsh Virginians might be in their judgment of others, they carried delicacy to an extreme in their treatment of each other. Even John Randolph and W. B. Giles, who seemed to put themselves beyond the social pale, were treated with tenderness and regarded with admiration.

The appearance of a rough and harshly speaking friend in such a society was no slight shock, and for that reason William Henry Crawford was regarded with some alarm; but Crawford was socially one of themselves, while Armstrong belonged to a different type and class. The faculty of doing a harsh act in a harsh way, and of expressing rough opinions in a caustic tone, was not what the Virginians most disliked in Armstrong. His chief fault in their eyes, and one which they could not be blamed for resenting, was his avowed want of admiration for the Virginians themselves. Armstrong's opinion on that subject, which was but the universal opinion of New York politicians, became notorious long before he entered the Cabinet, and even then annoyed Madison.[1]

[1] Madison to Jefferson, April 19, 1811; Works, ii. 493.

The newspapers gossiped about the mean estimate which Armstrong expressed for the capacities of the Virginia statesmen. So old and fixed was the feud, that from the first the Virginians lost no opportunity to express their opinion of Armstrong, especially in the Senate, whenever he was nominated for office. Madison unwillingly selected him for the post of secretary after Crawford refused it, but neither of the Virginia senators voted on the question of confirmation. In appointing Armstrong, Madison bestowed on him neither respect nor confidence. He afterward declared the reasons that caused him to invite a person whom he distrusted into a position of the highest importance.

" Should it be asked," wrote Madison ten years after the war,[1] " why the individual in question was placed, and after such developments of his career continued, at the head of the War Department, the answer will readily occur to those best acquainted with the circumstances of the period. Others may be referred for an explanation to the difficulty, which had been felt in its fullest pressure, of obtaining services which would have been preferred, several eminent citizens to whom the station had been offered having successively declined it. It was not unknown at the time that objections existed to the person finally appointed, as appeared when his nomination went to the Senate, where it received the reluctant sanction of a scanty majority [eighteen to fifteen]. Nor was the President unaware or unwarned of the temper and turn of mind ascribed to him, which might be uncongenial

[1] Works, iii. 384.

with the official relations in which he was to stand. But these considerations were sacrificed to recommendations from esteemed friends ; a belief that he possessed, with known talents, a degree of military information which might be useful ; and a hope that a proper mixture of conciliating confidence and interposing control would render objectionable peculiarities less in practice than in prospect."

Possibly Armstrong took a different view of Madison's conduct, and regarded his own acceptance of the War Department in January, 1813, as proof both of courage and disinterestedness. He knew that he could expect no confidence from Virginians ; but apparently he cared little for Virginian enmity, and was chiefly fretted by what he thought Virginian incompetence. No one could fail to see that he came into the Government rather as a master than a servant. According to General Wilkinson, he was quite as much feared as hated. " I am indeed shocked," wrote Wilkinson in his Memoirs,[1] " when I take a retrospect of the evidence of the terror in which that minister kept more than one great man at Washington." Wilkinson, who hated Madison even more than he hated Armstrong, evidently believed that the President was afraid of his secretary. Madison himself explained that he thought it better to bear with Armstrong's faults than to risk another change in the Department of War.

In that decision Madison was doubtless right.

[1] Wilkinson's Memoirs, i. 762.

Whatever were Armstrong's faults, he was the strongest Secretary of War the government had yet seen. Hampered by an inheritance of mistakes not easily corrected, and by a chief whose methods were unmilitary in the extreme, Armstrong still introduced into the army an energy wholly new.   Before he had been a year in office he swept away the old generals with whom Madison and Eustis had encumbered the service, and in their place substituted new men. While Major-Generals Dearborn, Pinckney, and Morgan Lewis were set over military districts where active service was unnecessary, and while Major-General Wilkinson was summoned to the last of his many courts of inquiry, the President sent to the Senate, January 21 and February 21, the names of two new major-generals and six brigadiers of a totally different character from the earlier appointments.

The first major-general was George Izard of South Carolina, born at Paris in 1777, his father Ralph Izard being then American commissioner with Franklin and Deane. Returning to America only for a few years after the peace, George Izard at the age of fifteen was sent abroad to receive a military education in England, Germany, and France in the great school of the French Revolution. As far as education could make generals, Izard was the most promising officer in the United States service. Appointed in March, 1812, colonel of the Second Artillery, promoted to brigadier in March, 1813, he served with credit under Hampton at Chateaugay, and received his promotion over the heads of Chandler, Boyd, and one or two other brigadiers his seniors. He was intended to succeed Hampton on Lake Champlain.

The second new major-general was Jacob Brown, who after receiving the appointment of brigadier, July 19, 1813, was suddenly promoted to major-general at the same time with Izard. The selection was the more remarkable because Brown had no military education, and was taken directly from the militia. Born in Pennsylvania in 1775 of Quaker parentage, Brown began life as a schoolmaster. At the instance of the Society of Friends, he taught their public school in New York city for several years with credit.[1] He then bought a large tract of land near Sackett's Harbor, and in 1799 undertook to found a town of Brownville. He soon became a leading citizen in that part of New York, and in 1809 was appointed to the command of a militia regiment. In 1811 he was made a brigadier of militia, and at the beginning of the war distinguished himself by activity and success at Ogdensburg. His defence of Sackett's Harbor in 1813 won him a brigade in the regular service, and his share in Wilkinson's descent of the St. Lawrence led to his further promotion.

Wilkinson, who regarded Brown as one of his enemies, declared that he knew not enough of military duty to post the guards of his camp,[2] and that he compelled his battery to form in a hollow for the advan-

[1] Memoir of Brown from the " Port Folio ; " Niles, vii. 32.

[2] Wilkinson's Memoirs, iii. 402.

tage of elevating the pieces to fire at the opposite heights.[1] Winfield Scott, who was one of Brown's warmest friends, described him as full of zeal and vigor, but not a technical soldier, and but little acquainted with organization, tactics, police, and camp-duties in general.[2] The promotion of an officer so inexperienced to the most important command on the frontier, gave a measure of Armstrong's boldness and judgment.

The six new brigadiers were also well chosen. They were Alexander Macomb, T. A. Smith, Daniel Bissell, Edmund P. Gaines, Winfield Scott, and Eleazer W. Ripley, all colonels of the regular army, selected for their merits. Armstrong supplied Brown's defects of education by giving him the aid of Winfield Scott and Ripley, who were sent to organize brigades at Niagara.

The energy thus infused by Armstrong into the regular army lasted for half a century; but perhaps his abrupt methods were better shown in another instance, which brought upon him the displeasure of the President. Against Harrison, Armstrong from the first entertained a prejudice. Believing him to be weak and pretentious, the Secretary of War showed the opinion by leaving him in nominal command in the northwest, but sending all his troops in different directions, without consulting him even in regard to movements within his own military department.

[1] Wilkinson's Memoirs, iii. 65.
[2] Autobiography, p. 118.

Harrison, taking just offence, sent his resignation as major-general, May 11, 1814, but at the same time wrote to Governor Shelby of Kentucky a letter which caused the governor to address to the President a remonstrance against accepting the resignation.[1]

At that moment Armstrong and Madison were discussing the means of promoting Andrew Jackson in the regular service for his success in the Creek campaigns. No commission higher than that of brigadier was then at their disposal, and a commission as brigadier was accordingly prepared for Jackson May 22, with a brevet of major-general.[2] Harrison's resignation had been received by Armstrong two days before issuing Jackson's brevet, and had been notified to the President, who was then at Montpelier.[3] The President replied May 25, suggesting that in view of Harrison's resignation, the better way would be to send a commission as major-general directly to Jackson : " I suspend a final decision, however, till I see you, which will be in two or three days after the arrival of this." [4] No sooner did Armstrong receive the letter, than without waiting for the President's return he wrote to Jackson, May 28 : " Since the date of my letter of the 24th Major-General Harrison has resigned

[1] Dawson, p. 436 ; Lossing, p. 563.

[2] Armstrong to Jackson, May 23, 1814; Madison's Works, iii. 376.

[3] Armstrong to Madison, May 20, 1814 ; Madison's Works, iii. 375.

[4] Madison's Works, iii. 375.

his commission in the army, and thus is created a
vacancy in that grade, which I hasten to fill with your
name." [1]

Armstrong's course was irregular, and his account
to Jackson of the circumstances was incorrect; for
Harrison's resignation had been received before, not
after, Armstrong's letter of the 24th. Madison believed that Armstrong wished to appear as the source
of favor to the army. Armstrong attributed Madison's hesitation to the wish of Madison and Monroe
that Harrison, rather than Jackson, should take command of Mobile and New Orleans.[2] Both suspicions
might be wrong or right; but Armstrong's conduct,
while betraying the first motive, suggested the fear
that the President might change his mind ; and Harrison believed that the President would have done
so, had not Armstrong's abrupt action made it impossible. "The President expressed his great regret,"
said Harrison's biographer,[3] "that the letter of Governor Shelby had not been received earlier, as in that
case the valuable services of General Harrison would
have been preserved to the nation in the ensuing
campaign."

Little as the President liked his Secretary of War,
his antipathy was mild when compared with that of
Monroe. The failure of the Canada campaign gave a

[1] Madison's Works, iii. 377.
[2] Kosciusko Armstrong's Notice of J. Q. Adams's Eulogy on
James Monroe, p. 32, *note.*
[3] Dawson, p. 436.

serious blow to Armstrong; but he had still recovered
Detroit, and was about to finish the Creek war.   His
hold upon the army was becoming strong.   His enemies charged him with ambition; they said he was
systematically engaged in strengthening his influence
by seducing the young officers of talents into his personal support, teaching them to look for appreciation
not to the President but to himself, and appointing to
office only his own tools, or the sons of influential
men.   He was believed to favor a conscription, and
to aim at the position of lieutenant-general.   These
stories were constantly brought to Monroe, and drove
him to a condition of mind only to be described as
rabid.   He took the unusual step of communicating
them to the President,[1] with confidential comments
that, if known to Armstrong, could hardly have failed
to break up the Cabinet.

"It is painful to me to make this communication to
you," wrote the Secretary of State Dec. 27, 1813;[2] "nor
should I do it if I did not most conscientiously believe
that this man, if continued in office, will ruin not you
and the Administration only, but the whole Republican
party and cause.   He has already gone far to do it, and
it is my opinion, if he is not promptly removed, he will
soon accomplish it.   Without repeating other objections
to him, if the above facts are true, . . . he wants a
head fit for his station.   Indolent except to improper
purposes, he is incapable of that combination and activ-

[1] Gilman's Monroe, p. 114.

[2] Monroe to Madison, Dec. 27, 1813; Monroe MSS. State
Department Archives.

ity which the times require. My advice to you, therefore, is to remove him at once. The near prospect of a
conscription, adopted and acted on without your approbation or knowledge, is a sufficient reason. The burning of Newark, if done by his orders, is another. The
failure to place troops at Fort George is another. In
short there are abundant reasons for it. His removal
for either of the three would revive the hopes of our
party now desponding, and give a stimulus to measures.
I do not however wish you to act on my advice, — con-
sult any in whom you have confidence. Mr. A. has, as
you may see, few friends, and some of them cling to
him rather as I suspect from improper motives, or on
a presumption that you support him."

Armstrong's faults were beyond dispute, but his
abilities were very considerable ; and the President
justly thought that nothing would be gained by dis-
missing him, even to restore Monroe to the War Department. Armstrong, struggling with the load of
incapable officers and insufficient means, for which
Madison and Congress were responsible, required the
firm support of his chief and his colleagues, as well
as of the army and of Congress, to carry the burden
of the war ; but he had not a friend to depend upon.
Secretary Jones was as hostile as Monroe. Pennsylvania and Virginia equally distrusted him, and the
fate of any public man distrusted by Pennsylvania
and Virginia was commonly fixed in advance. Armstrong was allowed to continue his preparations for
the next campaign, but Monroe remained actively hostile. In a private letter to Crawford, written prob-

ably about the month of May, 1814, and preserved
with a memorandum that it was not sent, Monroe
said : [1] —

> " There is now no officer free to command to whom
> the public looks with any sort of confidence or even hope.
> Izard stands next, but he is as you see otherwise en-
> gaged [on a court of inquiry on Wilkinson]. Thus the
> door is left open for some new pretender, and Mr.
> Armstrong is that pretender. This has been his object
> from the beginning. . . . The whole affair is beyond my
> control."

Thus the elements of confusion surrounding Armstrong were many. A suspicious and hesitating
President; a powerful and jealous Secretary of State ;
a South Carolinian major-general, educated in the
French engineers, commanding on Lake Champlain ;
a Pennsylvania schoolmaster, of Quaker parentage,
without military knowledge, commanding at Sackett's
Harbor and Niagara; a few young brigadiers eager
to distinguish themselves, and an army of some thirty
thousand men, — these were the elements with which
Armstrong was to face the whole military power of
England ; for Paris capitulated March 31, and the
war in Europe was ended.

In one respect, Armstrong's conduct seemed in-
consistent with the idea of selfishness or intrigue.
The duty of organizing a court martial for the trial
of William Hull fell necessarily upon him. Hull's
defence must inevitably impeach Hull's superiors ;

[1] Monroe MSS. State Department Archives.

his acquittal was possible only on the ground that the Government had been criminally negligent in supporting him. As far as Armstrong was interested in the result, he was concerned in proving the incapacity of his predecessor Eustis, and of the President, in their management of the war. He could have had no personal object to gain in procuring the conviction of Hull, but he might defend his own course by proving the imbecility of Dearborn.

The President ordered a court martial on Hull before Armstrong entered the War Department. A. J. Dallas drew up the specifications, and inserted, contrary to his own judgment, a charge of treason made by the Department. The other charges were cowardice, neglect of duty, and unofficer-like conduct. Monroe, while temporarily at the head of the Department, organized the first court to meet at Philadelphia Feb. 25, 1813. Major-General Wade Hampton was to preside.

Before the trial could be held, Armstrong came into office, and was obliged to order the members of the court to active service. Hampton was sent to Lake Champlain, and when his campaign ended in November, 1813, he returned under charges resembling those against Hull.[1] Finding that neither Wilkinson nor Armstrong cared to press them, and satisfied that no inquiry could be impartial, Hampton

---

[1] Wilkinson to Armstrong, Nov. 24, and Dec. 8, 1813. State Papers, Military Affairs, p. 480. Order of Arrest. Wilkinson's Memoirs, iii. Appendix v.

determined to settle the question by once more sending in his resignation,[1] which he did in March, 1814,
when it was accepted. Armstrong in effect acquitted
Hampton by accepting his resignation, and never publicly affirmed any charge against him until after
Hampton's death, when he attributed to the major-
general " much professional error and great moral
depravity." [2] Hampton's opinion of Armstrong could
be gathered only from his conduct and his letters to
the Secretary of War, but was not materially different from Armstrong's opinion of Hampton.

Meanwhile Hull waited for trial. During the summer of 1813 he saw nearly all his possible judges
disgraced and demanding courts martial like himself.
Hampton was one; Wilkinson another; Dearborn a
third. Dearborn had been removed from command
of his army in face of the enemy, and loudly called
for a court of inquiry. Instead of granting the request, the President again assigned him to duty in
command of Military District No. 3, comprising the
city of New York, and also made him President of
the court martial upon General Hull.

The impropriety of such a selection could not be
denied. Of all men in the United States, Dearborn
was most deeply interested in the result of Hull's
trial, and the President, next to Dearborn, would be
most deeply injured by Hull's acquittal. The judg-

[1] Defence of General Hampton; " National Intelligencer,"
June 7, 1814.
[2] Notices, etc., ii. 26.

ment of Dearborn, or of any court over which Dearborn presided, in a matter which affected both court and government so closely could not command respect. That Armstrong lent himself to such a measure was a new trait of character never explained; but that Madison either ordered or permitted it showed that he must have been unconscious either of Dearborn's responsibility for Hull's disaster, or of his own.

Hull offered no objection to his court, and the trial began at Albany, Jan. 3, 1814, Dearborn presiding, and Martin Van Buren acting as special judge-advocate. March 26 the court sentenced Hull to be shot to death for cowardice, neglect of duty, and unofficerlike conduct. April 25 President Madison approved the sentence, but remitted the execution, and Hull's name was ordered to be struck from the army roll.

That some one should be punished for the loss of Detroit was evident, and few persons were likely to complain because Hull was a selected victim; but many thought that if Hull deserved to be shot, other men, much higher than he in office and responsibility, merited punishment; and the character of the court-martial added no credit to the Government, which in effect it acquitted of blame.